NEW LITERARY HISTORIES

WITHDRAWN

MANCHESTER
UNIVERSITY PRESS

NEW LITERARY HISTORIES

New historicism and contemporary criticism

Claire Colebrook

MANCHESTER UNIVERSITY PRESS
Manchester and New York

distributed exclusively in the USA by St. Martin's Press

Copyright © Claire Colebrook 1997

Published by Manchester University Press
Oxford Road, Manchester M13 9NR, UK
and Room 400, 175 Fifth Avenue, New York, NY 10010, USA

Distributed exclusively in the USA by
St. Martin's Press, Inc., 175 Fifth Avenue, New York,
NY 10010, USA

Distributed exclusively in Canada by
UBC Press, University of British Columbia, 6344 Memorial Road,
Vancouver, BC, Canada V6T 1Z2

British Library Cataloguing-in-Publication Data
A catalogue record for this book is available from the British Library

Library of Congress Cataloging-in-Publication Data

Colebrook, Claire.
    New literary histories : new historicism and contemporary
criticism / Claire Colebrook.
        p.   cm.
    Includes bibliographical references.
    ISBN 0–7190–4986–5. — ISBN 0–7190–4987–3 (pbk.)
    1. Criticism.   2. Historicism.   I. Title.
PN81.C69   1998
801'.95—DC21   97–11953

ISBN 0 7190 4986 5 hardback
     0 7190 4987 3 paperback

First published 1997

01 00 99 98 97   10 9 8 7 6 5 4 3 2 1

Photoset in Joanna
by Northern Phototypesetting Co. Ltd, Bolton
Printed in Great Britain
by Biddles Ltd, Guildford and King's Lynn

Contents

Preface

Why is historicism a problem? Why do we need a *new* historicism? At first glance the answers to these questions seem easy enough. Historicism is problematic in the same way that all knowledge practices today are experiencing forms of legitimation crisis. How can a particular story or historical narrative be seen as definitive, valid or justifiable? Supposedly, a *new* historicism would be an historicism tempered by an awareness of this question, a critically self-aware form of historiography which took on board a sense of history as narrative, anecdote, power or discourse.

This book aims to show that the problem of historicism, and new historicism, is more than just a problem of knowledge-validity and that new historicism is not so much an answer to the difficulties of history writing but the opening of new questions. The very fact that this book begins with a historical narrative is a sign of the far-reaching implications of the question of historicism. Why, we might ask, do our current forms of explanation and understanding so often take the form of historical narrative? More importantly, would another mode of understanding be possible? In *The Order of Things* (1970) Michel Foucault demonstrated that historicism was a relatively recent phenomenon, part of a specifically modern way of thinking. But Foucault was only able to make this point by writing a history. In *The Order of Things* historical thinking was at once delimited by being recognised as contingent at the same time as it appeared as the only way to proceed.

In terms of literary criticism, history or historiography, ostensibly at least, looks less overwhelming. There is a strong, if much maligned, tradition of formalism which aims to interpret a text regardless of its historical position or context. But 'formalism' has, since the 1960s, been a constant target in discussions of literary theory. The main opponents of formalism, until recently, have been manifestly 'political' approaches such as Marxism and feminism which 'open' the text to its historical specificity. But if a text is more than its form, if a text bears a relation to something other than itself, then criticism will be presented with two problems. Firstly, how does a text relate to its outside? (This has been the question which, with varying degrees of sophistication, has occupied Marxist literary theory.) The second problem comes on the scene once the historical narrative which forms the text's context is itself considered: just what is it that a text relates to? Is history another text? A privileged narrative? Or is history something other than narrative? Is there something like 'culture' which could explain a text's historical specificity without positing context as either a brute fact or further text? It is this second problem which occupies the attention of the various approaches and movements considered in this book. The question is asked in a number of ways but in all cases the typically Marxist problem of relation (of text to objective context) is displaced. For if history itself is both narrative and a specifically modern form of narrative, then it may no longer be a question of relating a text to some context, but, rather, of asking how a text together with what is taken to be its context are produced. How do we establish a domain of aesthetic textuality which is seen as independent of other texts? How is history produced as a horizon within which texts are located? Are there other ways of thinking about a text's meaning which would avoid positing history as some pre-given fact without returning to formalism or collapsing into textualism?

These questions have provided the impetus for formulating new ways of thinking about history and textuality, and have led to the creation of a complex theoretical terminology. Foucault's concept of discourse can be understood, in part, as a refusal to posit anything as simply *given*, while at the same time recognising the positive and specific effects of the way in which things are given discursively. Clifford Geertz's theory of 'culture' is an explanatory rubric which is more comfortable than Foucault with giving a general account for the various forms of human life. But Geertz uses culture to place all events, meanings and practices (including analysis itself) within a complex whole, the complexity of which precludes any complete or external mapping. Pierre Bourdieu's concept of 'habitus' tries to think the meaning of events and practices according to what they enable (for participants) while at the same time recognising that theory itself is a habitus with its own conditions and effects. Michel de Certeau sees the positing of general explanatory horizons – such as culture, discourse or history – as strategies which can be avoided or short-circuited by local, specific and 'one-off' tactics.

In all this terminology there is a refusal of formalism – no event or text is meaningful in isolation – alongside an anxiety regarding generality. No overall totality, explanation or term can be set 'outside' events as their condition, cause or structuring principle. Accordingly, the appeal is frequently made to dynamic models. There is no overarching system but there are sets of interacting forces. Stephen Greenblatt's economic metaphors of exchange and negotiation, as well as his avoidance of explicit theoretical reflection, epitomises the post-historicist problem. Once we recognise that there can be no explanatory horizon which is not itself implicated in the field we wish to explain, how do we justify the task of interpretation? Perhaps the traditional problem of literary theory – the validity of interpretive method – is no longer possible. We just interpret, with a full recognition of the contingency and arbitrariness of our interpretive position. We no longer legitimate our practices through literary theory. The problem might now be the question of what we are interpreting. If there is no general theory of literature or literary criticism how do we decide what to read or what we find when we read? For traditional Marxism interpretation revealed the historical meaning of texts, and did so through a moral imperative. The moral narrative of Marxism and feminism and the idea that reading texts was a form of political enlightenment gave a relatively clear justification for reading canonic literature as the storehouse of power. But if history is no longer a non-textual or pre-textual outside which takes the form of ideology, then interpretation may no longer be the revealing of the meaning of a given text so much as a production. But what we are referring to when we call criticism a production of meaning is not at all clear. For if meaning is no longer intention, ideology or historical context, and if we also want to retain a sense that the text is more than its immanent form, then we might have to come up with quite new ways of undertaking interpretation or reading. The problem of what lies outside the text would still be important. The approaches to be considered in the following chapters provide a number of ways of opening the text to some 'outside' without seeing the non-textual as a brute fact. The idea that the 'outside' of a text is a simple given, such as history, is no longer seen as a possible response. It is this impossibility of history, as well as its perceived necessity, which the following chapters seek to explore.

1

History, historicism and new historicism

A sense of history

It is almost a commonplace that post-structuralism was a form of ahistoricism, and that new historicism marked something like a 'return' to history. After the supposed formalist relativism of the 1980s, literary criticism found history again, although now in a more rigourous and enlightened form. But it would be a mistake to see history as an unproblematic 'given'; and the fact that history has been rethought so thoroughly by new historicism is a consequence of certain moves made in post-structuralist thought. This is not to say that new historicism or current criticism are the effects of post-structuralism. The rethinking of history and historiography which is the focus of this study was prompted by a broad range of concerns which also motivated the post-structuralist endeavour. Problems of the narrative or inscriptive nature of all knowledge, problems of legitimation and situatedness, the contingency of disciplinary boundaries, a sense of political crisis and the absence of consensus and shared narratives all led to a questioning of history as the repository of truth. It would be naive to think that new historicism has arrived in literary criticism as an 'answer' or 'overcoming' of post-structuralist relativism. Not only does new historicism itself draw upon the work of Lacan, Derrida, Foucault and the broad range of post-structuralist thought, the questions raised by the *problem* of historicism have intensified rather than been resolved. If it is the case that the writing of history is a form of power – and a specifically Western and modern form at that – then new historicism may best be seen as a quite specific response within a larger field of questions. Rather than charting new historicism's influences, sources or emergence within the discipline of literary criticism alone, this book locates new historicism within the general question of historicism. It is perhaps new historicism's intense and sustained engagement with literature and its preoccupation with the Renaissance (when the category of literature as an autonomous domain was emerging) that grants the new historicist approach its specific value.

As the following chapters will argue, there has been a long tradition of attempting to *relate* literary texts to history (a tradition dominated by the Marxist enterprise). Not only does the problem of *relation* presuppose that the categories of literature and history are somehow already apparent, it also implies that there is an opposition between the two fields. While the writers considered in later chapters are united in their attempt to think history in terms other than that of a context or horizon to which texts would be related, there is often a sense that the literary or aesthetic will provide an 'other' to history. Literature is often seen as a privileged site where the determinism of history is disrupted, questioned or opened. New historicism, on the other hand, has constantly demonstrated the malleability, contingency and contested character of the category of literature. By demonstrating the complex relationship between the production of the categories of both literature and history, new historicism has contested the boundaries of traditional historiography and literary criticism. Paradoxically, perhaps, it has done so through the practice of literary history itself. Whether this practice provides a convincing response to the burden of historical legitimation is a question explored by this book. In order to see how new historicism has responded to the more general question of knowledge and power this book undertakes a genealogy of new historicism itself. By looking at the trajectory of this particular movement – and its shift away from an early Foucaultianism to a more 'formalist' position – new historicism can be seen as an indication that the problem of literature *and* history still retains a certain force.

The problem with giving an account of the contemporary problem of historicism lies in the fact that so much of our sense of the importance of history is itself historically determined. Our understanding of intellectual movements, theory and method is irreducibly historical. This book, like so many other texts about literary theory, takes the form of a historical narrative; and it does so precisely because our current practices of knowledge and justification operate with an assumption that the meaning of a practice lies in its historical location. Understanding intellectual movements, as well as the very notion of intellectual movement per se, seems to require a story about how that movement came about, its historical genesis, influences and reactions. It is difficult to imagine what literary study would be like if we did not have historical rubrics, such as 'Romanticism' or 'new criticism' which provide us with some fore-understanding of the work we are about to read. We continually acknowledge the inadequacies of general historical labels – we all know that Modernist poems exceed any broad definition of 'Modernism'. At the same time, the possibility of perceiving the complexity of particular works seems to presuppose the general movement within which, or against which, the specific poem is read.

Historical understanding and literary history are not new problems. The questioning of the validity of general historical terms goes back to A. O. Lovejoy's essay on Romanticism, which insisted on referring to 'Romanticisms' (Lovejoy 1924). But there is a sense in which the problems of history and historical labelling have now become far more intense. Not only are we aware – as Lovejoy was – that actual historical events were always belied by general descriptions. There is now a question surrounding the validity of thinking historically. For if we look back further than Lovejoy, to the earliest forms of literary criticism in the eighteenth century, we can see a remarkable ability of critics, such as Joseph Addison (1773) or Samuel Johnson (1781), to discuss texts without a sense of historical context. Shakespeare, Milton and Spenser were compared to each other – and then compared to Ancient Greek and Roman literature. Evaluations were made; the success of particular images discussed; comparisons of tone and vision and merit were made across historical boundaries without any sense of historical reference. Such discussions, of course, had their own historical condition. There had to be some specific domain – such as literature – and some particular practice – such as criticism – which placed diverse authors from a number of periods and genres within a single category of vision. Nowadays, comparisons between Spenser and Shakespeare may well take place; but it is more than likely that comparison would refer to the specificity of context and production. How it is that understanding a text also demands understanding its context is a question this chapter seeks to explore.

We are, we are constantly being told, post-modern: a term whose meaning implies a strong sense of historical sequence. Despite the fact that postmodernity is hailed as an incredulity towards meta-narratives (Lyotard 1984), most disciplines still rely, to a greater or lesser extent, upon some form of historical narrative in order to gain both justification and self-understanding. Post-structuralism is explained by referring back to its emergence from structuralism and phenomenology. Feminism is understood according to a historical trajectory from first-wave (equality) to second-wave (difference) approaches. Current literary practice concerns itself with the issue of post-coloniality. Analytic philosophy understands itself as a result of the 'linguistic turn' (Dummett 1993). Science practices are now consciously aware of their locatedness within historical paradigms (Kuhn 1962). Problems in epistemology and ethics are explained (or diagnosed) by tracing their origins back to the Enlightenment (Habermas 1987; MacIntyre 1981). Historians themeselves see their own methods as the result of historical development (White 1973). And it is this overwhelming sense of history which many of the theorists considered in later chapters feel the need to challenge.

Unfortunately, explaining why history is a problem seems to demand a historical explanation. Foucault's critique of historicism in The Order of Things begins by demonstrating that historicism emerged at a certain point in history. Foucault's own history of historicism can be seen as a challenge to historical method. By turning history against itself his practice of genealogy acknowledges that while we cannot simply step outside history, we can use history critically to demonstrate the specificity and contingency of our own knowledge practices. For Foucault, history is no longer an inevitable and necessary explanatory horizon, a way of revealing the inherent truth or meaning of an event. Not only are histories themselves open to contestation; it is also possible that forms of thought, truth and explanation might take a form other than that of historical narrative. While Foucault identifies historicism as a specifically modern achievement, Michel de Certeau has argued (1988:2) that the writing of history characterises a particularly Western mode of thought. History writing occurs through a 'labour of separation' which produces a division between self and other. De Certeau's response to the ways in which history was used in the processes of colonial expansion is to write a heterology: a thinking of history's 'other'. But if history has an 'other ' it is far from clear how such an other could be identified. As Jacques Derrida has argued in his essay on Foucault (1978a), as soon as one attempts to think of the origin or emergence of concepts such as those of reason, history or truth, one is already using the language of reason and history. History, while being acknowledged as specifically modern, Western, metaphysical or colonialist, has also been seen as an inescapable horizon.

It is with an awareness of history's specificity as well as its seemingly inevitable return that this first chapter charts a history of history. Questioning history might demand a quite conventional historical narrative in order to show just how contingent historical explanation is. But if historiography itself has a history, how ought such a history to be written? The problem of literary history is even more complex. We may acknowledge that all history takes some form of narration and that history is also style, metaphor and text; but how do we then relate literature to history, or history to literature, if the writing of history is now seen as a form of literature? In order to explore this question further we need to see the ways in which conventional literary history has understood itself.

The practice of writing literary histories, along with a strong sense of historical progress in general, emerged, in Europe, in the eighteenth century. While 'histories' had been written prior to the eighteenth century, the idea of history as a meaningful, progressive and developing series of changes began to take shape when writers felt that their present was qualitatively and historically different from their past. This sense of *historical difference*, or the emergence of historical consciousness is frequently attributed to an 'Age of Revolution' in which the goals of freedom were deemed to be obtainable only through a complete and radical break with the past. The writing of history was itself seen to be an act of emancipation. By *representing* the past historians could distance themselves from previous ages (de Certeau 1988: 36). The past could be figured as 'other', while the errors of the past could provide moral lessons for an age which had freed itself from the authority of God and ancient privilege. This sense of a liberation attainable through historical change was expressed forcefully in Thomas Paine's *Rights of Man* (1984 [1791–92]). For Paine each age had to decide for itself what constituted legitimate authority; there could be no power which was trans-historical:

> There never did, there never will, and there never can exist a parliament, or any generation of men, in any country, possessed of the right or the power of binding and controlling posterity to the 'end of time', or of commanding for ever how the world shall be governed, or who shall govern it; and therefore, all such clauses, acts or declarations, by which the makers of them attempt to do what they neither have the right nor the power to do, nor the power to execute, are in themselves null and void. Every age and generation must be free to act for itself, in all cases, as the ages and generations which preceded it. The vanity and presumption of governing beyond the grave, is the most ridiculous and insolent of all tyrannies. ... Every generation is, and must be, competent to all the purposes which its occasions require. It is the living, and not the dead, that are to be accommodated. (Paine 1984: 45–6 [1791–92])

According to the contemporary theorist of history, Hayden White, eighteenth-century or Enlightenment history was characterised by a feeling that the Age of Reason was a final and liberated detachment from the errors and superstitions of the past (White 1973: 51). Enlightenment thinkers saw their own post-Revolutionary present as a liberation from a previous history which was uniformly depicted as a series of injustices and

5

prejudices. This specific sense of history was in many ways a *secular* phenomenon. Reason, rather than faith, became the guiding principle of human life. The order of the world was no longer seen as preordained or justified by God's immutable law. An emphasis on historical change was entwined with a liberal humanism which declared the possibility of progress and rejected any present historical condition as either inevitable or insurmountable. A sense of history as *meaningful* was, according to Kant (1949), part of the very character of reason. As finite beings we cannot know for sure whether we really are progressing, but the idea of morality assumes that reason will achieve its aims. We imagine the world in such a way that reason will achieve its goals; only if we imagine the world in this way – teleologically – does it make sense to act at all. History was seen by Kant and others to be inherently *rational*. History proceeded as a series of breaks with a past in a movement towards emancipation and improvement. The very term 'Enlightenment' captures this sense of becoming.

The eighteenth-century novel, with its narratives of self-improvement, adventure, opportunity and liberation can (and has) been read as an allegory for Enlightenment emancipationism. Fielding's *Tom Jones* (1974 [1749]), which describes Tom's expulsion from the aristocratic structures of Squire Allworthy and Paradise Hall and his progressive journey of discovery and fortune, is both a secularisation of the story of Adam and Eve's banishment from Eden and an individualisation of Enlightenment progressivism. The subsequent crisis of this rationalism is clearly expressed in later Romantic literature. While the novel of individual development depicted a sense of history as the progressive realisation of rational order, the French Revolution (in works such as Blake's *French Revolution* (1791) or Wordsworth's *The Prelude* (1850)) became the motif of a shift in historical thinking. The violence and disorder which followed from this break with the past provided post-Enlightenment literature with an image of history as an apocalyptic break which could not be explained as another moment in reason's continued revelation. History would need to be rethought.

The nineteenth century, again according to White, modified the 'rationalist' view of history by acknowledging that previous 'ages' were not merely erroneous or superstitious; past cultures could be seen to operate according to their own logic or world-view (White 1973: 63). History was not just a line of progress, but was a series of qualitatively distinct wholes. Relations towards the past were no longer characterised by absolute difference and the overcoming of error. The past was granted its own unique value and form of understanding. Accordingly, the present was not just a fulfilment or improvement of the past. The historian's task therefore became interpretive: to make the past comprehensible for the present. Rather than emphasising a break with the past, nineteenth-century historiographers stressed a certain continuity; the gap between past and present could be bridged by interpretive understanding. It is not surprising – with this move away from 'rationalist' history – that literary works also shifted emphasis. The later Romantics, for example, had a strong sense of nostalgia regarding the past. Keats's 'The Eve of St. Agnes' and 'La Belle Dame Sans Merci' are typical of later Romanticism's celebration of mediaevalism, while his 'Ode on a Grecian Urn' meditates on the inevitable loss which comes with history, and the sense of the ineffable and transitory character of the past. The 'past' is both a golden age for which the present may yearn and an inevitably lost origin which can only be represented mythically. The figures on Keats's urn express the transitoriness of any moment; but the design also indicates a time when art was not burdened by a mythic past and was able to live fully in its present. Later nineteenth-century literature was less ambivalent about history. For Tennyson, history could only be loss. His evocations of the classical past had a sense of the value of that past, but this value was set off against the increasing barbarism of the present. In the historical novels of the time, history is no longer allegorised in the fortunes and achievements of an individual life; history is used directly to express social wholes or organisations. There is a sense of the distinctness of the past and its inherent value. Historical novels often looked back to earlier moments, the loss of which is seen as an indictment of the present. George Eliot's *Middlemarch* (1871–72) only had to turn back a few decades to posit a sense of community not yet torn apart by industrialism; James Fenimore Cooper's *The Last of the Mohicans* (1826), as the title implies, celebrates a natural unity of the American landscape and its indigenous culture which was no longer available in Cooper's present; while even the less overtly historical novels – such as those of Dickens – depicted their present less as an enlightened point of arrival than as moments of doubt and impending loss.

Despite these important differences, what characterises both eighteenth- and nineteenth-century historiography is a sense of the radical difference between past and present. Such differences require the historian, particularly as nineteenth-century historiography conceived its task, to understand or make sense of the past. If previous cultures differ significantly from our own then an act of *interpretation* is necessary to discover their logic. It is this *hermeneutic* approach to history, along with the idea of qualitative historical development, which becomes the target for contemporary criticisms of historical narration. To see the past as something to be interpreted suggests that the past harbours a *meaning*. While the rationalism of the eighteenth century may have been tempered by seeing the present as more than an endpoint of a line of progress, nineteenth-century uses of history still operated with an understanding that history was some horizon to be interpreted, a latent narrative, an inevitable site for understanding the present.

It may be argued, of course, that narratives about history – such as those of White and the one charted here – also serve to construct or separate a past from a supposedly more enlightened present. A number of recent studies which reflect on the uses and construction of history cannot but help positing the present as at least disburdened of the myth of history as some unproblematically given fact. Certainly, the figure of Hegel – the philosopher who saw reason *as* history (Hegel 1830: 126) – operates as something like a necessary figure in most accounts of historiography. History prior to Hegel, White argues, saw the past as *mere* error, contingency and a series of events. Only with Hegelian history does the past possess its own specific form of truth. Truth becomes dependent upon historical context, while history is not just a series of events but now forms a context, horizon or 'world' according to which events, meaning and truth are explained. But in writing such an account White himself has to rely on something like a Hegelian approach to history: 'we' are seen as Hegel's heirs, our practices of history writing are both different from and indebted to Hegelian historiography. The idea that history is an act of interpretation and that this interpretation will reveal something about human life is posited as a peculiarly nineteenth-century belief. At the same time, the historical narration of this nineteenth-century belief seems to have an indispensable function. In order to understand ourselves as critical and enlightened historiographers, we continually 'demystify' our past. The project of overcoming historicism, of no longer seeing the past as something that is either 'ours' to interpret or 'other' than our critical present itself depends upon a particular historical narrative.

The eighteenth century with its claims of reason, enlightenment and historical self-awareness is commonly the starting point for narrations, such as those of White, Foucault and de Certeau, who try to think history 'otherwise.' Such attempts to rethink historiography acknowledge the Enlightenment legacy of historicism and often turn to the Renaissance as a way of delimiting modernity and its belief in enlightenment. Similarly, new historicism has been dominated by a concern with Renaissance literature for a large number of reasons. But part of the appeal of the Renaissance must lie in the extent to which it is regarded as the limit point of our own historical horizon. If the enlightenment is characterised by its commitment to historicism, progress, self-understanding and continuity, then the Renaissance is both other – offering different ways of thinking about human life – and the same, close enough to our understanding to give a sense of historical emergence. Not surprisingly, Foucault begins *The Order of Things* with an analysis of Renaissance representation; de Certeau (1988) traces Michelet's Enlightenment historiography back to the Renaissance project of encompassing the New World through knowledge; while new historicism finds a certain *self-awareness* of power in the Renaissance which will later be obscured by Enlightenment rationalism. The Renaissance in general is seen as the origin of ways of thinking about power and knowledge which have not yet achieved the closed, rational and coherent form they will be given in the Enlightenment. Reading the Renaissance is, then, a way of getting past our own imbrication in eighteenth-century rationalism. But in order to see the Renaissance as a body of texts available for literary interpretation we already rely upon some already given understanding of literary history.

Literary history and the eighteenth century

The beginning of literary history in the eighteenth century has a similar structure to the development of Enlightenment historiography described above. Usually acknowledged as the first work of literary history in English, Thomas Warton's *History of English Poetry from the Close of the Eleventh to the Commencement of the Eighteenth Century* (1774-81; Vol. 4 1824) was an attempt to demonstrate the chronological development of literary forms from the first stages of literature in English to Warton's own present. While it has been convincingly argued that English Literature as an institutionalised discipline began in the British universities in the late nineteenth century (Baldick 1983), there was a widespread practice of literary criticism in the eighteenth century which occurred in 'gentleman's' journals and annotated editions, as well as in eighteenth-century poetry itself. This practice of literary criticism was strongly linked to a sense of nationhood and a perception of each nation's own specific history or destiny. One of the first authors to be 'studied' in the same way that the classics had been annotated and explained was the seventeenth-century English poet John Milton. Editions and studies of Milton in the eighteenth century sought to establish that Milton, just as much as Homer and Virgil, could be studied as a classic. As an epic poet Milton was seen to give the English language (rather than Latin or Greek) a sublime form of literary expression, as well as giving the English nation its own specific cultural identity. Similarly, literary histories, such as those written by Warton, sought to give English (or sometimes British) literature a sense of its own specific worth and development. Not only were sonnets and other poetic forms produced which 'hailed' great authors like Spenser, Shakespeare and Milton, there were also 'imitations' – poems written in the style and form of previous poets. Such works celebrated a specific tradition at the same time as they recognised the historical differences between literary styles. 'Imitations' consciously foregrounded 'archaic' or historically specific styles and forms which intensified the sense of literature as a historically developing phenomenon.

Literary-historical consciousness can, therefore, be seen in both the poetry and the literary criticism of the eighteenth century. The poetry of William Blake typically explored a sense of the past by drawing upon the many collections of English myths and fables (such as Percy's *Reliques* (1765)) which proliferated towards the end of the century. In addition to the 'imitations' he wrote of Spenser and Shakespeare, Blake also gave the earlier poet Milton a starring role in his later prophecy, *Milton* (Blake 1966 [1804–08]). Even Wordsworth, who seemed to reject history when he demanded that poetry be the 'spontaneous overflow' of feeling, wrote a eulogy to Milton (celebrating him as a figure of England's favoured destiny) and expressed a profound sense of historical crisis in his own epic *The Prelude*. Furthermore, as is often noted, the faculty of memory and a sense of the importance of the past was of profound importance for Romantic poets. Wordsworth's emphasis on childhood reacted against the scientific and rationalist view of nature as a mere object by seeing nature as always experienced through the memories of childhood; the past was inscribed in the very perception of any present landscape. The sense of literary history was not divorced from the personal history of memory. When Wordsworth begins *The Prelude*, which is an epic of his own poetic development, he echoes the closing lines of Milton's *Paradise Lost*: 'The world was all before them' (Milton 1971: 642 [1667]). Wordsworth's 'The earth is all before me' (Wordsworth 1987: 495 [1850]) serves to locate the poet's personal history within literary history; at the same time it invokes and pays homage to a specifically English tradition of epic.

Such acts of imitation and eulogy were typical of eighteenth-century literary nationalism and historical consciousness. Alongside the more conventional literary histories of the eighteenth century, poetic works such as those of Blake and Wordsworth produced a sense of cultural identity which was thoroughly historical. Like Enlightenment histories which celebrated their own privileged position of Reason in contrast to a misguided past, and while often seeing their own nation as the birthplace of Reason, these literary histories were a celebration of both the present and contemporaneous national identity. At the beginning of *Milton* (1966 [1804–08]) William Blake, despite his anti-enlightenment critique of Reason, still called for a literary renaissance in which the past (dominated by classical or non-English literature) would be superseded by a more self-consciously English present:

> The stolen and Perverted Writings of Homer & Ovid, of Plato & Cicero, which all Men ought to contemn, are set up by artifice against the Sublime of the Bible; but when the New Age is at leisure to Pronounce, all will be set right, & those Grand Works of the more ancient & consciously & professedly Inspired Men will hold their proper rank, & the Daughters of Memory shall become the Daughters of Inspiration. Shakspeare & Milton were both curb'd by the general malady & infection from the silly Greek & Latin slaves of the Sword.
>
> Rouze up, O Young Men of the New Age! … We do not want either Greek or Roman Models if we are but just & true to our own Imaginations…(Blake 1966: 480).

Romantic, or post-Enlightenment, poets had a sense that as poet-prophets they played a unique role in history. Their task was to awaken readers to the culmination of their nation's history and literary destiny. They saw their own present as in many ways an 'end' of history – the revolutionary present would open into a moment of eternal fullness and fulfilment. Such was the optimism of early Romanticism. Later Romantic poets may have had more of a sense of the 'fallenness' of the present in relation to a more golden past, but such a sense of loss was already a reaction against the earlier historical optimism.

Recent criticism has, however, challenged this traditional historical picture of Romanticism. We think of the early Romantics and their sense of liberation and political revolution as a golden age of historical hope inevitably surpassed by the awareness of revolutionary failure. The canonisation of Romanticism has reinforced this narrative. Wordsworth's *Prelude* – despite the fact that it was not published in his lifetime – is seen as the epitome of good Romantic poetry. The emphasis in *The Prelude* on the personal compensation gained through poetry is elevated at the expense of other, widely-read texts, such as Byron's *Don Juan* which sustain a demand for political and social transformation (McGann 1976). The contested nature of literary Romanticism demonstrates that the literary history of the eighteenth and nineteenth centuries, no less than the history of the

11

Enlightenment, is thoroughly determined by contemporary considerations of power and knowledge. The traditional history of Romanticism – in which hopes for a historical revolution are displaced by a more mythic, personal and spiritual sense of history – can be seen as a response to twentieth-century concerns. The depoliticisation of Romanticism is achieved by seeing its historical trajectory as mythic – the French Revolution is interpreted as a metaphor rather than an event – but this mythologisation has its own political and historical character. Romanticism, as it was constructed in America from the 1960s, 'mirrored' literary criticism's own preoccupation with post-structuralist questions of origin, time, tropes and subjectivity; at the same time, post-structuralism's appeal lay in its own 'Romantic' compatibility with current political concerns: in a postwar, cold-war, late capitalist and increasingly rationalised environment Romantic poetry 'offered'both a compensation and a justification for a retreat from political and historical concerns. Jerome McGann's criticism of the canonisation and unquestioned periodisation of Romanticism proceeds by writing another historical narrative. For McGann it is not a question of turning to the real *meaning* of Romantic texts so much as establishing other contexts. If we no longer see *The Prelude* as the key Romantic epic, then other concerns will construct other historical horizons. McGann's work on Byron, and the similarly forceful re-reading of Wordsworth undertaken by Marjorie Levinson, can still be seen as post-Romantic. For both McGann and Levinson (1986), engaging with a text demands engaging with its history. To this extent their work sees history as a context within which texts ought properly be read. This is not to deny that history is seen as a site of contestation and dispute; but it is history, nevertheless which forms the horizon for the text's political meaning. The Enlightenment idea that history and historical self-awareness is a vehicle of emancipation remains both the object, and the assumed premise, of contemporary re-readings of Romanticism.

Recent literary criticism and its concern with a text's historical location can be seen as a continuation of the earliest forms of literary criticism. The practice of literary criticism not only emerged once writers began to have a sense of themselves as existing within a particular tradition, the very sense of literary tradition was given through the practices of history writing and literary criticism. Milton, for example, was in many ways 'constructed' as a national epic poet in the eighteenth century both through literary criticism in the narrow sense and through literary works which emphasised his English and epic grandeur. The different genres – of literature, literary criticism and history writing – employed similar styles, figures, images and rhetorical techniques. Consequently, it would be naive to argue that literary Romanticism was 'apocalyptic' in tone *because* of the historical fact of the French Revolution, or that history writing was progressivist because it drew upon literary figures of eschatology and utopia. Literature did not simply 'borrow from', or reflect, the writing of history; as many writers have shown, history writing itself was profoundly 'literary' – employing all those features of narrative, metaphor and dramatisation which characterised more overtly literary texts (White 1987; Gossman 1986). To say that literary criticism was 'historical' is not to say that it began to draw upon some outside information or 'context' from which it was, essentially, separate; it is, rather, to note that these new practices of criticism and history were operating with the same sense of difference between the past and the enlightened and liberated present. Just as Romantic literature adopted an apocalyptic form in which the errors and prejudices of the past gave way to the illuminating freedom of the present, and just as enlightenment histories projected millenial triumphs of reason, so literary histories conveyed both a sense that literary history was not just a series of forms but a meaningful development and that the present was a different and privileged moment from which such differences could be surveyed.

Consequently, from the late eighteenth century, literature was profoundly aware of its own position in history, and in a specifically literary history. In a continuation of what is, essentially, still a Romantic view of literary history, the contemporary American critic, Harold Bloom, has even argued that modern literature (or literature since Milton) is characterised by an 'anxiety of influence'. According to Bloom (1973) a poet writes in order to respond to previous literary history and can only write great poetry if motivated by a desire to 'overcome' the influence of previous poets. Such a task will necessarily fail because the poet cannot but reveal his debt to the past; but English poetry is nothing other than a series of such failures. Bloom's vision of literary history, while crediting poets with a profound historical awareness, locates literary history in its own autonomous domain. The idea of the poet's own historical context (revolutions, wars, biography and society) are irrelevant to Bloom's 'line' of literary history. It is the influence of previous poets, rather than current surroundings, which marks a poet's place in history. While Bloom's theory of 'anxiety' represents an extreme version of the theory of the continuity of a literary tradition and the autonomy of literary history, a large amount of contemporary literary history still refers to nothing other than a writer's place within a 'line' of literary influence and innovation. One

13

could even argue that Bloom has merely reiterated Romanticism's own sense of history as a single line of development within an exclusively literary heritage. For both Bloom and many of the Romantics, history as an *external* context is left out of the picture. It is precisely this *displacement* of history which has been the focus for many recent cultural materialist and new historicist critics. For Anthony Easthope, Wordsworth's mourning of an irretrievable childhood or lost personal past conceals what is really a political predicament. The failure to achieve social liberation through the French revolution (Wordsworth's actual historical circumstances) is refigured in his poetry as a timeless and necessary loss of *subjective* unity (Easthope 1993: 32). Readings such as those of Easthope (and Marjorie Levinson and Jerome McGann) criticise not only the poem's failure to represent its historical conditions but also the subsequent tradition of criticism which has accepted Romanticism's displacement of political and social circumstances onto personal or subjective failures and losses.

It is possible, therefore, to consider some of the central theories of literary history as a symptom of Romanticism's reduction of history to personal memory or literary tradition. For example, many contemporary critics who *have* considered the role of such events as the French Revolution in the development of literary history, have gone on to argue that great poetry takes place when a poet abandons their hopes for salvation within history and instead turns to the compensations of imaginative or poetic resolution. The most well-known example of this argument was formulated by M. H. Abrams (1971) who argued that the best Romantic poetry was written when poets abandoned historical and political hopes for change and embarked upon purely aesthetic and spiritual resolutions. This relation between literature and history assumes the ability of literature to detach itself from some supposedly prior or independent historical context by turning to the realm of the specifically literary. In many ways this Romantic assumption of the autonomy of the literary sphere forms the target for the new historicist and cultural materialist re-readings of literature which we will examine later in this chapter.

Historical understanding and the nineteenth century

While the eighteenth century may have given rise to a historical consciousness in which qualitative temporal changes were seen as capable of affecting human life, it was in the nineteenth century that the *difference* of the past was seen not solely in the form of ignorance and error. Rather than seeing the past as so many failed or misguided attempts at a reason which was universal, the nineteenth century regarded past ages as possessing their own meaning and order. Relating to the past would therefore be an act of understanding rather than dismissal or overcoming. What makes this issue complex, however, is that this distinction between eighteenth-century Enlightenment historiography and nineteenth-century hermeneutic historiography is itself a product of the nineteenth-century's own historical self-awareness. Despite the claims of its historiographers, the nineteenth-century was not a complete break with the rationalist histories of the Enlightenment. In many ways Romantic and Victorian historiography continued the teleological (or goal-oriented) character of the eighteenth century. Just as Enlightenment historiography saw the present as the final point in a progress of reason, so nineteenth-century historiographers argued that history was not a random series of differing worldviews but had a definite end in view. The difference really lay in the character of the goal of history. Liberation was no longer conceived as the overcoming of the past through reason, but as an understanding of the past through history.

Rather than seeing the past as completely shrouded in error, nineteenth-century historians believed that they had overcome the rationalism of the eighteenth century by their attempt to understand and see a positive value in previous ages. The German philosopher, G. W. F.Hegel, provides the most celebrated example of a historiography which combines both teleology and an attempt to understand the past. Hegel, unlike the rationalist historians, did not see religion as a form of mystified superstition; rather, for Hegel, religion possessed a truth of its own (Hegel 1807). The idea of God represented a form of being which transcended the merely day-to-day existence of ordinary life. When individuals participate in religions they do so because they can (however inaccurately) sense a form of spirit which lies beyond their own limited experience. But this sense of transcendent spirit is destined to be more authentically understood as human history itself. Eventually, according to Hegel, consciousness will understand that ideas of 'God' are actually ways of representing the human spirit in an external form. Religion, therefore, is 'true', in so far as it provides an accurate picture of the way in which individuals relate to spirit; but these representations must be understood as stages on the way to a more rational historical awareness. The goal of all history, for Hegel, is historical understanding. By recognising the development and becoming of spirit, human life will no longer posit an external goal or value. Cultures will not be directed to a transcendent God but will see that historical development is the true aim of spirit. Earlier historical periods

15

will be recognised as stages on the way to historical becoming. To criticise or dismiss past forms of religious life misses the extent to which those forms of life take part in the qualitative historical development of human consciousness. Only when an actual overcoming of the distance between humanity and external spirit has occurred can a non-religious (and rational) understanding be formed. So, only when humanity recognises that God is a projection of its own spirit can philosophical awareness take place. Like Enlightenment secularists, Hegel's history had a goal – the recognition of all spiritual creations as human – although there were a number of ways in which this 'end' of history was conceived. But, unlike those who conceived of religion as error, Hegel recognised that religious culture was true for its time and that such a history of representations would need to have taken place for ultimate rational self-awareness to be eventually realised.

Enlightenment historiography and modern criticism

The continuity between an eighteenth-century historiography of enlightenment and a later historicism of empathy and interpretation can be seen in Hegel's philosophy of history, a theory which will be of central importance to Marx and subsequent Marxist theories of literature. Hegel shares with the Enlightenment the belief that the goal of history is reason and that reason will manifest itself as the overcoming of error and will issue in absolute self-understanding. However, Hegel's philosophy also acknowledges a relative, and in fact historically relative, 'truth' to previous forms of understanding. What Hegelianism allows is a recognition that historical truth is not a question of the accuracy of events but concerns the way individuals live those events. If an individual lives at a moment in history where there is no democracy and where he or she seems to have no control over their life, then it is not surprising that they will think that there is an external power, or God, which rules their existence absolutely and tyrannically. Not only can the historian understand belief in myth as in keeping with the alienation individuals might feel from the external world, the same historian would also have to acknowledge that these individuals could not believe otherwise. Given their position in history there is a certain 'truth' in the representations of an external God and an alien world. Only when reason is fully developed and the nation-state is formed in which all individuals are fully self-determining could humanity see that it is reason, not some external God, spirit or matter, which governs existence.

The idea of the relative truth of historical world-views is frequently used to interpret literary texts. If we take an existential novel for example, say Camus's L'Etranger (1957), it could be argued that the extreme isolation and angst experienced by the central character is not a universal condition of human alienation (as the narrative suggests); instead, the experience of alienation can be explained as an accurate representation of the way humans live their lives in a modern world deprived of the capacity to make political decisions or interact in a human community. A Marxist critic might go on to argue that this historically specific sense of alienation is due to economic circumstances. The control of capital, and hence social power, is no longer in the hands of the producer of commodities and so a sense of alienation or disempowerment appears natural and inevitable. For a Marxist, following Hegel's insight of the 'relative' truth of previous historical representations, the existential theory of angst would be true in so far as it accurately represents the lived alienation of the historical moment. But it would be an act of 'false consciousness' to represent such alienation as necessary or universal. Furthermore, the work of literature might be seen as ideological in so far as it takes a particular historical moment – post-war capitalist Europe – and universalises or naturalises that form of life as a representation of an essential and invariant human condition. Such interpretations of history and historical representation as just described rely upon some ultimate historical end (either Hegel's final embodiment of reason in the state or Marx's proletarian revolution) in order to read the deep or true historical meaning behind the ideological representations of the past.

In the Marxist literary criticism of the twentieth century, it is not only narrative content which is available for demystification. Literary forms themselves can be seen to represent ideology. Tragedy, it has been argued, because it pits human life against inexplicable and indomitable forces, accurately represents a pre-modern and theological world-view. The novel, on the other hand, in so far as it shows an individual 'hero' successfully making his or her way in a world of competitive but exploitable circumstances and other persons encapsulates the ideology of modern capitalism (Goldmann 1975). The Marxist critic Georg Lukacs (1981) argued that entire movements in literary history, such as Modernism with its emphasis on interior monologue, were acts of ideological concealment in which real historical forces were occulted. Similarly, Fredric Jameson (1984) has argued that postmodernism, with its abandonment of coherent narrative and determinate context, has lost all sense of historicity and, therefore, conceals its actual political and economic reality.

Although Marxist literary criticism has a long and conflicting tradition of questioning the relation between the literary work and the history from which it emerges, it is united by a commitment to a 'deeper' level of history operating in a text than at first seems apparent. History, as either the forces of production or the ideological superstructure which reflects them, is seen to provide some final and more authentic level of understanding. Like Hegel, Marxist critics see history as some ultimate explanatory horizon, which is capable of revealing the ideological truth of the work of art. Literary works are conceived as so many manifestations of ideology, the imaginary representation of actual historical existence. Even Marxist critics who have attempted to go beyond Hegel's 'expressivist' relation between history and literature (in which the text reveals or expresses a historical form of life) have still had to rely on some historical explanation to relate economic and social circumstances to literature.

Post-structuralist forms of Marxist criticism have attempted to incorporate the insights of Louis Althusser, who sought to overcome the vestiges of Hegelianism within Marxism. In his most influential essay, 'Ideology and ideological state apparatuses', Althusser (1971) argues that areas of cultural life (traditionally, the superstructure) are not entirely caused or determined by the economic forces of production (the base or infrastructure). Arguing against mechanical or expressivist causality, Althusser puts forward a notion of 'structural causality' in which ideological functions have a necessary and integral role in maintaining relations of power. Ideology no longer merely *reflects* economic circumstances; it plays an active role in enabling those circumstances. (Althusser's theory will be explored more fully in a later chapter.) Whereas critics like Goldmann had argued that the structure of the novel reflected the individualism of modern capitalism, Althusserian critics have shown the ways in which literature can *produce* individuals in order that the capitalist forces of production may continue. Ideas of the self, morality, propriety and subjectivity are, according to this picture, *effects* of literary production.

Critics have differed as to how the production of such subjects occurs. Some have argued that by presenting coherent narratives in which individuals are depicted as autonomous moral agents, authors perpetuate the ideology of modern subjectivity (Belsey 1980). Others have argued that the nature of writing can itself either reinforce or, if it is 'revolutionary', destabilise subjectivity (Easthope 1983). The process of narrative itself, it is claimed, can provide a symbolic resolution to concrete historical contradictions and hence enable the system of relations of production (Jameson 1981). Despite their reaction against Hegelian explanations of the relation between representation and lived relations to history, all these post-Althusserian critics rely upon a historical narrative of the shift between pre-modern, or feudal, societies and modern, capitalist cultural formations. The idea of the individual as a necessary outgrowth of capitalist ideology and the task of demystifying this ideology in the name of some deeper historical truth is still present to a greater or lesser extent. Indeed, the attack on the individual, subjectivity and humanism is still a principle motive in contemporary cultural materialism. While Althusserian Marxists and cultural materialist critics frequently reject the idea that there is any truth outside ideology, they still engage in a critique of literature in the name of some non-literary idea of social change, if not revolution. Following the work of Pierre Macherey, it is often argued that the contradictions inherent in the representation of ideology will of themselves bring about the overcoming of that particular ideology. However, even this reliance upon 'contradiction' (as opposed to some ultimate historical truth in the Hegelian sense) needs to be validated by a historical narrative in which the relations of capitalism and capitalist ideology are seen as in some ways distortions of a more proper form of social relations.

The 'overcoming' of Hegelian teleology has been one of the major problems for both literary theory and social theory (Descombes 1980; Young 1990). And the Hegelian approach to literary history has not occurred solely within the Marxist tradition. One of the more influential works in Shakespeare and Renaissance literary studies is E. M. W. Tillyard's *The Elizabethan World Picture* (Tillyard 1943) – a work against which new historicist and cultural materialist critics have often defined themselves. While Tillyard does not go so far as to posit some ultimate form of historical truth or revelation against which the past can be read, his work does employ an 'expressivist' theory of history which, like Hegel, interprets imaginative forms and representations by demonstrating the ways in which they reflect the social world from which they emerged. Presupposed in Tillyard's reading is the Hegelian idea of a uniform 'mind-set' or 'spirit' which characterises a specific historical age. The feudal world, Tillyard argues, is characterised by a sense of natural order and hierarchy. Just as the serf is naturally below the lord who is naturally below the king who is naturally below God, so this age had a philosophy of the 'great chain of being' in which every different being or form of life had its own essence and its own place in a divinely-ordained hierarchy. This sense of order is then reflected in Renaissance literature. In the dramas of Shakespeare, for example, there are quite definite ideas about natural order – the chaos of the comedies always resolves in the end with a return to hierarchy in

19

which the sovereign powers again take control; the disruptive forces of youth are stabilised within marriages and nature returns to its normal course. Tragedies on the other hand are concerned with violations of natural order; because, for example, there is an initial transgression (Macbeth kills Duncan) the bonds and ties of social order are disrupted and chaos ensues. Only when such transgressions have been paid out or expiated can the social order return to normal. The sense of tragedy reveals the frailty of human order and the necessity for a divine order to intervene and redress the failure of human power to live up to natural law. In the history plays, Tillyard (1944) argues, Shakespeare presents a cycle of history in which the transgressions and denials of natural justice by one ruler are eventually paid for in a series of tragedies. The cycle of history then culminates in the divinely-ordained and 'natural' rule of a just king. Tillyard therefore accepts that literature faithfully expresses something like a 'world-picture' which is itself directly related to a period, in this case Elizabethan England. Similar arguments have been made by critics such as Ian Watt (1957) in relation to the novel – that it, too, expresses the economic and social realities of the modern world – and by other critics in relation to other historical circumstances. In all of these cases it is assumed that literature is deeply embedded in something like a historical context, that that context can be reawakened by an act of literary interpretation and that the study and reading of literature is appropriately a historical activity. Furthermore, while social forms and ideas may differ through history it is assumed that each period or era forms a single and coherent whole; difference is acknowledged between but not within periods.

For the most part, then, some idea of 'expressive' causality (whereby literature reveals, mirrors or even enables a similarly structured economic base) has dominated Marxist literary studies. But the relationship between literature and history in general, and not only within specifically Marxist forms of criticism, has usually posited a similar relationship between the 'world-picture' and its literary expression. To speak of either 'ideology', 'world-picture' or 'mind-set' is to have already some idea of history as a series of coherent cultures, each with a particular and more or less uniform world-view. Even philosophies of history which reacted against the teleology and rationalism of Hegelian history still retained some notion of ideology or world-view which referred to a framework of concepts or a way of thinking which would typify a culture. In the post-Hegelian Marxism of Althusser, ideology need not be a mere reflection of the economic base; it could possess a 'relative autonomy'. But in Althusserian criticism the increased role of ideology only emphasises the idea of a cultural totality. In extreme cases of such criticism, there is no 'outside' to ideology, and historical change can only be brought about by contradictions inherent within ideology. If as subjects, so the argument goes, we are nothing other than a 'nexus of discourses' produced by ideology, then resistance cannot come in the form of any natural or pre-existing freedom or Reason. Rather, change occurs when ideology itself (as it were, of its own accord) reveals its incoherence. Granting ideology this importance or semi-autonomy only increases the extent to which culture or a worldview can be examined as an ostensible totality.

Similarly, even non-Marxist reactions against the totalising narratives of Hegelian history, did not depart significantly from the idea of historically specific cultural consciousness. The movement of historicism or *Weltanschauung* ('world-view') philosophy is identified primarily with the work of the German thinker Wilhelm Dilthey (1976). Dilthey argued that historical study required Einfuhlung ('empathy') on the part of the historian. While rejecting the economic determinism of Marxist historiography, as well as the trajectory which would imply historical progression to a higher form of revolution, demystification and enlightenment, Dilthey's historicism gave each culture its own value, logic and coherence. The historian would no longer exercise a hermeneutics of suspicion which would reveal the hidden truth behind a culture (as in the Marxist critique of ideology). Rather, the culture of the historian was no more enlightened than the culture under examination and therefore possessed no epistemologically privileged ground from which the historian could survey and demystify history. In fact, 'truth' was historically relative; there simply was no trans-historical standard from which the historian could judge the representations of past cultures. Because it was the very character of human life to make and interpret its own world and create its own circumstances, history was no longer something that a prior human essence (reason, humanity) went through. On the contrary, human life was historical in its very essence and only existed in so far as it occurred historically. There would, therefore, be no trans-historical or universal law which could explain or judge history: such notions as law and universality were themselves the products of culture and history. Because Dilthey located all knowledge, practices and representations within human 'life', and because that 'life' was in its very nature historical, there could be no appeal to some law or first cause outside history. Historiography would be, therefore, not an act of demystification or critique but a practice of interpretation, where one culture encounters and uncovers the meaning of another historical formation. No ultimate truth or reality could be gained or revealed through the study of history. The historian's task would always be conditioned and delimited by his or her own historical position which would not in itself permit of ultimate explication. History could increase understanding of one's culture by revealing its difference or specificity; but in so far as history was the final court of appeal, the first and last word of human life, it could no longer be used to lead to some 'higher' enlightened truth.

This radical historical relativism was an attempt to understand cultures on their own terms and not according to some predetermined set of values, such as Hegel's reason or Marx's theory of economic development (Marx 1867). Historicism of this type presented a challenge to the interpretive enterprise. The act of encounter or empathy was seen as inherently valuable; but it was also important that the specificity of the past be retained. Because the past *was* different it would demand interpretation, but this hermeneutic leap should not be a reduction of the difference of the past. The idea that human life was nothing other than historical differentiation was seen as a way of overcoming the limits of the present. But the difference of the past was understood within a single horizon – history – while different periods were still seen as integrated wholes. The world-view was no longer a 'reflection', but it was seen as a coherent cultural totality which delimited the possibilities of experience within a culture. While there was no brute reality seen as prior to, or determinant of, this world-view, life was apprehended as an examinable cultural whole which could be interpreted, described and reawakened by historians in a subsequent culture.

While Dilthey's version of historicism may have had no direct effect on English literary studies, the practice of historicism (in contradistinction to a Marxist explanatory or demystificatory model) has usually been the only form other than Marxism undertaken by literary-historical enquiry. Indebted firmly to a nineteenth-century historiography of interpretation, such non-Marxist studies in literary history have intersected with the 'history of ideas' and have set as their goal descriptions of 'wholes' such as 'the Elizabethan world-picture', 'the eighteenth-century background', 'the age of revolution' and even 'postmodernism'. While not locating literature within its own autonomous historical development, in the manner of critics like Bloom and Abrams, these histories of ideas see the text as part of a culture and as expressing that culture in the way that a historical document reveals forms of life. A traditional example is the series of studies by Basil Willey (1940, 1949, 1950), who locates literary works within a general background of *ideas*. But there are more recent, and influential, examples which argue that works can be understood by referring them to a set of background assumptions which characterise a historical epoch. Jurgen Habermas, for example, explains post-structuralism as a development of the ideas of Nietzsche, Heidegger and Bataille. The position of writers like Derrida and Foucault, he argues (Habermas 1987) can be explained by situating them within modernity. But for Habermas, this historical picture is one of texts and ideas; the authors he locates are situated according to their philosophical and literary heritage. Historical understanding does not refer to events but to the development of thought. The approach of historicism and the history of ideas locates texts within a general horizon of understanding – a background, world-view or tradition – without supposing that these texts can be explained by non-textual causes such as the economy, progress or technological change. Such approaches differ from Marxism in their refusal to posit any extra-historical rationale or cause, but they share with Marxism an emphasis on the meaning, unity and relevance of historical periods.

From all this it can be seen that the relation between the literary text and history can be theorised in a number of ways. There can be arguments that there is a direct causal relation between the environment in which a text is produced and the ultimate product. Or, the text can be seen as mere propoganda creating a 'false consciousness' which conceals the real truth of history. Theories of greater complexity have also been formulated which argue (a) that texts reflect social forms, (b) that texts are symbolic resolutions to intolerable social conditions, (c) that texts are valuable in so far as they reveal social conditions, (d) that texts produce social conditions and (e) that texts are part of the culture which is itself like a text. All these theories tend to posit a relation between history and text in which history, to a greater or lesser extent, is seen as a 'context' against which the text can be interpreted. It is this relational model, along with the idea of ideology or world-picture as the entity which relates the text to history which will be challenged by new historicism.

New historicism

Unlike other critical practices such as deconstruction, structuralism, Marxism, or even feminism, which have relied upon developments in philosophy and social theory, new historicism has been reluctant to identify itself with any particular theorist or theory. Indeed, new historicism had, until recently, remained an ostensibly untheorised practice with its main exponent, Stephen Greenblatt, declaring that new historicism was actually

23

'no doctrine at all' (Greenblatt 1989: 1). This reluctance to theorise is not accidental to new historicist practice; such reticence stems from both a calculated rejection of any unified theory of meaning and new historicism's debt to theorists, like de Certeau and Foucault, whose work in many ways problematised the primacy and possibility of any general philosophical discourse. Ostensibly, then, new historicism seems to proceed in a rather *ad hoc* manner – drawing texts from various domains (science, jurisprudence, travel writing, etc.) in order to seek the resonances and distinctions which operate among discourses. Relying heavily upon archival material and historical documents, new historicism can be seen as a form of textual inductivism – dealing directly with sources and particulars rather than pre-given totalities such as a 'world-picture' or 'ideology'.

Perhaps the best description of new historicism could be achieved by concentrating on its reaction against those earlier forms of literary history which relied upon general models in order to relate the text to history. Indeed, it is this supposed division between text and history (however complex either of these terms is seen to be) which is challenged by new historicism. New historicism is neither a fully-fledged textualism (where the world exists only as a consequence of discursive construction); nor is it something like a Marxism which would see the history of economic forces as a primary or pre-textual determinant. Rather than seeing the text, or culture, as dependent upon or distinct from history, new historicism focuses on the way in which social forces produce such boundaries between reality and text, or history and culture. There is no 'cultural' domain as such which is either produced by, or productive of, history; rather, the cultural/aesthetic domain is an area of contestation where various forces (aesthetic, political, historical, economic, etc.) circulate. The idea that an autonomous aesthetic domain is neither pre-given nor transhistorical has also been a central tenet of cultural materialism. Drawing upon the earlier work of Raymond Williams, Alan Sinfield has even seen the enquiry into how art is recognised and categorised as a feature which sets cultural materialism apart from new historicism. As Sinfield argues, 'Insistence on the process through which a text achieves its current estimation is the key move in cultural materialism, and a principal difference in emphasis from new historicism' (Sinfield 1994: 28). This 'insistence' on the processes of art's legitimation goes a long way to explaining the cultural materialist concern with Shakespeare whose work, since the eighteenth century, has been inextricably intertwined with projects of producing and defining British national identity. But despite Sinfield's claim that this concern with the construction of the aesthetic sphere is unique to cultural materialism, new historicism has also frequently explored the ways in which cultural boundaries are produced. In fact, Joel Fineman has explicitly argued that the categories of both the literary *and history* are immanent to, and formed by, particular historical formations and particular ways of writing (Fineman 1994: 116).

In the closest thing new historicism has to a manifesto, 'Towards a poetics of culture', Stephen Greenblatt (1989) sets himself against both Marxism and post-structuralism by drawing attention to the ways in which new historicism refuses any general theory of the relation between art and history. According to Greenblatt, Marxists, such as Fredric Jameson, are critical of capitalism because of the ways in which it divides experience into various domains (such as the autonomously aesthetic) – domains which the Marxist wants to reunite by relating all events back to a historical ground. On the other hand, according to Greenblatt, post-structuralists, such as Lyotard, see capitalism as totalising in its reduction of all experience to 'a single language and a single network' (Greenblatt 1989: 4). For Greenblatt, however, neither of these ways of approaching a historical period is satisfactory because both Marxism and post-structuralism define the relation between text and history as singular and monolithic. Greenblatt, however, sees the cultural domain as a contradictory site: a place where capitalism is both enforced and challenged; an arena in which history is both revealed and produced; and, most importantly, an area which is both carved out as autonomously aesthetic and as ideologically determined. Consequently, a work can have neither a unified ideology (such as 'Elizabethan', 'bourgeois' or 'subversive') nor an entirely aesthetic function. While there may be a distinction between the political and the poetic (1989:3), Greenblatt argues that this distinction will always be the effect of a dynamic 'circulation' in which cultural boundaries are produced through 'practical strategies of negotiation and exchange' (1989:8). Like Greenblatt, Louis Montrose also argues for the hybridity of social formations:

> A closed and static, singular and homogeneous notion of ideology must be succeeded by one that is heterogeneous and unstable, permeable and processual. It must be emphasised that an ideological dominance is qualified by the specific conjunctures of professional, class and personal interests of individual cultural producers (such as poets and playwrights); by the spectators, auditors and readers who variously consume cultural productions; and by the relative autonomy – the specific properties, possibilities and limitations – of the cultural medium being worked. (Montrose 1989: 22)

25

Consequently, the relation between text and history cannot be given in a pre-formulated theory; on the contrary, the interaction between text and world, between the materiality of the text and its produced meaning and between art and history should be the object of investigation in each critical practice. The idea of a 'relation' between text and history, then, becomes highly problematic. Whereas Marxist and post-structuralist theories argue for a specific relation between text and history or between aesthetics and politics, the new historicist reading proceeds by investigating the ways in which texts produce such boundaries. The relation between the text and its historical context becomes dynamic. Not only is history itself only accessible as text, the text itself is also the result of certain non-discursive forces (highly-material determinants such as printing, performance conditions, distribution, etc.). Consequently, Greenblatt argues that critical practice should focus on the 'negotiation and exchange' by which the representation of history is made possible. Similarly, Louis Montrose has also drawn attention to the 'dynamic, unstable, and reciprocal relationship between the discursive and material domains' (Montrose 1989: 23). The text can no longer be a reflection or epiphenomenon of the pre-textual world (however complex or dialectical such a process of reflection is understood to be). This principle is also stated by Catherine Gallagher:

> Although there has been a certain amount of controversy over just what the new historicism is, what constitutes its essence and what its accidents, most of its adherents and opponents would agree that it entails reading literary and nonliterary texts as constituents of historical discourses that are both inside and outside of texts and that its practitioners generally posit no fixed hierarchy of cause and effect as they trace the connections among texts, discourses, power, and the constitution of subjectivity (Gallagher 1989: 37).

This problematisation of the relationships between art and power, text and history, or aesthetics and ideology is one of the reasons why new historicist critics have focused so attentively on Renaissance drama. Because such texts are performed, and because of their central role in public life, critics can investigate the material divisions which produce the conceptual divisions between the real and the aesthetic. By describing the architecture of Renaissance theatres, critics have shown the way actual spatial divisions produced the boundaries between the fiction on stage and the 'real' world surrounding the stage (Orgel 1975). At the same time, critics have concurrently demonstrated the ways in which Renaissance drama worked against such divisions. One need only think of the common 'play within the play' motif as it is used in *Hamlet*, or the projection of the fictional world onto the 'real' audience at the close of *A Midsummer Night's Dream* to see the ways in which Renaissance drama worked against the very conditions which made it possible: the distinction between the stage's world of artifice and the supposed reality surrounding it. Many Renaissance dramas also reveal the extent to which real political power is itself based upon skilful performance. Two figures who have received a great deal of new historicist and cultural materialist attention – Prospero of *The Tempest* and Hal of *Henry IV Part 1* – reveal the extent to which kingship is conceived as dramatic performance. But not only do such plays reveal the historical practice of the performance of power, critics have also demonstrated that the performances of such plays were themselves parts of the ruling structures of spectacle. Pardon scenes, executions, trials and pageants could appear in plays as forms of spectacle but they could also borrow from the effects such scenes could have in the real world, which was itself considered to be a form of stage. The king or queen very often attended Renaissance masques or plays and their presence at the performance was often built into the significance of the work as a whole (Orgel 1975: 8; Montrose 1988: 32).

The actual material and spatial conditions in which a work is produced are, therefore, not considered as extraneous but as productive of the play's very meaning. In *Measure for Measure*, the final scene in which the Duke pardons Angelo can be interpreted as either a repetition of the demonstration of power by a ruler which occurs in the 'real' world (in which case the play would borrow materials from reality), or as a critical reflection upon power's dependence on spectacle (in which case 'reality' would be revealed as another mode of performance). New historicism's problematisation of the relation between the text and its context has meant that it has often taken both such possibilities simultaneously, such that texts are often read as both constructions and negotiations of the relation between art and life. *Measure for Measure* would produce the boundary between the 'real' pardon and its dramatic replication at the same time as it worked upon the very 'dramatic' effect of the real. To what extent the performance reinforced or undermined the legitimacy of social spectacle would have to depend on its particular location. The effect of a play would lie in its possible reception; there would be no inherently subversive or reactionary meaning. The processes of subversion and containment are mutual rather than mutually exclusive. Because a text can be read and performed in a number of situations its meaning is necessarily multiple. Texts both produce *and* reveal mechanisms of power; it is the location and condition of each particular performance or reading which will distribute such contradictory forces. The consumption and production of texts are not external contexts which can be brought to bear upon a text's central meaning. Such processes are central to the text's capacity to mean. Moving away from seeing meaning as inherent in the text, new historicists see the text as a work which manufactures its meaning through various procedures (including production, consumption and circulation).

New historicism in many ways defines its practice against any theory of meaning in which the text would have its own single and determinate semantic content and moves towards the idea of the text as practice: the critic focuses on the material effects and circumstances produced by the text and in which the text is produced. Against interpretation which would reveal a text's hermeneutic depth, new historicism concentrates on a description of the discursive and material domains in which a text is situated. This anti-interpretive stance is a clear reaction against all those previous accounts of literary history which would see the text as possessing a meaning which could be related to, or explained by, a somewhat extraneous history.

While Greenblatt rejects any overarching theory of the relationship between art and society under capitalism – neither Lyotard's theory of phrases nor Jameson's Marxism – he still retains the historical context of capitalism itself. The processes of 'negotiation and exchange' are not explanations of the way texts work in general; they are, he argues, specific to capitalism:

> from the sixteenth century, when the effects for art of joint-stock company organization first began to be felt, to the present, capitalism has produced a powerful and effective oscillation between the establishment of distinct discursive domains and the collapse of these domains into one another. It is this restless oscillation rather than the securing of a particular fixed position that constitutes the distinct power of capitalism. The individual elements – a range of discontinuous discourses on the one hand, the monological unification of all discourses on the other – may be found fully articulated in other economic and social systems; only capitalism has managed to generate a dizzying, seemingly inexhaustible circulation between the two. (Greenblatt 1989: 8)

Greenblatt does not, therefore, 'universalise' the process of capitalism as some of his critics have claimed (Graff 1989: 180; Wilson 1992: 10). His focus on the production of culture as a separate aesthetic domain relies upon a recognition of the 'contradictory' nature of capitalism which, it is argued, both divides experience into separate domains and dissolves such distinctions into totalising categories. However, Greenblatt's reaction against any monolithic theory of the way capitalism operates still relies upon the general idea of capitalism as a historical phenomenon with a specific characteristic contradiction. If new historicism claims a theoretical self-awareness which precludes it from accepting any unproblematically prior historical context, how is it able to invoke a category as general as capitalism and why would it wish to do so? In many ways we could see this commitment to the background of capitalism as a residue of Marxism. While rejecting any specific Marxist picture of the relation between art and history new historicism accepts the general historical category of capitalism and its distinction from feudalism. It is not only Greenblatt's work which employs this general category; the British and more avowedly Marxist cultural materialists also still accept the idea of capitalism as valid in referring to historical change, however mediated that process of change might be. Even when capitalism is not explicitly mentioned, the focus on metaphors of economy, exchange, circulation and profit demonstrates a concern with a particular historical shift in which such forces become prominent. As the Renaissance is marked as the moment at which such capitalist motifs begin to circulate, new historicism's reading of the Renaissance can be seen an examination of its own (capitalist) historical conditions. This might also explain why new historicism so frequently 'recognises' its own arguments in the very texts which it sets out to examine. The dependence upon some idea of capitalism does however raise the question as to whether a descriptive, non-totalising history which does not subsume particulars into general categories is possible. Greenblatt's rejection of monolithic world-pictures (those of Jameson and Lyotard, for example) is enabled by his appeal to a larger historical category: capitalism is such that no general theory can account for the relation between art and text. We could also see this appeal to capitalism as the consequence of a thoroughgoing historicism. If Greenblatt did not locate his argument for negotiation and exchange within the frame of capitalism he would be in the position of arguing for the ways in which meaning operated in general. Rather than provide a universal theory of the relation between text and history Greenblatt locates his practice within the distinct category of capitalism. But how is capitalism itself theorised? Is this not the result of some greater historical narrative? Is it possible to write a history of the present which neither universalises the present nor defines all historical differences within a general theory of history? How can an historicist theory resist totalisation if even the claim to historical relativity itself is specific to a particular period and its conception of a broader historical picture?

29

The attempt to think the radical historicity of texts and events without appealing to history as a general interpretive category was one of the main tasks of Michel Foucault and it is his work that has arguably been the single most important source for new historicist practice. The very construction of Foucault as a 'founding father' of new historicism is itself contradictory, for if there is any unifying feature of Foucault's complex and diverse *oeuvre* it is a resistance to the idea of a single author as a generator of intellectual developments in a history of ideas. The idea of influence, in this sense, was anathema to Foucault's project. In spite of this fact Foucault's work – his methodology, practice and terminology – has been of significant importance for new historicism. Typically, perhaps because of the paradox outlined above, the effect of Foucault in the reading of literary history is evidenced not in appeals to his work as offering a theory of meaning and history, but rather in replications of his actual method. Despite the reticence of new historicists either to theorise their work or to appeal to any specific theorist as providing a ground for their practice, new historicism is, in its own description, methodologically 'self-conscious' (Greenblatt 1989: 12). Those moments in which new historicism's methodological exemplars, such as Foucault, de Certeau and various cultural anthropologists, do theorise their practices can be important in illuminating the procedures of new historicism. The work of Foucault and his theorisation of discourses, practices and history will be the focus of the next chapter.

2
Michel Foucault: archaeology, genealogy and power

The impact of Michel Foucault upon literary studies has been felt most strongly, perhaps, in the new historicist and cultural materialist movements of criticism. The later chapters of this book will look at these movements directly. Here, we will be concerned with the large number of challenges Foucault's work presents for any project of history or interpretation. Assessing the impact of Foucault's work is no easy task. Not only is the complexity of his work capable of yielding a large number of conflicting interpretations; Foucault's corpus itself is by no means a unified whole. His work changed direction several times throughout his career while his own reassessments of his past work were far from reliable. Rather than seeking to provide yet another interpretation of Foucault's work as such, this chapter will be limited to the possible uses and implications of his work for the practice of literary-historical enquiry.

At its most general level Foucault's work provides a way of thinking about literature and history which does not presuppose the coherence or unity of historical periods; nor does it see ideas or ways of thinking in terms of historical development. Most importantly, perhaps, it problematises the relationship between the text and history. Unlike previous historicisms, Foucault's histories did not view documents as a means of access to some psychological or cultural entity such as a world-view or ideology. From the beginning, and throughout the diverse forms of text which he produced, Foucault's work was set against what he saw as a predominance of hermeneutic approaches. Not only Foucault's work, but many of the approaches which will be considered in the following chapters, can be seen as reactions against the phenomenological and hermeneutic approaches to meaning.

Although phenomenology is usually regarded as having been

founded by Edmund Husserl, it is the work of Martin Heidegger which most clearly joins the tradition of hermeneutics (the interpretation of the text's 'deeper' meaning) to phenomenology (strictly, the study of 'appearances'). For Heidegger, we can only know a world because it is given, or appears, or is revealed in a certain way. Rather than accept that a subject simply encounters a world, phenomenology asks how a 'world' is possible, or how a world is given. From the question of how the world is given, phenomenology comes up with the notion of a horizon. There must always be a background to any perception, and this background will be meaningful. We do not just encounter an object; it is always encountered *as* some specific thing. Experience is, for phenomenology, meaningful. To see the world *as* a world already involves an act of original interpretation. What this entails for Heidegger is that experience is no longer an object set over against a subject; the separateness of the world follows from an act of interpretation. Prior to the interpretation of the world as a separate thing, experience is already within the world and meaningfully located. Experience, for phenomenology, has a certain depth and meaning. Phenomenology, in its various forms, works upons this idea that experience, or the given, is more than is immediately presented. The world and all experience is like a text. It conceals meanings, conditions and histories that are not immediately present.

From this we can see how Heideggerean phenomenology provided a sympathetic extension of traditional historicism. For Dilthey, the past was an object of interpretation and objects of the past – such as texts – were expressions or reflections of the meaning of previous cultural horizons. Heidegger himself radicalised the study of history of philosophy but he did so by seeing previous texts as the articulation of a historically specific relation to the world. It made no sense to examine a text, such as Descartes's *Meditations*, in terms of its correctness or the value of its method. In reading past philosophy, Heidegger uncovered the relation to the world which, for him, was the deeper and more profound meaning of any philosophical text. What Heidegger discovers, when he reads Descartes, is not the beliefs of a particular philosopher, but a calculative and mathematical comportment which supposedly characterises modernity in general (Heidegger 1967). To read a text is to reveal the character of an epoch. For Heidegger history is no longer a particular discipline but the way in which all meaning and experience is understood. The meaning of any text is ultimately the expression of a specific historical moment.

Heidegger was not alone in seeing history as the horizon for meaning in general. Many studies in anthropology, ethnography, psychoanalysis, linguistics and other disciplines all operated with the assumption that to study a culture involved interpretation, and that the object to be interpreted was historically determined. Within literary study there was both the Marxist tradition of literary analysis which regarded texts as ultimately explicable in terms of their historical moment, as well as forms of historicism, which referred to world-pictures, mentalités or world-views. The text was seen as a vehicle or expression which harboured a depth or meaning which was neither immediately apparent nor adequately presented. The task of interpretation was ongoing and itself marked by its own moment of historical specificity. Texts were seen in terms of what they revealed, while the object which was revealed was seen as coherent only in terms of historical understanding.

In all this emphasis on history and historical interpretation there was a deep sense of both the specificity of Western history and its particular moment of crisis. Phenomenology was only one example of a more general attention to history and meaning. Historical interpretation was seen as an urgent task precisely because there was no longer a clear feeling of cultural coherence. Heidegger demonstrated this tendency explicitly. He termed his method of interpretation destruktion: the texts of the past would be pulled apart to reveal the more profound history of Western thought which had 'forgotten' its relation to Being. But you didn't have to read Heidegger to get a sense of the urgency of interpreting the present as a moment in a meaningful history. Apart from the large number of apocalyptic studies, such as Oswald Spengler's The Decline of the West (1926), which presaged the collapse of culture if it did not have more awareness of its historical direction, there were also clear movements in literature and criticism which argued for a historically attentive appoach to the past as an issue of moral urgency. Modernism can, in many ways, be seen as an attempt at historical and interpretive retrieval. Eliot's The Waste Land (1922) (like Pound's Cantos (1917–70), Joyce's Ulysses (1922) and Woolf's To the Lighthouse (1924)) suggest that the lack of meaning in the present can only be redeemed by turning back to a past, a past which is both meaningful and textual. When Modernism 'looks back' it sees the texts of a tradition and their meaning, rather than events as such (just as Heidegger considered the past as a series of philosophical encounters). Literary criticism of the time also expressed a sense of cultural crisis which, similarly, could only be averted through a textual study of tradition. Eliot's 'Tradition and the individual talent' and Leavis's The Great Tradition may be particularly English expressions of the need for historical reassessment through interpretation, but there were more subtle forms of historicism as a moral imperative. Even American literature, which had a tradition of throwing off the burden of the past, started producing texts with a sense of historical crisis. Theodore Dreiser's *Sister Carrie* (1965) was typical of the naturalism which picked up on Spengler's *Decline of the West*. In this novel humanity is seen in a position of decline, a decline all the more certain because of the deep lack of historical awareness and direction. The forces of capitalism, rather than historical action and agency, were seen to govern life. Freud's *Civilization and its Discontents* (1973) is both an instance of early European Modernism and a classic example of the intimate connection between meaning, history and crisis. For Freud, civilization in general was becoming neurotic; its only hope was an attention to its own history, through analysis, interpretation and a less neurotic relation to its origin. In a large number of ways, Modernism and its legacy reiterated two key assumptions of historicism: the world is not an object but a site of meaning; and this meaning is irreducibly historical.

Foucault's earlier work not only criticised such forms of historicism; he saw the idea of historical hermeneutics as itself historically determined. His work sought to provide new approaches to historical understanding which would not assume that current ideas about mind, ideology, history or interpretation could be adequately used to describe the past. If such ideas were, as Foucault argued, the products of a specifically modern way of thinking then the historian's practice would be one that concentrated less on understanding, continuity and coherence and more on difference, disruption and discontinuity. Ideas such as ideology and mind would no longer be methodological resources; it was their historical particularity that was going to be questioned. According to Foucault, the usual practice of the history of ideas was united by a belief in a coherent human subject whose various manifestations would be the object of study. Dilthey's emphasis on 'empathy', for example, presupposed a unified human understanding such that difference would always be understood against a backdrop of continuity.

The aim of Foucault's work – to rethink history as discontinuity – led to a number of approaches in his own work as he continually revised his project in the face of the difficulty of overcoming nineteenth-century historiography and hermeneutics. But despite Foucault's continual revision of his own methodology, his entire corpus can be considered as an ongoing challenge to the phenomenological and structuralist emphases on meaning and interpretation. And this challenge is by no means over: whether there can be a historical and critical project which is not ultimately unified by understanding and interpretation is still an open question. It is the difficulty of Foucault's task – to at once think 'otherwise' and have a sense of the locatedness of one's position – which accounts for the varied nature of his methods and focus. Foucault's theorisation of his project shifted from archaeology to genealogy; from power to the subject; and from discursive practice to ethics. Because Foucault undertook a number of projects, and because of his changes of strategy, there is no single 'example' of Foucaultian literary criticism. His theorisation of discourse presented a challenge to Marxist notions of power and ideology; his work on the sexual subject provoked responses in feminist theories of gender identity; while the problem of genealogy offered a way of rethinking historiography for all knowledge practices.

As a consequence, it is not only new historicism, which no longer assumes that there is something like historical context to which a text can be related, but forms of Marxist and feminist criticism which have altered through an encounter with Foucault's work. Earlier forms of feminist literary criticism concerned themselves with discovering a female aesthetic or women's tradition of writing (Showalter 1977). But recent examinations of the problem of history writing have argued that historical interpretation produces, rather than uncovers, identities and traditions (Crosby 1992). Further, the idea of 'discovering' a feminine aesthetic assumes that there is something like the feminine which exists independent of social and historical construction. But what Foucault's work and its critique of hermeneutics set out to do was disrupt the idea of any meaning, identity or entity which was simply 'there' to be interpreted. On the contrary, for Foucault it is only through practices, such as history writing and interpretation, that identities are produced. What this questioning of hermeneutics and historicism leads to, then, is an emphasis on discontinuity. The 'discovery' of a tradition may have more to do with contemporary strategy than it does with some continuous, concealed and pre-existing past. In terms of literary history, an emphasis on contingency and discontinuity will have both a critical and productive dimension. At the critical level, ideas of uncovering the 'origin' of genres or the 'rise' of historical movements, can now be questioned according to the present demands such histories would serve. Jerome McGann, accordingly, has argued that the construction of Romanticism as a unified movement helps to reinforce our present beliefs about individualism, imagination and the relation between politics and art. In a positive sense, Foucault's attention to discontinuity may provide different ways of looking at texts and events. If we no longer accept that the novels written by Defoe will 'develop' into

35

fully-fledged mature English realism, we may begin to read those novels in terms of difference. We might ask how the early novel marks new ways of thinking and writing, and how this discourse might challenge the way we currently understand what literature is.

Only a moment's reflection will reveal the extent to which literary-historical enquiries have been dominated by ideas of continuity. In terms of genre, for example, the novel is frequently explained as having 'developed' or 'evolved' from the earlier form of romance to become the extended prose narrative we recognise today as the novel. Within the novel itself there is assumed to be some common form which unites works as diverse as *Tom Jones* and *Women in Love*. (Studies such as those of Ian Watt (1957), F. R. Leavis (1960) and Raymond Williams (1970) describe the development or 'rise' of a genre.) Continuity also operates powerfully in the idea of 'influence' where studies such as *Milton, the Metaphysicals and Romanticism* (Low and Harding 1994) or *Poetry and Repression* (Bloom 1976) show the links between literary movements and authors. Romanticism is frequently explained as a reaction against the enlightenment and the ideas central to such movements (such as the notion of the 'individual' or the 'imagination') are seen to transform, develop or even progress through history to greater forms of sophistication. Authors can be seen to operate in a 'line of vision' (Wittreich 1975) whereby ideas are handed down and refined. Leavis's 'line of wit' (Leavis 1936: 17–39) refers to a series of poets who developed a progressive literary technique. Other literary techniques, such as stream-of-consciousness, are explained as 'arising' from earlier styles such as free-indirect style, itself an extension of nineteenth-century realism.

As Foucault argued, such an emphasis on continuity presupposes that all historical differences can ultimately be understood within a terrain of similarity. In the case of literary history, the continuities of genre, influence, style and period can be used to describe a development and evolution of literature. Even Marxist critics who concentrate on the historical shift from feudalism to capitalism rely upon the progress of technological/economic change which can then allow texts to be read as examples of, say, 'nascent capitalism' or late monopoly capitalism. Even a Marxism as 'sophisticated' as that of Fredric Jameson (which attempts to incorporate post-structuralism) sees literature as an allegory of historical development. *Wuthering Heights*, according to Jameson, expresses the historical transition from aristocratic feudalism to bourgeois familialism in the relations between characters. Significantly, Jameson sees history as the ultimate interpretive horizon for the literary text and, even more significantly, history is regarded as a meaningful process, a transition or development in the stages of capital:

> the text would necessarily be read or rewritten, not as the story of 'individuals', nor even as the chronicle of generations and their destinies, but rather as an impersonal process, a semic transformation centering on the house, which moves from Lockwood's initial impressions of the Heights, and the archaic story of origins behind it, to that final ecstatic glimpse through the window, where ... a new and idyllic family takes shape in the love of Hareton and the second Cathy. (Jameson 1981: 127)

Jameson's emphasis on history as a history of capital is typical of a historicist emphasis on continuity. Despite the fact that the object is historical change (from feudalism to capitalism), transitions are understood as ultimately meaningful and developmental. Change is interpreted within an horizon of continuity; for Jameson this continuity is the series of modes of production; for liberal historians history is the progress towards human emancipation; for literary historians change takes place in terms of influence or legacy. Such continuity, Foucault argues, is reassuring; it provides historical enquiry with a benchmark against which various historical changes can be understood and supports the idea of a unified human subject:

> Continuous history is the indispensable correlative of the founding function of the subject: the guarantee that everything that has eluded him may be restored to him; the certainty that time will disperse nothing without restoring it in a reconstituted unity; the promise that one day the subject – in the form of historical consciousness – will once again be able to appropriate, to bring back under his sway, all those things that are kept at a distance by difference, and find them in what might be called his abode. (Foucault 1972: 12)

Against this emphasis on continuity, recent criticism has taken up the challenge and opening of Foucault's discontinuous history. It has done so by showing that history is not a logical and coherent narrative but proceeds in an *ad hoc* manner and by also showing that certain events which did happen could have been otherwise. To show how recent literary history emphasises discontinuity we could take the example of the 'rise' of the novel. Both Marxist and non-Marxist critics have attributed a certain historical necessity to the form of the novel. Accordingly, so the story goes, just as the modern world focuses more and more intently on the concept of the individual and away from forms of community, so literature moves towards a consideration of everyday life and away from grand mythic forms (epic and tragedy). The novel would therefore become the appropriate expression of this historical/cultural development. As the ethos of individualism is intensified so the novel concentrates to a greater and greater extent on psychology. Eventually, it is argued, the novel becomes a direct transcription of experience; from being the recounting of the objective data of an individual's life and times it becomes a record of experiential data.

More recent work on the novel, however, has shown that the writing of novels was not the result of a unified ideology (individualism) finding its adequate expression. The emergence of the novel was not the result of some disembodied 'idea' but was a consequence of new forms of writing and discursive exchange. New types of text were produced alongside concrete and material practices. Davis, in *Factual Fictions* (1983), shows the way novels were part of a discursive field which included the narration of individual criminals' lives in news broadsheets. The emergence of this discourse had a juridical function; it produced the criminal as a type and object of study. Early novels, such as *Moll Flanders*, which chart the moral dissolution, imprisonment and subsequent reform of their central character can be read as part of a discursive network which took as its object criminality, individual moral discipline and reform. To see the novel as having 'emerged' from the previous genre of romance (as do, for example, Scholes and Kellogg (1968)) is to glide over the important discursive and material conditions and changes which characterise the novel's various features. The notion of discourse functions here to open up the literary text to a wider field of practices. The novel does not just 'emerge'; to write a novel the author draws upon new forms of language (ways of speaking about individual lives, about criminality and about personality) and new relations between practices: in the novel literature is no longer a text performed in a court or read in a drawing room; it is printed and distributed. The novel is a discursive event. It does not *reflect* history; it *is* history. The novel is a collection of new relations. The text now produces new objects (the individual life), is situated alongside other texts (the broadsheet), and is specifically located (consumed privately, rather than performed publicly).

As an example of what a discursive analysis might look like we could take Samuel Richardson's *Pamela* (1740). In this novel the narrative depends heavily upon a single term – 'virtue'. Now what virtue *does* in this text is very different from its use in, say, traditional or pre-modern ethics. Virtue, in its classic sense, is an ethical propensity, an ability of citizenship and part of the formation of a life. The word 'virtue' in the Greek *polis*, for

example, was connected with a series of practices: of household manage-
ment, self-discipline and political self-formation. In *Pamela* the term
'virtue' no longer refers to self-management, the way one forms oneself
and organises one's life. The term is privatised and is seen less as an activity than as a possession and a commodity. Pamela's life is defined according to how she uses her virtue. Virtue is something she *has* (her virginity)
and not a practice or goal. What 'virtue' does in *Pamela* is to create a new
'ethical substance': a new object which will be monitored and evaluated.
The term connects with a series of practices – bourgeois marriage, the
focus on one's inner sexual worth, the formation of female sexuality and
novel writing – which are discursive precisely because they depend upon
certain conditions of articulation. The way 'virtue' works in *Pamela* is not
caused by capitalism. Bourgeois marriages and social structure are nothing
other than these new practices which depend upon certain discursive formations.

New historicist works have also used the history of genres to emphasise the role of literature as a political practice, rather than seeing literature
as developing from within its own autonomous history. Stephen Orgel
(1975) has shown that the masque was part of a construction of power in
the Elizabethan and Jacobean courts. The drama did not 'reflect' an ideology; by acting out the role of a mythic character like Neptune (who was
capable of controlling natural forces) the king was able to produce certain
power relations. He could present himself as a natural and divine ruler.
Drama was, therefore, a directly social and discursive practice. It took part
in its historical moment not as a mere reflection or expression but as a
practical component in a field of discourses invested with power (Orgel
1975: 57). Publicly performed works, such as masques, were not the only
literary forms which had a productive social discursive function. Joel Fineman's work on Shakespeare's sonnets argues that the modern subject was
invented and constructed in the Renaissance through literary forms which
performed the very privacy and interiority which was, ostensibly, their
object of examination. In both writing and reading a sonnet one undertakes self-reflection. But, it could be argued, it is precisely through the discourse of self-reflection that the subject is produced. In the act of writing
(or reading) the 'I' within a discourse of the passions and affects, the site
of the interior subject is carved out through its exploration. Not only did
the subject not precede its literary expression and performance, Fineman
(1986) argues that the modern theories which are used to analyse modern subjectivity (such as psychoanalysis) are also effects of the Renaissance
invention of the literary subject. In this type of criticism, rather than relat-

ing the literary text as an autonomous unit back to some pre-textual origin (as, ultimately, does Jameson's reading of *Wuthering Heights* in terms of
capital), the work is related to other texts from a variety of domains. But
such relations do not aim to understand a society in its totality by coming
up with a 'world-picture'. Rather, new historicism concentrates on the
discrete historical particulars which signal disruption, change and discontinuity. There is no longer a single historical process which literature
would either reveal, produce or enable. Texts and discourses themselves
take place *as history*.

Foucault's idea of 'discursive practice' has, therefore, been central to
rethinking the relation between text and history. It shows that literature
can work in a social formation, as opposed to simply reflecting it. Working against ideas of reflection, expression or ideology, the notion of 'discursive practice' considers the text as a material, active and powerful
component amongst others in a field of forces. The publication of a gyne-
cological treatise, for example, does not just tell us about the way Renaissance societies viewed the female body; the treatise itself was a way of
producing anatomy (and therefore woman) as an object of study. Its articulation of theories of sexual difference took part in a series of actions
(including the juridical determination of sex differences, regulations
about clothing and performances of cross-dressing) which produced individuals as gendered. A text is therefore part of a discursive practice; it is
both textual and active. It does not need to be related to some idea of its
historical background; it is already an active player in that history. In order
to understand the use of 'discursive practice' as a critical concept we need
to turn to Foucault's method of 'archaeology'.

Archaeology

In *The Archaeology of Knowledge* Foucault described his historical method
as 'a pure description of discursive events' (Foucault 1972: 27). In doing
so he distanced himself not only from Hegelian forms of continuous and
teleological history, but also from Dilthey's historicism of 'interpretation'
and from 'static' forms of structuralist analysis. According to structuralist
thinking a statement or individual speech act (*parole*) can only occur within
an already existing system of signs (*langue*). The possibilities of meaning
are therefore dependent upon the system as a whole and a specific utterance can only be understood in relation to the total linguistic structure.
Given this model of meaning, it is impossible to see how any single utterance could alter or produce new meanings. On the structuralist paradigm,

any text would be referred to a general system of which it would be an instance. Just as Hegelian history posits a unity and continuity through time (in its history of reason or spirit); and just as Dilthey's distinct *Weltan-schauung* can always be understood and reactivated by the human subject; so structuralism posits a unity and uniformity at the level of atemporal structure.

So a text would, in structuralist terms, no longer be seen as an exemplar of some 'external' history (of capital, literature or human development) but the text would be an instance of a general system of signs. Structural analyses of literature tended, not surprisingly, to be remarkably ahistorical and formalist. The text was considered as a system of relations. The Cathy–Heathcliffe relation in *Wuthering Heights* would be read as fulfilling a function in a system of narrative relations. And when structural analysis tried to combine its methods with historical interpretation it did so by taking the internal structure and relating it to historical structure. (Jameson's analysis of *Wuthering Heights* is such an equation: Heathcliffe is to Lockwood what nascent capital is to aristocracy). Avowedly structuralist-Marxist criticisms were less schematic but no less confident that a text was a system of relations. (Macherey (1978) saw literary texts as repetitions of ideological systems of signs.) It is against all these attempts to reduce the particularity and difference of local statements to some ultimate coherence that Foucault sets his notion of *discursive event*.

While Foucault inherits from structuralism a refusal to locate meaning within the consciousness of an isolated author, or in the unique site of a single text, he adds to the structuralist notion of discursive field the specificity of the statement (which is not equivalent to the structuralist *parole*). In arguing against Hegelian and Diltheyan forms of history which locate all historical meaning and development within the arena of human consciousness, Foucault adopts the structuralist notion that subjects do not produce meaning; meaning is, rather, an effect of the discursive system within which individuals are placed. This, however, creates the problem of the *event*. From a purely structuralist point of view the 'closure' of a discursive system would preclude the possibility of any radically new statement. An event would be unthinkable. Foucault's reaction against structuralism in many ways centres on his attempt to think the possibility of events, which are not directly reducible to, or determined by, a pre-existing structure. He does this by trying to think beyond structuralism's *langue/parole* distinction.

A specific utterance is, for Foucault, more than an instance; it is at once a rupture, a break and (because it is also an instance) a reconfigura-

41

tion. So a text *may* be related to all those historical and literary continuities which it sustains, but perhaps what makes the text an event is *what it does* and the new relations it brings into play. We may now think certain relations are inevitable – the connection between lyric poetry and introspection for example – but from a different perspective such a connection could be seen as an event. What if the whole possibility of introspection, an inner self, the significance of memory, the notion of an intensely private and meaningful past were part of a discursive event? The Romantic lyric could be seen as the production of new entities (narcissistic interiority, poetic reflection, personal depth) through new discursive relations (between nature, text, poet, personality). We may read Wordsworth's 'Intimations of Immortality' ode as an example or reflection of Romantic individualism; but it is also the case that Romantic individualism is nothing other than the discourses which produce it. And those discourses include not just poetry but psychology, history writing, criticism and social relations. So while historicism and stucturalism both refer a text to some explanatory horizon (of development or structure), seeing a text as discourse situates it as an event. Here, texts work, perform, function and act in a dynamic field; they are not just expressions or instances.

At the same time, Foucault does not want to revive Hegelian or phenomenological ideas of human spirit or imagination to account for the ways in which discursive structures change. While historical change is undeniable, any reference back to a human reason which is responsible for such change would have the effect of returning the differences of history back to the arena of a sovereign consciousness. Because a discourse is a system of competing forces where rules govern what is valid, sayable and possible, a system of signs has a specific and historically determinate structure of relations. While the structuralist notion of *langue* was of a static unity of equally exchangeable elements, Foucault's idea of discursive formation operates by exclusion. Ideas of 'truth' and validity are produced by rules which govern a discourse; such rules are located in institutions and practices. It is not the case, therefore, that discourse is reducible to structuralism's *langue* or language system. At any given time certain types of statements are capable of having a truth function while others are excluded. Today, for example, the discourse of astronomy is institutionally divided from the discourse of astrology. The truth effect of the former is achieved by the location of the discourse (in universities, laboratories, research foundations) and the positions of those who speak (as scientists, specialists). The exclusion of astrology from science is achieved by its location in another domain (television, magazines, popular culture). However, this discursive division was by no means always the case; prior to the Renaissance, many forms of now legitimate science (chemistry, astronomy, biology) were intertwined with what are now considered to be abnormal practices (alchemy, astrology, physiognomy). Even today we can see how boundaries between true and authoritative discourses and those which are excluded as illegitimate are produced juridically or institutionally: the incorporation of naturopathy or home-opathy into medicine only occurs if and when these 'alternative' practices are legally sanctioned and located within dominant institutions. What constitutes a 'literary' text and 'literary value' is also effected through processes of discursive legitimation and exclusion. Texts once considered ephemeral are now granted value and legitimation; the very novels which are now canonised were once seen as a threat to the institution of letters. Both D. H. Lawrence and Gustave Flaubert were the subject of legal pro-ceedings which sought to establish whether their novels were forms of art or obscenity. But this does not mean that these texts possess an inher-ently transgressive potential. These texts were events that realigned the institutional boundaries which determined the category of literature. Now that *Lady Chatterley's Lover* (1928) and *Madame Bovary* (1857) are central texts in the canon of modern literature, they are both institutionalised as valuable and serve as boundaries or markers as to what constitutes litera-ture as such. As a discursive formation the category of 'literature' is effected through a dynamic process of institutional exclusion and inclu-sion.

Discursive formations, therefore, grant some statements a force, validity and truth effect which is achieved *inter alia* by the exclusion of other statements. Discursive formations include extra-linguistic phenom-ena such as institutions, practices and the material sites of production for their legitimation. For Foucault, a discursive event is an utterance which realigns or alters the configuration of force which operates in a discursive formation. In this mutation different types of statement are granted a validity; new divisions between discourses are made and 'truth' is attrib-uted to a new type of utterance. Such discursive events are not, however, referred back to an originating consciousness – say, the genius of a partic-ular scientist or author. The character of a discursive event is marked by its position within a field of already existing utterances. The discursive event reorganises, redistributes, displaces and produces a 'mutation' in dis-course (Foucault 1973: xi). The possibility of a discursive event can be linked, then, to new relations in power.

In Foucault's *Madness and Civilization* (1965), for example, the incarceration of the insane in the eighteenth century is related to a new conceptual division between reason and madness. Once incarceration produces physical limits between reason and madness, unreason can be thought of as reason's 'other': it can be objectified, distanced, studied, known and talked about. Furthermore, one could even suggest that such material and conceptual divisions produce objects of knowledge. After writing *Madness and Civilization*, Foucault went so far as to deny any pre-linguistic, transhistorical phenomenon known as madness which is then recognised, labelled and practised upon. There is no pure reality or single cause (either linguistic or spatial/material) which can explain the eighteenth-century theorisation of madness. A series of accidents and *ad hoc* procedures, rather than a rational development, leads to new configurations of space, force and language. Here, literature would not be a reflection or expression of new ways of seeing but would be coterminous with their production. If, in the eighteenth century, there was a proliferation of texts concerning madness, these texts would have been part of (and productive of) a new discursive formation. It is possible to see late eighteenth-century literature with its emphasis on gothic, madness, addiction and unreason as part of new discursive relations. Only with the production of autonomous reason in certain discursive practices (such as science, hospitalization, criminology, education and Enlightenment philosophy) is it possible to produce madness, delusion and unreason in literature. But this 'new' division between reason and madness (or science and literature) is not a complete break with some prior unity. Reason is divided from madness by a redistribution of existing boundaries. Power moves within already existing structures and redistributes relations.

In *Madness and Civilization* Foucault narrates the shift from a society that had excluded its 'other' by placing outcasts such as lepers on its boundaries, to a society which could contain its 'other' by studying an incarcerated madness – making madness an object. On this model, there is no logical or ideal development of knowledge; practices simply work upon already existing discursive structures. Discontinuity occurs in the form of mutations and redistributions rather than discoveries or complete breaks. Nor is knowledge a single and unified field which develops as a coherent whole. Rather than saying that new ideas emerge because of material determinants, or that material determinants are the result of 'thought', the concept of discursive formation shows a number of complex interactions and exchanges between linguistic and non-linguistic events. Any practice is already a statement; words and things produce each other. In the process of incarceration, the eighteenth century already marked a certain conceptual division, but concepts and language are themselves made possible only by specific practices.

A discursive practice is neither a purely linguistic nor a purely material phenomenon. Factors such as architecture and bodily disciplines intersect with systems of classification and definition. The relation between text and world is neither one of expression nor reflection nor determination. Discourse and practices are part of the same system of force:

> Discursive practices are characterised by the delimitation of a field of objects, the definition of a legitimate perspective for the agent of knowledge, and the fixing of norms for the elaboration of concepts and theories. (Foucault 1977a: 199)

After describing the ways in which discursive practices delimit and define knowledge, Foucault stresses that they cannot be reduced to discourse alone:

> Discursive practices are not purely and simply ways of producing discourse. They are embodied in technical processes, in institutions, in patterns for general behaviour, in forms for transmission and diffusion, and in pedagogical forms which, at once, impose and maintain them. (Foucault 1977a: 200)

It would follow from this that a text could not be considered in isolation. The idea of hermeneutics, in which the text is in some way conceived as containing or revealing a meaning, would be set aside in favour of considering a text within a network – not just of other texts, but of institutional and disciplinary boundaries. A text would not be referred to some prior historical context; it is already part of a discursive formation – the linguistic, material and practical conditions of its occurrence. Foucault argues against a tradition of 'commentary' which would reveal the inner meaning or intention of a text. Archaeology, on the other hand, is nothing more than the description of a text as an event, considered in relation to other discourses as events:

> Is it not possible to make a structural analysis of discourses that would evade the fate of commentary by supposing no remainder, nothing in excess of what has been said, but only the fact of its historical appearance? The facts of discourse would then have to be treated not as autonomous nuclei of multiple significations, but as events and functional segments gradually coming together to form a system. The meaning of a statement would be defined not by the treasure of intentions that it might contain, revealing and concealing it at the same time, but by the difference that articulates it upon other real or possible statements, which are contemporary to it or to which it is opposed

45

in the linear series of time. A systematic history of discourse would then become possible. (Foucault 1973: xvii)

Nor can a discursive formation be likened to a world-view or *Weltan-schauung*. While Foucault uses the concept of 'episteme' to characterise historical periods, this notion is quite different from earlier notions of *Weltanschauung* both in its emphasis on difference and contradiction within the episteme and in its anti-psychologism. An episteme is not located at the level of mind or world-picture; it occurs as a distribution of discursive effects; its nature is institutional and positive, rather than psychological and foundational. A discursive formation lacks the coherence and unity of a 'mind-set' or world picture; different discursive rules may operate at the same historical moment for different domains. The notion of femininity in the nineteenth century, for example, differs radically according to whether one is reading English Romantic poetry or gynecology; it is the contradiction and heterogeneity of such differences which characterise a discursive formation. A world-view is a coherent and ideal structure which can be related to a material context. (For example, 'the great chain of being' supposedly reflects a feudal/pre-capitalist society.) A discursive formation, on the other hand, is neither ideal nor material; rather, it is an intersection of forces in which certain statements and practices dominate. Whereas historiography has traditionally tried to play down differences (by locating all forces within a single 'age' or era) and has sought to *explain* change (by showing causes and developments of concepts), Foucault's archaeology focuses on the chance emergence of events and the contradiction and heterogeneity within any historical moment:

> What one must characterize and individualize is the coexistence of these dispersed and heterogeneous statements; the system that governs their division, the degree to which they depend upon one another, the way in which they interlock or exclude one another, the transformation that they undergo, and the play of their location, arrangement and replacement. (Foucault 1972: 34)

Against the depth hermeneutics which operates in Hegelian and nineteenth-century forms of history, designed to study and reveal the meaning concealed within the texts of the past, Foucault's archaeology seeks to *describe* rather than interpret. A text itself is not the bearer of a meaning; it is an occurrence and an intervention within a field of forces. There is no deeper truth behind a text which can be recovered in order to demonstrate the ultimate coherence of ostensible historical difference. Such interpretations only confirm to the present-day historian that the otherness of the past can be made meaningful to the present. Such acts of

historical interpretation are a comforting form of retrieval which annihi-
late the disturbing possibility that ideas, such as reason or 'man', may not
have a trans-historical and essential unity:

> There is the notion of 'spirit', which enables us to establish between the
> simultaneous or successive phenomena of a given period a community of
> meanings, symbolic links, an interplay of resemblance and reflexion, or
> which allows the sovereignty of collective consciousness to emerge as the
> principle of unity and explanation. We must question those ready-made syn-
> theses, those groupings that we normally accept before any examination,
> those links whose validity is recognized from the outset; we must oust those
> forms and obscure forces by which we usually link the discourse of one man
> with that of another; they must be driven out from the darkness in which
> they reign. And instead of according them unqualified, spontaneous value,
> we must accept, in the name of methodological rigour, that, in the first
> instance, they can concern only a population of dispersed events. (Foucault
> 1972: 22)

A historical event should, therefore, not be referred back to the consciousness of a governing subject or author who expresses some interior
meaning. Foucault avowedly seeks to rid his work of any unity of 'man':
such unity would take the form of what he refers to, pejoratively, as 'anthropologism' (Foucault 1972: 16). The idea of description, as opposed to
interpretation, accepts the discursive formations as they appear without
positing a prior meaning (neither of a creating subject nor linear history).
Rather than seeing the text as a means to reveal a historical context, world-
view or mode of production, the text itself is focused upon as an operation
that *makes possible* its object or referent. But this is not mere textualism either.
Discursive formations are not just language in the narrow sense. Discourse
includes the relations between practices, institutions, norms, actions and
spatial distribution. In this sense we could see a building as discursive. A
modern theatre which divides an audience from the action, which illumi-
nates the stage and darkens the auditorium and which grants the dramatic
work an aura through its august architecture and elaborate design is discursive in the same way that a text (in the strict sense) is discursive. What is, is
produced through a dynamic set of relations. In the same way, an asylum is
as discursive in its production of the division between reason and madness
as is Descartes's *Meditations*. The word 'discourse' is used in these cases to
avoid the idea of representation: the text or building does not reflect or
represent ideas. There are not self-present 'things' which are then negotiated
and encountered. Discourse is the encounter itself. Ideas are nothing apart
from their discursive, or positive, instantiation. As Foucault argues:

47

But what we are concerned with here is not to neutralize discourse, to make it the sign of something else, and to pierce through its density in order to reach what remains silently anterior to it, but on the contrary to maintain it in its consistency, to make it emerge in its own complexity. What, in short, we wish to do is to dispense with 'things'. ... To substitute for the enigmatic treasure of 'things' anterior to discourse, the regular formation of objects that emerge only in discourse. (Foucault 1972: 47)

Consequently, the notion of a 'history of ideas' becomes highly problematic. A number of classic arguments have traced ideas such as the individual, the sublime, natural law and virtue in uninterrupted developments of influence, progress, development and culmination. Such instances of development and change are charted within a unified arena of human history. Works which employ this evolutionary or developmental model have been written in historical, philosophical and literary disciplines. Charles Taylor's *Sources of the Self* (1989), as the title implies, charts the decline and fall of the Aristotelian conception of the political self as ideas of the individual become theologised and progressively privatised in the modern state. Such histories rely upon a notion of continuity, such that the concept of 'self' is said to have gradually altered its meaning through time. The alterations in meaning are attributed to a logical process of human development, or fall, (from ancient times to modernity) and it is assumed that the phenomenon of the present can be explained and made meaningful by a historical narrative which reveals its origin.

Other studies, such as A. O. Lovejoy's *The Great Chain of Being* (1964) have charted the movement of an idea from Aristotle to Shakespeare, while standard works of literary 'influence' assume that 'ideas' can have a transhistorical identity. Literary works can then be explained by locating their origins in former works of the tradition. Some studies of influence have even gone so far as to trace 'lines of vision' (Wittreich 1975; Wittreich 1979) in order to show how authors apparently draw upon ideas or 'visions' of the past and reawaken them in later works. Such studies obviously dehistoricise the particularities of utterances. The relation between Shakespeare's and Milton's notion of virtue might be better illuminated, not by charting a continuity between two 'great names' in the literary canon, but by referring to the historically specific circumstances in which each notion is articulated. Such specificity would not be achieved by referring the work to some unity, such as 'the seventeenth century'; it would, on the Foucaultian model, be achieved by setting the text alongside other texts. The new historicist practice of setting canonical works alongside some seemingly marginal works — such as those of geography, travel and reportage – can be seen as a way of presenting discursive formations in their heterogeneity. The idea of influence (whether Shakespeare actually read Machiavelli) would then be beside the point. Texts are already part of a more general discursive network. This is not to say that texts can be considered in relation to each other because they share an identical ground (of history or ideology). Rather, the text is already a relational phenomenon; its identity and meaning is an effect of a system of differences and similarities. Focusing upon differences rather than similarities disrupts the traditional notions of identity and continuity which miss the true historicity of utterances. Such utterances cannot be referred back to a history of ideas, as the developing products of human subjects; nor can they be isolated within a particular world-view conceived as a coherent and interpretable system. In Foucault's archaeology, discourse itself is the object of attention and any forms of *exteriority* (such as the creating subject or the historical or material world) are effects of a discourse which is anonymous in so far as it produces (rather than being produced by) subject positions:

> I do not wish to take as an object of analysis the conceptual architecture of an isolated text, an individual *oeuvre*, or a science at a particular moment in time. One stands back in relation to this manifest set of concepts; and one tries to determine according to what schemata (of series, simultaneous groupings, linear or reciprocal modification) the statements may be linked to one another in a type of discourse; one tries in this way to discover how the recurrent elements of statements can reappear, dissociate, recompose, gain in extension or determination, be taken up into new logical structures, acquire, on the other hand, new semantic contents, and constitute partial organizations among themselves. These schemata make it possible to describe – not the laws of the internal construction of concepts, not their progressive and individual genesis in the mind of man – but their anonymous dispersion through texts, books and *oeuvres*. A dispersion that characterizes a type of discourse, and which defines, between concepts, forms of deduction, derivation and coherence, but also of incompatibility, intersection, substitution, exclusion, mutual alteration, displacement, etc. Such an analysis, then, concerns, at a kind of *preconceptual* level, the field in which concepts can coexist and the rules to which this field is subjected. (Foucault 1972: 60)

Foucault's question is, then, 'What makes a discourse possible?' This question is not answered by reference to a thinking subject's intention, nor by referring to the logic of historical development, but by focusing on 'the economy of the discursive constellation' in which certain statements are permitted or excluded (Foucault 1972: 67). The rules which govern such a discourse should not be seen as some hidden political meaning as in the classically Marxist model of ideology. A discursive formation cannot be interpreted to reveal a pre-discursive or ideal meaning. The 'rules' of discourse are nothing other than the configuration of possible statements at any moment in time. Foucaultian history is neither interpretive nor hermeneutic – revealing the rules behind discourse; it is *descriptive*. For discourse itself is a process of delimitation and exclusion. These limits and exclusions are located neither in thought (psychologism) nor in a coherent world-view (historicism). Against these ideas of discourse as expressing some prior meaning, Foucault sets the idea of discourse as a system of regularities with no reference to a prior exteriority (a historical context) or interiority (a human meaning):

> One is not seeking, therefore, to pass from the text to thought, from talk to silence, from the exterior to the interior, from spatial dispersion to the pure recollection of the moment, from superficial multiplicity to profound unity. One remains within the dimension of discourse. (Foucault 1972: 76)

Remaining within the dimension of discourse cannot be equated with a crude 'textualism' (the idea that outside language there is no world). Rather, the 'world' is itself part of the system of discourse. Non-linguistic phenomena (the housing of the insane in asylums for example) are discursive in so far as they are part of a system of relations. Actions are discursive: the position of a king in a masque, the architecture of a prison, the geography of eighteenth-century London are part of, not external or prior to, a system of relations in which texts are produced and consumed.

Foucault's aim in The Archaeology of Knowledge is to remain totally within the realm of discourse, seeing all forms of exteriority as an effect of that discourse, and this precludes referring a text or statement back to either an individual author or to any idea of human experience in general. In many ways his method here is purely 'immanent': all forms of 'exteriority' are produced by the discursive formation and no prior or foundational cause is permitted consideration. Foucault proposes that 'we no longer relate discourse to the primary ground of experience, nor to the a priori authority of knowledge; but we seek the rules of formation in discourse itself' (Foucault 1972: 79).

Such a methodology might seem to be a pure form of structuralism, limiting all phenomena to occurrences within a system that encompasses all possibilities. If all phenomena are to be examined as elements in a discursive system, then the position of the description of that system has to remain unaccounted for. In this sense the discursive formations in The

Archaeology of Knowledge can be seen as a form of positivism: the position of the observer of the discursive formation is neither questioned nor explicitly thematised. However, against this, Foucault refers to the discursive formation as a 'problematic unity' which suggests that any simple notion of structure cannot be used to explain his concept of discourse. Where Foucault's position differs most markedly from an entirely systematic and positivist structuralism is in his emphasis upon the statement.

A discursive formation is not an abstract and neutral langue; its character and rules are determined by the occurrence of statements. The discursive formation cannot be infinitely manipulated; it is delimited and restricted by statements which characterise what is to count as true and valid. In *The Order of Things*, for example, Foucault analyses certain statements which make possible new entities for examination. Foucault refers to 'new empiricities' which are produced by the statements of the modern human sciences. Marx did not 'discover' the notion of economy; Marx's discourse was, Foucault claimed, 'an event that any archaeology can situate with precision' (Foucault 1970: 262). This is not to say that there is no difference between the classical idea of wealth and the modern idea of economy employed by Marx. But it is to say that these ideas were produced from within particular discursive arrangements and that the change in 'ideas' was the result of new disciplinary and institutional structures which were themselves enabled by reconfigurations in the discursive formation. Therefore, as Foucault argues in *The Order of Things*, what matters is not a history of ideas in which various individuals discover, invent or imagine new ways of thinking; such events have to be accounted for within an already existing discourse: 'What is important, what makes it possible to articulate thought within itself, is its internal conditions of possibility' (Foucault 1970: 275). Such *internal* conditions of possibility refer to the character, relations and distribution of discourse itself and not external conditions such as history, reason or progress.

In *The Order of Things* Foucault shows the way in which the modern idea of 'man' did not just 'emerge' in the late eighteenth century. The previous classical discursive formation in which all being was considered to have a knowable and taxonomic order eventually produced the question of the knower of that order. Focus on knowledge shifted from a world of facts to a study of 'man'. A new discourse – the human sciences – took the question of knowledge and directed it towards, not an external table of facts, but to 'man' himself. Consequently, there is no radical historical break in which the modern concept of the individual is born; nor is there an essential continuity in which the individual is gradually and logically discovered. Rather, there is a discontinuity which demonstrates that systems are never closed structures; they alter according to the shifts in emphasis and force operating within them. But such discontinuity comes in the form of discursive events. A statement can alter the character of a discursive formation but it cannot occur outside that formation in a moment of pure invention.

We can see the way such shifts operate in literary texts. The concept of the sublime has a rich and varied history. But any historical tracing of the notion from Longinus to the present would restore the notion to a horizon of homegenity. If, however, we related the articulations of the sublime to their discursive locale we could see the various uses of the term – which would have less to do with its inherent meaning and more to do with its strategic employment. In the eighteenth century, when the term went through a revival, the concept was articulated in terms of the subject and its relation to nature. Discourses on the sublime both made possible, and intersected with, a number of concerns and problematics. The French Revolution, and its description, was seen as a break or disruption from the past; but it was also seen as the destruction of a limit. The discourse of political events, and the discourse of literature produced the notion of a subjective limit. When early Romantic poetry articulated the sublime it did so through the production of an introspective subject who would discover human finitude in its incapacity to comprehend nature. Shelley's 'Mont Blanc' (1970: 532–5) inscribes the limit of the subject in its description of a 'spirit' which the subject both senses and is unable to represent. The discourse of the sublime here is part of a discursive formation – including practices of political emancipation, scientific reflections on the origins of life, philosophical theories on the limits of knowledge and the distinction of the private domestic sphere – which inscribes and produces the finite, private subject of modernity who is both empirically separate (limited) and ideally capable of thinking beyond that limit (unlimited). The sublime here would be crucial in the specifically modern production of what Foucault, in *The Order of Things*, refers to as the empirical-transcendental double. 'Man' is both a finite being (empirically) and a being capable of reflecting upon the limit of his finitude (transcendentally). The sublime, from Burke to its articulation in contemporary theory, both concerns a common object – the modern 'doubled' subject – and differs in its discursive articulation. The Romantic sublime was inscribed in discourses of human life and intersected with political movements and the production of human finitude as an ethical substance. Today, rather than being concerned with a soul, spirit, sentiment, feeling or affects (which is 'sensed' beyond the limit), the current discourse of the sublime concerns the limit itself (Lacoue-Labarthe and Nancy 1988; Lyotard 1994). By adopting a discourse of writing, line, limit and inscription, the current theorisation of the sublime forms part of the postmodern discursive formation which takes textuality as its problematic object.

Even after Foucault moved on from a focus on archaeology to genealogy and ethics, his work still retained an attention to history as a series of discursive shifts (rather than complete breaks or continuous developments). In his later work, The History of Sexuality (1978–88), Foucault shows how the practices of sexual and erotic ethics in ancient times altered when they were taken up by the Christian church. From being a mode of exercising and demonstrating will and self-discipline, sexual ethics became a system of moral codes in themselves. Abstinence was no longer valued as a form of self-regulation; it was a virtue in a Christian morality which attributed a negative value to sexual pleasure per se. Such a historical shift used the same practices and divisions and did not occur by completely breaking with the ancient model. New questions were asked within the same discursive formation, producing new statements, new problems and, most importantly, new entities – eventually, in the nineteenth century, the idea of an 'inner' sexuality 'essential' to each individual.

On a Foucaultian analysis, then, even the most material phenomena such as desire and bodies are always located within historically specific discursive practices. There is no general system which accounts for subjective production; rather, bodies and desires are produced in particular and contested textual and institutional procedures. According to the cultural materialist critic, Francis Barker, 'Rather than an extra-historical residue, invariant and mute, [the] body is as ready for coding and decoding, as intelligible both in its presence and in its absence as any of the more frequently recognized historical objects' (Barker 1984: 13). Barker's work on Hamlet shows the ways in which the modern bourgeois subject was textually constructed as a domain of psychological interiority set against a body. Whereas pre-Renaissance societies had been public and specular and had seen the self as an embodied object to be worked upon through physical forms of power and coercion, the modern 'subject' is created in discursive practices as a site of self-regulating subjectivity. Hamlet's 'crisis' is not part of a timeless existential dilemma (as traditional criticism had argued) but is historical, political and discursive. The 'old kingdom' of centralised power, public legitimation, court rule and spectacle is being eclipsed by modern forms of self-discipline and subjective introspection.

53

And this discursive conflict takes place in the textual construction of Hamlet's subjectivity:

> If we have identified in *Hamlet* a *historical* register of modernity, the Oedipal prince is, as they say, ahead of his time when he calls on the 'too too solid flesh to melt' (I.ii.129). His desire to refine away the insistent materiality of the body is the necessary complement to that interiority of soul which would otherwise realize itself utterly in him. ... A struggle is being fought out in these texts, and this is the lot of discourse, and of social life, in any polity organized under forms of domination. ... As modern subjectivity begins to emerge, it turns destructively on that older body from which it struggles to free itself. (Barker 1984: 41)

What Barker's reading of *Hamlet* demonstrates is that subjects are effects of discursive relations and that these relations are historical and fragmented. The subject's disunity is an effect of the competing discourses within which it is defined. Foucault's notion of discourse, within which bodies and desire are effected, is therefore more diverse or multiple than ideology. In any given discursive domain there are a number of different practices and forms of desire. In fact, power works by the organisation and *differentiation* of desiring practices. There is no capitalist subject in *general*; rather, there are a number of related forms of desire, embodiment and sexual practice which are produced through processes of regulation, normalisation, exclusion, marginalisation and difference.

Foucault's account of historical change as located within discursive formations has also provided new ways for thinking about shifts in traditional literary-historical eras. The shift from the Enlightenment to Romanticism, for example, is usually explained by literary historians taking up Romanticism's own images of apocalyptic and violent change. Romanticism is often seen as a movement which promotes 'imagination' in contrast to the enlightenment's 'reason'. But rather than arguing for either a complete break with enlightenment reason, or its development toward Romanticism, it could be argued that relations of both continuity and discontinuity were at work. Whereas the Enlightenment used the idea of reason to be critical of any external authority (Church, State, tradition, law, etc.), the Romantics argued that reason itself was yet another form of exteriority applied tyrannically to human life. But in doing so the Romantics were continuous with the Enlightenment critique of external authority. Furthermore, far from being distanced from enlightenment reason, their questions and anxieties were statements only explicable within Enlightenment terms. The revolutionary character of Romanticism was highly ambivalent; it had rendered problematic Enlightenment reason but could not do away with that discursive structure in general. Romanticism had, therefore, as its historically prior condition, the discourse of the Enlightenment which it turned against (Colebrook 1994). The representation of Romanticism as the complete overcoming of all limits to the self is the consequence, not of a discovery or unveiling, but of a shift in relations of a discursive formation. Any present day history of the nineteenth century would therefore be compelled, like Foucault's The Order of Things, to acknowledge that the present, too, is part of this very discursive formation. There can be no detached historical knowledge of the shift from Enlightenment to Romantic thought, only further explications of the discursive field. Such explications would themselves take part in the reconfiguration of discursive relations and determinations.

Consequently, new historicist critics shift the focus away from the origins of a text in terms of its authorship or position within an autonomous literary history. Rather, the text is a discursive event; it is formed in relation to available statements within a network of possible statements and, as such, acts in history. For Foucault, a text is not reducible to a structure but as a statement it acts upon and realises the forces of that structure:

> The statement is not therefore a structure (that is, a group of relations between variable elements, thus authorizing a possibly infinite number of concrete models); it is a function of existence that properly belongs to signs and on the basis of which one may then decide, through analysis or intuition, whether or not they 'make sense', according to what rule they follow one another or are juxtaposed, of what they are the sign, and what sort of act is carried out by their formulation (oral or written). One should not be surprised, then, if one has failed to find structural criteria of unity for the statement; this is because it is not in itself a unit, but a function that cuts across a domain of structures and possible unities, and which reveals them, with concrete contents, in time and space. (Foucault 1972: 86–7)

The performance of a Renaissance play, the publication of a text on hermaphrodites, the reporting of a crime in a newspaper, the transcription of a legal proceeding: such events may not have been read or known by an author but, in so far as they realign discursive relations, they can be used to discuss a particular text. Because an author works within a discursive formation of which he or she is not the originator, the texts and events which can be brought to bear on a text are not limited to the author's reading or influence.

While the concepts central to Foucault's notion of archaeology carried through to his later work and are still used in new historicist criticism, Foucault was subsequently critical of an implicit positivism in his works of archaeology and later moved towards the idea of genealogy. In genealogy the idea of a pure description of the discursive formation shifts in emphasis to become a 'history of the present' or effective history. Here, the interests and historical position of the historian/critic receive more attention.

Genealogy

Foucault's emphasis upon archaeology as description, rather than interpretation, can be seen as a form of positivism – an attempt to remove normative or evaluative criteria from the writing of history. While Foucault's work always problematised the structuralist paradigm of a static system of differences, his desire to remove all forms of commentary or interpretation from the presentation of the past shares the structuralist impulse of objectivism. However, even while writing *The Archaeology of Knowledge*, it seems that Foucault felt uneasy about the status of his own position as a writer of history. While exposing the historical conditions which underpinned other discourses, the conditions of his own discourse were left unexamined.

In many ways the logic of archaeology had to leave its own position unexamined. In *The Order of Things* Foucault had demonstrated that the 'transcendental' move, by which a subject comes to know and understand the conditions which ground his or her own existence, was the final instance in the modern study of 'man'. Prior to the classical age 'order' was assumed to reside in nature; in the classical age order is seen as an act of the representation of nature; 'modernity' begins when questions regarding the knowability of that order lead to a study of 'man' as a knowing subject. But if knowledge is seen as dependent upon, or refracted through, a knowing subject then it is important that the subject come to know itself. This move towards self-knowledge results in a 'transcendental' mode of enquiry: the subject asks how it is possible for subjectivity to be. In doing so the subject overcomes its finitude (the fact that it can only know the world as it is mediated by a subject) by knowing itself (how the subject produces that world). Given Foucault's clear critique, in *The Order of Things*, of this 'transcendental' tradition – in which the subject examines and knows the grounds for its discourse – it is not surprising that he leaves his own position unexamined. His attempt at a pure description of the 'historical a priori' which make various discourses possible ostensibly removes the subject from both sides of the enquiry: neither the 'minds' of the authors studied nor of the historian is to be considered. There is no 'empathy' between two human 'world-views'. There is, in its place, a presentation of the system of discourse and its reconfigurations.

However, this ideal of pure description still leaves the motivation and historical conditions of Foucault himself unexamined. It is clear that Foucault perceives the problems inherent in his attempt at a pure and objective description. In the concluding section of The Archaeology of Knowledge Foucault declares that, far from providing a coherent and single philosophical position which could examine other discourses, his work avoids the positing of itself as a 'starting point':

> my discourse, far from determining the locus in which it speaks, is avoiding the ground on which it could find support. It is a discourse about discourses: but it is not trying to find in them a hidden law, a concealed origin that it only remains to free; nor is it trying to establish by itself, taking itself as a starting-point, the general theory of which they would be the concrete models. It is trying to deploy a dispersion that can never be reduced to a single system of differences, a scattering that is not related to absolute axes of reference; it is trying to operate a decentring that leaves no privilege to any centre. (Foucault 1972: 205)

Foucault's subsequent response to such problems, however, is not to take a transcendental move and expose and validate the grounds of his own method. Instead, he brings the specificity and historical situatedness of his own discourse into greater relief. Rather than being a pure description of system, his method, in the form of genealogy, will provide a history of the 'present'. Beginning from the Nietzschean recognition that there are no facts but only interpretations of facts, Foucault's genealogy emphasises the political interest in all forms of knowledge, including his own. There is no act of 'knowledge' which is not also an act of power. Foucault's emphasis upon knowledge as power marks a shift away from structuralism towards the more Nietzschean notion of genealogy.

Reacting against the totalising (and what he saw as paralysing) character of nineteenth-century historiography, Nietzsche argued that modern man had 'become a strolling spectator' in the gallery of history (Nietzsche 1983: 183 [1873–76]). According to Nietzsche, in his essay 'On the uses and disadvantages of history for life', a complete knowledge of the past, an over-commitment to the past, would preclude any radical movement towards the future. While it is true, Nietzsche admitted, that humanity cannot live in a moment of pure presence like a cow grazing in a field, it can relieve the burden of the past by a process of willed and *active* 'forgetting'. History should be used to counter the paucity of the present. This does not mean that the historian should seek great examples in the past. On the contrary, the historian should create a past which will produce a more vigorous present. To write history is, therefore, an act of power:

> If you are to venture to interpret the past you can do so only out of the fullest exertion of the vigour of the present: only when you put forth your noblest qualities in all their strength will you divine what is worth knowing and preserving in the past. Like to like! Otherwise you will draw the past down to you. Do not believe historiography that does not spring from the head of the rarest minds; and you will know the quality of a mind when it is obliged to express something universal or to repeat something universally known: the genuine historian must possess the power to remint the universally known into something never heard of before. (Nietzsche 1983: 94)

On this model, of course, there can be no 'pure' description of a discursive formation, historical era or any aspect of the past whatsoever. Accepting Nietzsche's idea that no historical description can be complete (an aim for such completion locks the historian into the past), Foucault's genealogy focuses on the connection between history, use and power. It is now power, interest and will, rather than discourse, which is foregrounded in Foucault's genealogy. History is a history of the present in so far as it is written to disrupt the self-evidence or feeling of progress which enables satisfaction with the present as the inevitable outcome of the past. Whereas conventional history would show all events leading naturally and logically to the present, the genealogist shows the chance, the heterogeneity and the forces of power (including accidents) which have produced the present in its own heterogeneity. Referring to Nietzsche's distinction between the metaphysician and the genealogist, Foucault argues:

> In placing present needs at the origin, the metaphysician would convince us of an obscure purpose that seeks its realization at the moment it arises. Genealogy, however, seeks to reestablish the various systems of subjection: not the anticipatory power of meaning, but the hazardous play of dominations. (Foucault 1977a: 148)

History, the shift of discursive formations, becomes a play of competing forces:

> In a sense, only a single drama is ever staged in this 'non-place,' the endlessly repeated play of dominations. The domination of certain men over others leads to the differentiation of values; class domination generates the idea of liberty; and the forceful appropriation of things necessary to survival and the

imposition of a duration not intrinsic to them account for the origin of logic. This relationship of domination is no more a 'relationship' than the place where it occurs is a place; and, precisely for this reason, it is fixed, throughout its history, in rituals, in meticulous procedures that impose rights and obligations. It establishes marks of its power and engraves memories on things and even within bodies. (Foucault 1977a: 150)

While Foucault's theory of the statement had always given each discursive formation a set of rules dominated and determined by certain forces, his more explicit theorisation of power in the concept of genealogy explains both the position of the genealogist and the ways in which statements have effect. The 'immanent' analysis of the archaeology is sustained; there is no invention, imagination or birth which produces historical formations. The power and forces which play themselves out in history are not reducible to the will of individuals. Power is a network of forces through which individuals, institutions and discourses are formulated.

This notion of power was important in Foucault's genealogical histories: *Discipline and Punish* (1976) and the first volume of *The History of Sexuality* (1978). It was these works, and their notion of power as the productive distribution of forces, which inspired much new historicist and cultural materialist criticism of the 1980s. And it could even be argued that the ficto-critical aspect of new historicism and contemporary criticism has a genealogical dimension. By injecting personal anecdote, reflection and self-description into criticism, the author foregrounds her own position, desire and will without using this foregrounding as a form of general legitimation. Through Foucault's emphasis on genealogy, power was no longer seen in negative terms – as power 'over' a pre-existing entity; power did not merely repress, contain and delimit. Power existed at all levels – including control and resistance – and was positive and productive. Entities such as the individual, discourses, institutions and events were the effects of, and enabled by, the network of power.

Foucault and new historicism

Stephen Greenblatt's 1980 study, *Renaissance Self-Fashioning*, was heavily indebted to the Foucault of *Discipline and Punish* and *The History of Sexuality* (Vol. 1). In this work Greenblatt charts a genealogy of the modern self and argues that the idea of a private and interior subject is an effect of new modes of surveillance and new performances of power which emerged in the Renaissance. This historical shift is exemplified, for Greenblatt, in the career of Thomas More who is divided between, on the one hand, a yearning for a thoroughly communitarian, socially-defined self, and on the other, a private subjectivity which is set against social performance. The torture of heretics, according to Greenblatt, in its rituals of surveillance, confession, examination and questioning produced the sense of interiority which characterised the Renaissance – an era which was both aware of the status of selves as products of public performance and profoundly anxious that the self might be nothing other than performance (Greenblatt 1980: 102). Paradoxically, this new sense of interiority was only meaningful when asserted against public performance; but such a private self was also an effect of, and not a creator of, its corporeal and social acts. According to Greenblatt, 'There is a powerful ideology of inwardness but few sustained expressions of inwardness that may stand apart from the hated institutional structure' (Greenblatt 1980: 85). The Renaissance subject was fashioned according to a public performance which it also negated in order to posit its private interiority. This follows Foucault's argument that the discursive construction of the private subject is achieved through various social practices of self-observation and personal introspection. As Foucault had argued in *Discipline and Punish*, modernity is characterised by a shift in power relations; no longer subject to public and corporeal forms of discipline, the modern subject is produced as the effect of procedures of self-discipline (such as the confessions, acts of faith, testimony and poetry examined by Greenblatt in *Renaissance Self-Fashioning*).

If Greenblatt follows *Discipline and Punish* in arguing that the self is constituted through practices of surveillance, he appears as an even more dutiful Foucaultian when he discusses Renaissance representations of sexuality. For Foucault in the first volume of *The History of Sexuality*, sexuality is not something which is discovered in modern analysis. Sexuality is produced through the rules which organise it; there is no 'natural' sexual desire prior to its discursive delimitation and prohibition. Greenblatt seems to follow this emphasis on the co-production of desire and prohibition in his analysis of Spenser. Spenser's description of the Bower of Bliss (the site of alluring sensuality) in the *The Faerie Queene* produces a desire alongside the containment and prohibition of that desire. According to Greenblatt, the discourse of sexual excess produces the same discourse of renunciation. The domain of 'civility' is constituted by the very power which divides the sexual from the civilized. For Greenblatt, Spenser writes in a full awareness of the role of power as constitutive of knowledge, desire and value:

The Bower of Bliss must be destroyed not because its gratifications are unreal but because they threaten 'civility' – civilization – which for Spenser is achieved only through renunciation and the constant exercise of power. If this power inevitably entails loss, it is also richly, essentially creative; power is the guarantor of value, the shaper of all knowledge, the pledge of human redemption. (Greenblatt 1980: 173)

Unlike Foucault, Greenblatt *recognises* in the Renaissance his own (Foucaultian) sense of power and attributes that awareness of power to those texts he studies. This may be what makes Greenblatt's work both highly problematic and productive. Unlike Foucault, who uses the notion of power as a strategic term to overcome an emphasis on intention and meaning, Greenblatt locates power as an intention within a historically specific political formation. Having read Foucault, who argues for power as the productive motor for subjects, relations and action in general, Greenblatt *finds* this theory of power in the specific awareness of Renaissance texts. (Rather than arguing that Greenblatt has got Foucault wrong we could see his work as symptomatic: what if Foucault's theory of power was itself historically determined and part of the modernity described in Greenblatt's Renaissance?)

A similar move of 'recognition' also characterised earlier cultural materialist work on Shakespeare. Jonathan Dollimore, in *Radical Tragedy* (1984), sees Renaissance drama as a literary movement which can reveal the 'truth' of the critic's own theory of power and ideology. Writers like Machiavelli and Montaigne (who are also important for Greenblatt's study) were, according to Dollimore, exemplary of the 'period's developing awareness of ideology' (Dollimore 1984: 11). The success of new historicist and cultural materialist readings (and the penchant for Renaissance literature) can be explained in part by this recognition effect. The Renaissance, it is argued, is a privileged object for analysis precisely because its texts express the very theory of power or ideology which we, today, use to criticise the present. In looking back at the emergence of modernity the critic can see, in the transition from feudalism to capitalism, the relativity and instability of modern social formations. The new historicist reading of the Renaissance is a reading of the present. But in the Renaissance – particularly in those writers who have an insight into power – the critic finds a series of critically distanced texts, texts which bear a heightened awareness of the workings of power or ideology.

This recognition can be seen as a form of genealogy where the past is used to describe the character of the present. Foucault explicitly argues that history and its presentation is effective precisely in so far as it is used as both a form of self-analysis and self-distancing. The aim of genealogy is, for Foucault, 'to examine both the difference that keeps us at a remove from a way of thinking in which we recognise the origin of our own, and the proximity that remains in spite of that distance which we never cease to explore' (Foucault 1985: 7). But Foucault's descriptions, while enabling a 'recognition' also aim to show the distance we have travelled. In *The History of Sexuality: The Care of the Self* (Vol. 3 1988) Foucault charts the formulation of early Christian ethics but points out that while there is an extreme vigilance towards sexual activity in Hellenistic writings and an increasing pathologisation of sex, this approach is not yet a hermeneutics of the soul in the modern sense: 'this attention does not lead to a decipherment of that activity in its origin and unfolding' (Foucault 1988: 142). Such a decipherment emerges with the Christian practices of confessional and is fully explored in the first volume of the History. The effective character of Foucault's genealogy of the modern sexual subject is described in the second volume: 'The object was to learn to what extent the effort to think one's own history can free thought from what it silently thinks, and so enable it to think differently, (Foucault 1985: 9).

Greenblatt's focus on self-fashioning also demonstrates the production of subjects in discursive formations and, like Foucault, attempts to show the specifically modern conditions and character of the post-Renaissance subject. Where the two accounts differ most is in Greenblatt's attribution of power *as an ideology* to those authors he studies, while for Foucault power is 'anonymous'. While *Renaissance Self-Fashioning* seems to still work with a notion of power as ideology (that is, power is an idea used by a particular individual or group) Foucault's notion of an anonymous and diffuse power is not locatable within a specific ideology or group of individuals. There is a clear methodological difference here. For Foucault, power is a methodological strategy, a way of reading and an explanatory device which attempts to avoid referring texts, acts and practices to some domain (intention, ideology, interests other than themselves). For Greenblatt the notion of power is already implicated in the texts studied; the critic does not 'have' a notion of power which is then used to read the texts. 'Power' is found both as something of which Renaissance authors were themselves aware and a term which was used in Renaissance discourse. Greenblatt argues that Spenser sees power as a guarantor of value. Here, 'power' itself has its own effects; it is part of a discursive formation, and not just an analytic tool. What this reveals is perhaps the difficulty of any term — such as Foucault's discourse or power — which presents itself as something other than a general explanation, ground or horizon. As the uptake of Foucault's work showed, not only does 'power' fall back into being an idea used to explain some hidden meaning, it also has its specific history of use and representation.

This point of difference can be made more clear if we return to Greenblatt's reading of Spenser in the above quotation where he argues that civility 'for Spenser is achieved only through renunciation and the constant exercise of power' (emphasis added). Here, Greenblatt is not speaking about his own theory of power; he is articulating Spenser's vision of power. This is made more explicit in a following sentence when he aligns Spenser with Freud 'in the great Western celebration of power' (1980: 174). What happens here is not that we have an examination of the self as an effect of power (as in Foucault). Rather, power is an ideology, an idea or representation through which individuals (like Spenser, Bacon, Freud, Shakespeare and Marlowe) construct themselves. One could argue that Greenblatt sees Renaissance authors as particularly self-aware, such that literary texts are not effects of the workings of power but themselves manifest a Nietzschean/Foucaultian awareness of the operations of power as the positive condition of knowledge. (This is precisely the position of many cultural materialists who favour the Renaissance for its more critical attitude towards authority.) But there is also a sense in which power for Greenblatt is nothing other than a representation, or a fact of ideology and not, as in Foucault, an anonymity which precedes any ideological identification. If it is a display of power which produces an inner self, a seeming distance between the subject and its performance, then it is also the case that power for Greenblatt is nothing other than a performance. So, power would be one motif among others, within Greenblatt's general theory of the self as performance, rather than a radical theoretical method. Commenting this time upon Shakespeare, Greenblatt argues that the 'theater is widely perceived in the period as the concrete manifestation of the histrionic quality of life, and, more specifically, of power ...' (1980: 253). That is, power is part of the perception of the period. It is a representation, an ideology; and it is in so far as power is a representation that it is able to act in the formation of subjects.

Greenblatt, who distances himself critically from this period, at the same time as he sees his own history as a history of the present, posits performance and representation – and not power – as the explanation and explanandum of Renaissance self-fashioning. The literary mode does have a privileged specificity – not because in its awareness of power it reveals the true workings of modern life – but because literature foregrounds representation. Only in literature is that dependence of the immediate inner voice on text and discourse made explicit. As an example, Greenblatt cites a historical shift which occurs in modernity whereby the form of representation alters: from the self as constituted through public performance, the modern subject is dependent upon the text; the book replaces the communal body (Greenblatt 1980: 159). 'Power' is central to this argument as an idea or theme which the critic studies, and does not provide a new way of reading. It is argued that the texts of Spenser and Shakespeare reveal a shift from publicly grounded legitimation to a power operating in the domain of the subject. Not surprisingly, then, there would be a concern with power. Where is power? How does it work? Who owns it? These are the questions Greenblatt finds in the Renaissance texts under examination. Foucault's work could then be seen as part of the tradition analysed by Greenblatt and Renaissance critics; power becomes a problem when there are new modes of representation. Representation is no longer public production and spectacle; it takes private forms of reading, writing and reflection. In this shift the self is represented in a different mode; differences of history and the self are differences in modes of representation. Power in the Renaissance is nothing other than a certain forcefulness of representations: 'one of the highest achievements of power is to impose fictions upon the world and one of its supreme pleasures is to enforce the acceptance of fictions that are known to be fictions' (Greenblatt 1980: 141). Power, for Greenblatt is, then, very different from Foucault's attempt to write in terms of positivity (the conditions of knowledge which lie outside subjective representation). In fact, power for Greenblatt becomes another prior ground, the condition for the possibility of representation, or 'the enabling condition of representation itself' (Greenblatt 1988a: 3). At the same time, this ground is seen as a specific theorisation of the Renaissance. Greenblatt speaks, as it were, in a free-indirect style which inhabits Renaissance self-awareness. The Renaissance sense of power is found in literary texts and then turned back upon them.

The point in articulating this difference between Foucault and Greenblatt is not in order to say that Greenblatt has misread or disobeyed Foucault. It is, rather, to point out that if, for Greenblatt, power is a mode of representation and performance then the affinity between new historicism and Foucault is not a strict identity. The differences could be summarised by remarking that the idea of representation in Greenblatt's work sustains the sense of human intentionality (a distance between the self and its representations) – an idea directly challenged by the anonymity of Foucault's notion of power. For Greenblatt the notion of power is not used critically to disrupt any transcendental grounds of interpretation (as it is in Foucault); on the contrary, power as the performance of representations enables an idea of culture in general (Pechter 1987; Patterson 1988: 95) at the same time as this theory is critically located as a response to the Renaissance. While Foucault was highly critical of the notion of representation – in so far as it sustained the theory of 'man' as a thinking subject – new historicism and cultural materialism have combined their analytics of power with a focus on representation and culture. This difference between both new historicism and cultural materialism and Foucault can be further illuminated by examining other theoretical movements which have been important for recent criticism. In particular, an awareness of the position of the critic within a specific culture (Western/European) has also been a feature of new historicist and cultural materialist work. In order to understand this emphasis it is necessary to go beyond the work of Foucault and consider the theorisation of the notion of culture which has taken place in anthropological and ethnographic theory.

3

Culture and interpretation: anthropology, ethnography and understanding

The concept of culture has become prominent in recent literary criticism – most obviously in cultural materialist and new historicist criticism. While the concept of culture has been a part of literary enquiry since, at least, Matthew Arnold's *Culture and Anarchy* (1869), the term as it is currently employed differs significantly from its previous usage. F. R. Leavis had used the idea of culture to describe highly-valued and privileged social forms (such as religion, art and knowledge). For new criticism, works of art were defined in opposition to social purposes; 'culture', here, was that which resisted anything other than purely aesthetic forms of justification. Recent literary criticism has taken on a broader definition of culture – taking up some of the inflections it has received in anthropology and social theory. By paying attention to anthropological theory, recent criticism has challenged the narrow autonomy which traditionally shielded works of art (or 'culture' in Leavis's sense) from general sociological enquiry.

This chapter will look at how recent uses of 'culture' differ from those methods, such as Marxism and sociology of literature, which *relate* a text to some outside. By thinking of texts as aspects of culture, rather than as being related to culture, recent criticism has replaced 'context' with the more dynamic notion of symbolic exchange. One of the distinguishing traits of new historicism has been a use of anthropological theory and terminology – in particular the work of writers such as Clifford Geertz and Mary Douglas. (The use of 'culture' in cultural materialism will be the subject of a later chapter.) Having, to a large extent, done away with or problematised mediating concepts such as 'world-picture', 'ideology', 'mind-set' or '*mentalité*', – ideas which relate texts to some context – new historicists more frequently adopt the use of 'culture'. The idea of 'culture' may appear to be just one more mediating concept among others but its prominence in new historicist practice can be atttributed to an attempt to overcome the process of relating a text to a world.

The idea of culture in its anthropological sense also enables new historicism to be a 'history of the present'. While the discipline of anthropology has usually been associated with the study of other cultures, the location of English literary texts within the framework of anthropological theory enables a study of English literature as a specific and determined practice with its own culture and history. As a result, the meaning of a text is no longer referred to supposed universals such as 'the human condition', 'tragic spirit' or 'aesthetic value'. Such literary-philosophical concepts are now seen as specifically located within a particular (Western or British imperialist) culture. In the past, even historical criticism which resisted such universals by focusing on temporal difference neglected to focus on the cultural specificity of Western or European history. Marxism as a critical practice, for example, accounts for the text within a movement of history determined by the economy in the last instance. The possibility of other historical trajectories in societies not determined by capitalist production is normally left out of account. The idea of culture and the use of anthropological theory, on the other hand, places the literary critic in the position of accounting for the specific practices of English and European society. Ideas of 'tragedy', 'individualism' and 'capitalism', for example, cannot be accepted as natural developments in a history of civilization but are specific to European culture. Not only should such notions not be accepted as universal or inevitable; their formation and understanding by European culture may also be investigated. Thinking of cultural specificity enables critical reflection upon literary criticism's own central ideas, such as imagination, value, affect and even history. Because such ideas are never simply given or immutable, a closer look at culture can question the way concepts need to be worked at or produced – including the concepts of 'culture', 'history' and 'literature'.

If new historicism has also been called cultural poetics, this is because of the way both terms – culture and poetry – have been expanded in meaning. Culture is not just the domain of art or understanding as it has traditionally been considered. And the 'poetics' of a culture includes not just its literary texts, but the creation of meaning through practices, ritual, events and structures. From this new understanding, a text is not related to a culture in the way in which a work is related to a historical background. Texts produce culture. Culture is nothing other than the values, self-understandings and ways of thinking achieved by such practices

67

as the writing of texts, the performing of ceremonies, the exacting of punishments and the formulation of prohibitions. Cultures do not sit 'above' the world in the way that ideologies are seen to be determined by, or expressive of, prior economic conditions. Nor are cultures ideal or psychological entities like a 'world-view' or 'mind-set'. Cultures are not used to relate texts to worlds because cultures are already texts, persons, practices and rituals. The text is not an expression or reflection of its world; it plays an active part in producing and acting within that world. To say that Jane Austen's *Pride and Prejudice* (1873) is a form of culture is not to say that it has some inherent artistic merit which separates it from other objects. *Pride and Prejudice* is culture because it has certain effects, creates certain relations, interacts with other texts and repeats rituals, values and practices. If we were to understand romance or romantic love in contemporary Western culture, we would have to consider not only the way individuals act – the giving of flowers, the exchange of looks, the interaction of bodies, the utterance of certain statements – but also the symbols exchanged. Part of the cultural complex of romance would have to include texts like *Pride and Prejudice*. These texts are revived, read and understood as exemplary of romance; but they are exemplary only because they create the culture of romance. It would be a misunderstanding to say that Jane Austen discovered and expressed the essence of romantic love, or that her novels are timeless because they tap into some eternal qualities of human nature. *Pride and Prejudice*, as much as the novels of Barbara Cartland, the practices of Valentine's day or romance films are all cultural acts. They constitute patterns of behaviour, constitute the value of symbols and organise understanding.

Because the idea of culture sets texts *alongside* practices, rituals and disciplines, it enables critics to consider a text according to any number of variables. Architecture, the theatre in which a tragedy is performed, film adaptation, the use of boys to play women in Renaissance drama, the presence of royalty at a performance, the publication of a novel in a certain binding, the reading of a poem at a public gathering and new scientific and medical practices are placed within the same field of meaning as the literary text: all are seen as various aspects of a single field of 'culture'.

Clifford Geertz

In his essay 'The impact of the concept of culture on the concept of man' Geertz (1973) argues that cultural difference and diversity should not be seen as something that overlays a pre-cultural phenomenon of 'man'. For Geertz there can be no pre-cultural universals (such as the presence of some form of religion, ethics or society) when considering different cultures; the attempt to describe such universals in substantive form always fails because the differences between the various types of society or religion preclude any unified definition. For Geertz, no single idea can define what constitutes human culture.

The challenge that presents itself once we accept this argument is clear. How do we understand the term culture itself? If there is no unifying feature which collects all societies, and we use this lack of unity to say that we are all instances of culture, what stops 'culture' from becoming another unifying term? A simple answer would be that culture is whatever form human life takes, regardless of difference. But this throws the burden back on the concept of human life, a concept which, according to Geertz, takes a severe beating once we recognise that there are no universal human characteristics. If there is no essence or single feature which defines what it is to be human, how can we define culture as the various forms of human life? Geertz rejects the concept of man – for this would imply an essence – but he confidently assumes the category of human life in order to investigate the variety of cultural configurations. For the most part Geertz works as though the idea of culture itself were broad enough to operate without the need to define what a culture is. Geertz seems to answer this problem by using culture as a family resemblance. There is no single feature, or essence, which would unite all cultures – neither religion, ethics, incest taboos nor technology – but there is a collection of different characteristics which create cultural configurations in different ways. We call all these groupings cultures because some share certain characteristics (such as writing) while others share other features (religion, ethics). There is no single feature which they all share but they are recognised as instances of 'culture' because we understand the term culture through these various uses. At other times Geertz implies that there is a general characteristic which defines culture in general. Indeed, in order to have a theory of culture some notion of culture in general would seem to be a minimum requirement. Geertz's general definition of culture as a form of exchange mechanism is largely defined by refuting earlier understandings of what a culture might be or how it might be analysed.

Geertz argues against the view that cultural formations are like rules or patterns which individuals subject themselves to in order to take part in a social whole. Such rules are usually posited by anthropologists who observe regularities of behaviour and then assume that individuals possess a mental content or psychological conditioning which produces such behaviour. Such explanations of society posit regular and coherent patterns which individuals internalise in order to behave in a certain way. But this pattern would be a result of what Geertz refers to as the 'illusion of quiddity'; that is, we observe a certain regularity and then go on to posit some thing (ideology, human nature, structure) which causes or produces the regularity (Geertz 1995: 22). Geertz, on the other hand, argues that cultures can not be reduced to such patterns and that there is no simple underlying pattern which produces behaviour. Rather, behaviour itself operates by its own mechanism irrespective of any psychological content. Instead of likening a human being to a puppet which is organised from within by behaviour patterns, Geertz argues that human action should be likened more to computer programs, where the mechanism itself is its own ordering. Whatever order the observer subsequently discovers is achieved after the fact, and should not be posited as the cause of events (Geertz 1995: 23).

Doing away with the universal notion of mind which would then be ordered by social patterns, Geertz posits cultural 'control mechanisms' which produce varieties of behaviour. Culture is a way of doing things, a form of achievement or a mode of activity rather than an internalised pattern or scheme. It is not that there is something like human life or mind which then enters into culture, or becomes enculturated. There is no prior mental space where rules are either formulated or deposited. Human life is nothing apart from its ways of behaving:

> culture is best seen not as complexes of concrete behaviour patterns – customs, usages, traditions, habit clusters – as has, by and large, been the case up to now, but as a set of control mechanisms – plans, recipes, rules, instructions (what computer engineers call 'programs') – for the governing of behaviour. (Geertz 1973: 46)

What Geertz's rejection of concrete patterns emphasises is that cultures are not rigid sets of pre-given rules which are then followed. Geertz's model of culture is a form of immanence; a culture should not be explained or analysed through some external cause, but should be understood according to its own recipe for order. Observed behaviour cannot be explained by some larger external or imposed pattern such as custom. Behaviour is a complex phenomenon with its own internal logic; an event is not just the result of a given tradition imposed upon individuals; behaviour possesses its own plan or 'recipe'. But such regularities, Geertz argues, should not be explained by positing the mental intentions of the agent who acts.

Rules and instructions are public; they are continually reproduced in processes of interaction and exchange. In keeping with Geertz's rejection of mind (or some mental site where rules are internalised) the medium for cultural exchange is the symbol:

> The 'control mechanism' view of culture begins with the assumption that human thought is basically both social and public – that its natural habitat is the house yard, the marketplace, and the town square. Thinking consists not of 'happenings in the head' (although happenings there and elsewhere are necessary for it to occur) but of a traffic in what have been called, by G. H. Mead and others, significant symbols – words for the most part but also gestures, drawings, musical sounds, mechanical devices like clocks, or natural objects like jewels – anything, in fact, that is disengaged from its mere actuality and used to impose meaning upon experience. (Geertz 1973: 45)

Geertz's idea of thinking as 'traffic in significant symbols' can be likened to Greenblatt's concept of 'negotiation and exchange' in which a culture exists and sustains itself by circulating symbols. The forms of a society, for Geertz, are neither static nor pre-determined by a unified whole, such as 'tradition' or ideology. Cultures occur as dynamic systems in which various signs – texts, actions, rituals – occur as public events which negotiate with other signs. This is one way in which culture avoids becoming another general concept which would unify the differences of human life. For there are differing ways in which cultures form themselves and different forms of symbolic exchange. The character of a culture is not predetermined by a general theory of meaning production. On the contrary, the various ways in which meaning is produced, the differing forms of exchange, are precisely what is in question. So there is no single trait or essence of culture as such other than the production of cultural differentiation itself. Culture functions here as a general term which problematises the process of generality. But even this very loose definition of the term seems to make some claim regarding all human life: the ideas of symbolic traffic and representation do appear as features of any possible form of life. So Geertz's attempt to use culture to resist universal definitions of 'man' or 'culture' is perhaps only successful if we attend to the differences enabled by the term, rather than the generality which would stem from any concept – be it culture, history, man or representation. Whether 'culture' is a better term than others for playing up difference rather than similarity depends upon how much room the concept allows for the undermining of its own generality. This is similar to the problem of history: to acknowledge that all life is historically specific at once opens up a field of radical difference at the same time as history is posited as the unifying feature of all life. Unlike Foucault, who persistently reformulated his writing strategies in order to resist overarching horizons – which were inevitably perceived in his use of power, history and discourse – Geertz's methodological reflections focus on emphasising cultural difference without explicitly theorising how culture itself might avoid functioning as a unifying concept. The idea of culture as continual exchange without a general underlying pattern seems to be sufficient for the task Geertz sets himself. The differences in the form of exchange carry the burden of disrupting the idea of underlying unity.

But if culture in general is a traffic in symbols how do we locate difference and how might we cope with those symbols which seem to be qualitatively unique? Geertz's metaphor of the computer program may seem to reduce cultural artifacts – such as literary texts – to mechanistic functions. There may be no extra-artistic structures (such as ideology or history) which the work of art replicates; but even if its order is posited as an internal mechanism or recipe, it is still seen as ordered. If a poem is like a computer program it is because it does not follow rules. When Shakespeare writes a sonnet he writes in a certain way which creates a form; the observational error would be to count the syllables, work out the rhyme scheme, notice regularities and then assume that Shakespeare somehow possessed a series of guidelines for the 'Shakespearean sonnet'. There may be a recipe-like function of the sonnet form. An author may have to be aware of certain features which would enable the creation of a sonnet, to be recognised *as* a sonnet. But these recipe-rules are enabling and productive and not imposed from without. The 'rules' for a recipe are internal to the creation; they enable what it is I want to make. They are not rules in the sense of external laws. If I want to make a chocolate cake I must use chocolate – but this has to do with the nature of what I want to make, and so the rule is internal. It is not motivated by a demand to obey the cookbook. Of course, this distinction between external and internal rules is difficult because the boundary is quite fluid. I might start cooking by obeying recipes in a literal and slavish manner, not having a sense of the practice and doing everything 'by the book.' Only when I become skilled do the rules seem like guides rather than laws. Similarly, if I want to start writing poetry I might get the schema of a sonnet and follow it as though it prescribed what I ought to do. But it is the subsequent improvisation, creation and malleability of the schema which defines culture in Geertz's sense. When poetry is composed we seem to do it for the sake of the poem itself – and not because we obey patterns. We do not follow rules; our traffic in symbols has a regularity but this is always an effect of observation after the fact. The sonnet is nothing other than its own form; it possesses, rather than adheres to, a pattern. Geertz, unlike Foucault (and Bourdieu and de Certeau, who will be considered later), does not explicitly refer to literature in his theory. But it follows from his explanation of culture, and the uses made of it by literary critics such as Greenblatt, that what makes the term culture valuable is precisely its ability to deal with 'complex and contradictory fields of significative action' (Geertz 1995: 49).

Culture is not the background of a text because it is already a form of text. Art works would not be essentially different from other forms of symbol. There is no problem of relating a text to a culture, because texts are explained as instances of culture. They may have complex internal programs, but what makes them aspects of culture is still their character as meaningful items of ordered exchange. There would be no *essential* difference between reciting a sonnet or waving a traffic flag. A poem could be interpreted by setting it alongside any other form of cultural exchange. The meaning of a text would lie in its surroundings rather than its inherent depth. The status of certain symbols – a sonnet, an icon or a totem – is achieved through the specific mode of traffic in which they are circulated. But these artifacts are still symbols: what they are is effected and produced culturally, through exchange. The performance of a play is neither reducible to the intention of the playwright, nor is it a reflection of its historical locus; the play itself is a player in the complex games and exchanges by which a culture makes itself. It cannot be explained by a static system of rules; for the regularities which characterise the traffic in signs are also subject to exchange and renegotiation.

The concept of culture allows an 'immanent' analysis of its fields. The text is not explained or interpreted by being referred to some external rule, ideology or background. The text is already part of a larger story. While its meaning is not posited as some inner depth, the significance of a text or any event is still more than the text itself. An event is not self-evident; for the observer from another culture (either geographically or historically) a simple description of the event in isolation will not suffice to reveal its meaning. Nor does meaning reside 'behind' the event in the intentions of the participants. But the event is meaningful in terms of its location within a whole system of other events. In this way we can see that, like Foucault's idea of discursive practice, Geertz's anthropological theory of culture enables an expanded view of the text without positing a separate 'background' or context. The text is its culture and does not have to be subsequently related to a background or context by a critic or

73

anthropologist. Culture is already likened to a text; for the understanding of a way of life is seen as a certain capacity of story-telling. But the rules of this form of narrative are immanent to its practice; and anthropological understanding is also part of a way of life which is already a form of story. A general narrative is not imposed, nor is the data merely assembled. According to Geertz, cultural understanding is a form of story-telling which relates to other stories:

> Understanding a form of life, or anyway some aspects of it to some degree, and convincing others that you have indeed done so, involves more than the assembly of telling particulars or the imposition of general narratives. It involves bringing figure and ground, the passing occasion and the long story, into coincident view. (Geertz 1995: 51)

This recent statement by Geertz reiterates the central features of his early notion of thick description. Here, an event or text is seen as being more meaningful than its isolated observation would suggest. But this meaning is still immanent because it is not located in a text's 'outside' (structure or ideology) but within a field of texts and events. A text's complexity can be seen as immanent only if we take the text to already possess a certain 'thickness'. Through his concept of 'thick description' Geertz suggests that a symbol or action is not immediately coherent; but this is not because there is some deeper hidden meaning. Thickness is simply all that is presupposed by, and coextensive with, the exchange of a symbol.

Thick description accepts that the meaning of a cultural event is not self-evident. The behaviour which an observer notes cannot be reduced to some immediately apparent function or efficiency. But despite this obvious complexity it is not legitimate to assume immediately that there is some mental or psychological component which accompanies behaviour which it is the duty of an anthropologist to describe. The 'taboos' of a community, for example, do not reside in the minds of the members; taboo is nothing other than the expected repetition of certain practices. Such practices can only be understood in relation to other practices. Understanding an action is not about finding out what the agent really thinks; it is about relating that action to other actions which a community also undertakes. Explaining why the Balinese grant a certain importance to cock-fights is not a matter of ascertaining the mental content of participants but rather the role such fights play in a network of practices. Like Foucault, Geertz's work is set against psychologism and mentalism. Practices possess an order but this is the result of a certain regularity which is a social phenomenon and not an ideal content. A text's meaning is not considered in isolation and referred back to an entity like 'mind'; meaning is a complex and material event. As Geertz argues:

> To set forth symmetrical crystals of significance, purified of their material complexity in which they were located, and then attribute their existence to autogenous principles of order, universal properties of the human mind, or vast, a priori *weltanschauung*, is to pretend a science that does not exist and imagine a reality that cannot be found. Cultural analysis is (or should be) guessing at meanings, assessing the guesses, and drawing explanatory conclusions from the better guesses, not discovering the Continent of meaning and mapping out its bodiless landscape. (Geertz 1973: 20)

This rejection of explanation of intention places an emphasis upon description. Such descriptions can never be final in so far as they will continually have to take into account new variables and new events. The interpreter is not above and beyond the culture to be interpreted; he or she also has a culture. Acts of anthropology are acts of cultural encounter rather than interpretation or explanation. The description of a culture is 'thick' not only because it seeks the fullness of any particular event in terms of the original culture. 'Thickness' also derives from the resonance of the anthropologist's own cultural specificity:

> anthropological writings are themselves interpretations, and second and third order ones to boot. (By definition, only a 'native' makes first order ones: it's his culture.) They are, thus, fictions; fictions, in the sense that they are 'something made,' 'something fashioned' – the original meaning of fictio – not that they are false, unfactual, or merely 'as if' thought experiments. (Geertz 1973: 15)

If we sought to apply Geertz's concept of 'thick description' to literary criticism we might come up with something very like new historicism. Rather than seeking the meaning of a text in the intention or mental content of either the author or the work, we could focus on the effect of the text in a network of practices. We could see the text as an effective symbol: a social fact which makes action meaningful and is part of a culture's way of performing its actions in an ordered and understandable way. Descriptions of texts would be 'thick' if they referred to the social and cultural forms in which the text operated.

The concept of 'thick description' might also provide a way of thinking beyond the common distinction between formalist and political approaches to a text. An immanent analysis of a poem in the formalist sense would account for the features of the poem in their purely textual relations. Blake's poem 'The Sick Rose'might be analysed according to the way terms play off each other.

> O Rose thou art sick
> The invisible worm,
> That flies in the night
> In the howling storm:

> Has found out thy bed
> Of crimson joy
> And his dark secret love
> Does thy life destroy   (Blake 1966:213)

Here, a symbol of beauty and desire – the rose – is set against images of decay and destruction – the worm, the storm, sickness. The only two lines that rhyme end with 'joy' and then 'destroy' which heightens the dichotomy between the affirmative life of the rose and its destruction. But the duality of the poem is also troubled by the penultimate line's paradox of 'dark secret love'. The rose is usually a symbol of love, but it is the worm's 'love' which is the rose's destruction. Within the poem alone the meaning of darkness and secrecy are troubled and enriched. The very associations of love – its secrecy and darkness – are also its destruction. The sickness of the rose, which initially appears in the poem as an external accident is, through the invisible worm, seen as already within the rose itself. And this complex of meaning is achieved by the relation of terms within the poem. A formalist analysis such as this is immanent because it accounts for the poem's significance without referring to context or intention.

This type of immanence would be set against forms of interpretation which referred to the author's intent. Blake's inclusion of this poem within 'Songs of Experience', along with his views on the paralysing effects of seeing desire as a form of destruction and the subsequent utterances by Blake's characters in later works might lead us to read this poem as ironic. Blake would be showing us the limits of a certain way of viewing sexual desire, and the weakness of conventional images – such as the rose – to describe love. Or, the poem could be read in terms of its historical location. The image of the sick rose could be likened to a whole series of Romantic images of failed desire and destruction. Natural beauty is frequently seen as in a process of immediate loss. The idea of an original natural innocence is inevitably problematised through its internal destruction. Wordsworth's 'nature' is similarly lost as soon as it is found. And this retreat of the Romantic natural origin could be accounted for by referring to a general historical sense of failure, alienation and demise. No longer is nature seen as a simple ground of beauty and innocence. The French Revolution, the development of science, the growth of industrialism all explain an increasing sense of distance from a nature which is no longer simply present in its innocence.

Thick description would differ from traditional formalism by locating a text's meaning neither in the text alone nor in some general pre-existing background. Blake's poem, for example, would still be seen in its specificity. Rather than being the reflection of Romanticism as a general historical phenomenon we might look at the poem as an event. What surrounds the poem would not be a general explanatory ground – history or intent – but further cultural events. Thick description here would be a continuous task. We might describe the poem alongside the circumstances of its production and circulation: how the poem was engraved by Blake, the differences in the forms of engraving, the ways in which the poem was read. Or, thick description might look at other exchanges: how understandings of natural symbols such as roses gained a certain currency in Blake's culture. 'The Sick Rose' as the production of a symbol would interact with other symbols of nature – including other poems, landscape painting, contemporary science, theological tracts – which create nature as a symbolic currency. There would not be a general mind-set, such as Romanticism (and its complex notions of alienation, origins and meaning) which the natural symbol expresses. Blake does not write a Romantic poem. His poem takes a symbol (with a storehouse of narratives already surrounding it) and exchanges it in a certain way. What we later understand as Romanticism is an effect of taking a particular exchange of symbols – of roses, landscapes, mountains and hedgerows – and then positing a general narrative. But Romanticism is nothing other than these acts of exchange and cannot be posited as their cause or explanation. The poet's intent is similarly posited after the fact. We begin with description – Blake's works, the stories of his life – and intent is then posited as the causal feature. Thick description does not begin with a general narrative (of, say, Romanticism or Blake's life) but creates a number of dynamic narratives from particulars. And, in the case of a literary text, the particulars would be continually renewed by new responses and events.

Alongside notions like 'thick description', which move away from ideas of intention towards seeing the text as a social event, recent literary criticism has also placed an emphasis upon the effective powers of texts as forms of ritual. Although such an emphasis can be explained by using Geertz's notion of culture as an exchange in symbols, the very different work of Mary Douglas is also useful for describing the text as a form of ritual.

Mary Douglas

While the work of Clifford Geertz has emphasised the local and particular practices of agents (against 'totalising' or 'mentalist' approaches) there have also been more 'structural' approaches to anthropology which have been taken up by literary criticism. Mary Douglas's *Purity and Danger* (1966) is an influential and exemplary instance of anthropological work which tries to identify systemic cultural rules. At the same time, Douglas, like Geertz, insists that such rules should not be located in the private space of an individual's thought. Nor do such rules sit 'above' a culture and remain alien to human interests. On the contrary, cultural practices such as taboos, ritual, magic and ceremony are effective modes of social organisation. Rather than seeing ritual and magic as 'primitive' forms of religion which had not yet 'developed' into properly 'spiritual' beliefs, Douglas argued that all rituals – primitive or otherwise – were forms of enabling social practice. The Eurocentric and traditional division between primitive societies (dominated by magic and ritual) and developed societies (dominated by reason and 'purified' religion) is problematised, if not entirely abandoned, in Douglas's work.

In *Purity and Danger* Douglas argues that our most basic moral divisions are thought through material boundaries. That is, ostensibly irrational taboos and prohibitions (regarding food, cleanliness and so on) enable us to think of social oppositions. And by creating social and material divisions societies can organise themselves. Douglas's discussion of dirt, for example, shows that even before modern ideas of hygiene were articulated the control of dirt enabled certain boundaries which could produce 'symbolic systems':

> If we can abstract pathogenicity and hygiene from our notion of dirt, we are left with the old definition of dirt as matter out of place. This is a very suggestive approach. It implies two conditions: a set of ordered relations and a contravention of that order. Dirt, then, is never a unique, isolated event. Where there is dirt there is system. Dirt is the by-product of a systematic ordering and classification of matter, in so far as ordering involves rejecting inappropriate elements. This idea of dirt takes us straight into the field of

symbolism and promises a link-up with more obviously symbolic systems of purity. (Douglas 1966: 35)

Social divisions between castes, classes and gender are made (and made comprehensible) by symbolic systems. Such systems use material boundaries or taboos to inscribe social and cultural divisions. Taboos and sanctions which operate around virginity, menstruation and childbirth, for example, reinforce gender divisions. Physically confining or marking off menstruating women from the general social space enables a conceptual division between order and disorder, and a practical cultural division between genders. As Douglas argues, much of our social symbolism focuses on the body and its limits. Experiences such as childbirth, menstruation and defecation transgress the limits of the body. Because they can confuse symbolic boundaries these phenomena are usually placed under taboo and sanction.

Douglas's work in the 1960s anticipated many arguments of the 1990s which have drawn attention to the significance of the inscription of the body. Contemporary feminist criticism has shown the ways in which bodies are not brute cultural facts, but are sites of cultural coding. A body is 'written' – not only in the explicit cases of tattooing, piercing and adornment – but also through cultural representations of body images . And it is the body as bounded image which enables the production of identifiable and limited subjects (Grosz 1994; Gatens 1996). What Douglas's early work brings to light is the importance of boundaries and their continual re-enactment through ritual and transgression. It is not that boundaries represent or symbolise ideal differences; we do not have a distinction between purity and danger which is then represented through an integrated or repressed body respectively. Rather, purity itself is produced through boundaries. The Western medieval understanding of purity, it could be argued, is achieved through the continual inscriptive ritual of a female body: the statues of the virgin Mary, the religious practices and festivals that consecrate this image, and the literature of courtly love. The opposition between purity and danger is further enforced in the drawing of limits around the impure female body: not only in the explicit expulsion of witches, but in the anxiety surrounding those female bodies which blur limits – in childbirth, menstruation and sexual desire. And the inscription of cultural order through corporeal boundaries is by no means a pre-modern phenomenon. Modern horror films have recently been analysed as cultural events which work through the limits of the female body (Creed 1993). By representing monstrous female bodies which transgress boundaries, contemporary culture ultimately reinscribes and restores constitutive cultural limits.

Cultures, according to Douglas, are systems of order and organisation; but a sense of order can only be achieved by boundaries which exclude and marginalise disorder. Before any abstract or conceptual distinction between desired order and threatening disorder can be thought, material boundaries are brought into play and continually re-enacted through ritual. Places of complete purity – such as churches – are dominated by symbols of cleansing, order, borders and sanctification. They are directly opposed spatially and conceptually to those other places where dirt, chaos and confusion are dominant. (Think of the medieval opposition between the church and the marketplace.) Abstract concepts, therefore – such as that between the soul and the body – are enabled by these material and spatial divisions. As another example, Douglas points to contemporary Western practices of 'spring cleaning' which can be seen as ritualised ways of marking a difference between a past and a hopefully renewed future.

The importance of seeing symbolic divisions or conceptual boundaries as dependent upon the physical drawing of limits can be seen in the ways texts are now considered as acts of delimitation. The oppositions in a text are not just conceptual; they are ways of thinking which also occur materially. In the Renaissance, for example, the power and authority of legitimate rule was performed by the inscription of boundaries. Literary critics have focused on stage-plays as symbolic markings which divide the just from the unjust, the legitimate from the illegitimate. Such divisions are enabled by dividing and excluding all those categories considered as chaotic or disruptive of the sense of social order. Thus in Shakespeare's *Coriolanus* the 'mob' is associated with animality, dirt, disorder, the body and misrule, while the virtuous Romans are associated with the mind, the respect of proper boundaries and order. The play therefore has as its condition certain material divisions but it also ritually re-enacts and grants further symbolic meaning to those divisions. The play is a cultural event both in its repetition of materially ordering boundaries and in the symbolic weight it grafts onto those divisions.

The further significance of arguments for the materiality of symbolic distinctions lies in the refusal to see forms of ritual and magic as superstitious, misguided and irrational forms of behaviour. Douglas argued that ritual had its own social efficacy. In ritual it is not that the performing agent believes that a particular practice will necessarily cause a certain outcome; rather, she argued, the practice of ritual enables ways of re-thinking or re-ordering reality and divisions. Tying a knot in a handkerchief does not make us remember a thought, but it does give a thought a material symbol. Acts of sacrifice, at the same time, cannot undo acts of transgression but they can help to reinscribe disturbed social boundaries. Douglas discusses a large number of forms of ritual: those that re-draw boundaries, those that externalise conceptual oppositions, those that mark temporal borders, those that tame contingency and those that recognise and exclude disorder. In all cases, Douglas argues that symbols, rituals and practices have a social efficacy. Religions and forms of belief are not metaphysical systems to which individuals submit. Spiritual systems are responses to practical and social problems. As such they are institutional – neither ideal nor psychological:

> the metaphysic is a by-product, as it were, of the urgent practical concern. The anthropologist who draws out the whole scheme of the cosmos which is implied in these practices does the primitive culture great violence if he seems to present the cosmology as a systematic philosophy subscribed to consciously by individuals. (Douglas 1966: 91)

While Douglas's work focuses on structure and divisions, her work differs from structuralism proper in several respects. To begin with, Douglas sees all 'ideal' or symbolic divisions as dependent upon materially and culturally inscribed boundaries. It is not just that (as structuralists would argue) one needs an idea of 'evil' to think about 'good'; it is also the case that one needs concrete oppositions between dirt and cleanliness to think these more 'spiritual' oppositions. This production of social and conceptual boundaries is also a part of cultural organisation. Phenomena such as witchcraft, and the devaluation of border-blurring experiences (such as defecation, madness, incest and so on) demonstrate the ways in which societies recognise and exclude disorder. Alongside any system of conceptual divisions is the possibility of the disruption of those divisions. Cultures therefore have to think of ways of excluding the liminal and the ambiguous. As Douglas argues:

> by settling for one or other interpretation, ambiguity is often reduced. For example, when a monstrous birth occurs, the defining lines between humans and animals may be threatened. If a monstrous birth can be labelled an event of a peculiar kind the categories can be restored. So the Nuer treat monstrous births as baby hippopotamuses, accidentally born to humans, and, with this labelling, the appropriate action is clear. (Douglas 1966: 39)

Insofar as symbolic divisions precede and enable thinking, they can be considered unconscious. But Douglas's idea of symbolic thought differs from the Freudian or psychoanalytic unconscious in two respects. Firstly, symbolic thought is social and interactional and does not occur at the level of individual psychology. Secondly, Douglas's 'unconscious' divisions have their basis in material boundaries and not in mental space.

If a culture is organised by rituals which reinforce boundaries, it is also the case that a culture can be disrupted by experiences which threaten such divisions. Much new historicism has, in fact, focused on those liminal cases which disturb a culture's conceptual ordering. In his essay 'Fiction and Friction' Stephen Greenblatt (1990) shows the ways in which court proceedings determined the specific gender of otherwise indeterminate gender boundaries. A focus upon cases of ambiguity is at the same time tamed through processes of juridical or institutional differentiation. According to Greenblatt the occurrence of hermaphroditism and marginal cases – the muddying of borders – was dealt with by a social performance which reinscribed those borders:

> The Fascination with all that seems to unsettle sexual differentiation – hermaphroditism, gender metamorphosis, women who conceal the inward form of men, men who conceal the inward form of women – never actually threatens the proper generative order, which depends upon the stable distinction between the sexes. ... Even the much rarer cases of authentic hermaphroditism are not permitted to remain ambiguous; judges order that such people decide which sex arouses them more and on this basis choose their gender once for all. (Greenblatt 1990: 42)

While Douglas's work has been one of the main texts which have inspired literary critics to see cultures as systems of divisions enabled by forms of symbolic ritual, these ideas have been articulated in areas other than anthropological theory. The work of the Russian thinker Mikhail Bakhtin has also been used to show that social divisions between order and chaos both dominate societies and are continually threatened by disruption. In his work on Rabelais, Bakhtin (1984) cites the carnivalesque example of a peasant urinating from a cathedral spire. At such moments the conceptual division between purity and chaos which is represented by the opposition between the Church and the marketplace is transgressed. The political meaning of this act of disorder is by no means determinate, but the cultural significance of such borders provides a way of thinking through the process of sustaining and subverting social order. According to both Bakhtin and Douglas, societies are made possible through acts of material ordering which are at once symbolic and political. Divisions are produced through symbols which have a cultural instantiation in the form of boundaries, hierarchies and order.

Drawing on the work of Bakhtin, Stallybrass and White (1986) have shown the ways in which material and ideal oppositions in a culture are produced through physical symbolism. Once again, 'ideal' oppositions such as those operating in literature no longer need to be related to a material or historical context, for the oppositions at work in all these domains are mutually constitutive. Stallybrass and White, for example, demonstrate that the literary term 'classic' derives from a division in Roman law denoting a higher tax band. This evaluative division is initially economic and material. They go on to conclude that

> cultural categories of high and low, social and aesthetic, like those mentioned above but also those of the physical body and geographical space, are never entirely separable. The ranking of literary genres or authors in a hierarchy analogous to social classes is a particularly clear example of a much broader and more complex process whereby the human body, psychic forms, geographical space and the social formation are all constructed within interrelating and dependent hierarchies of high and low. (Stallybrass and White 1986: 2)

New historicism's focus on the disturbance of borders and margins cannot be attributed to any single influence. Along with the work of Douglas and Bakhtin, Foucault had also shown that institutional divisions (the housing of the insane in asylums) were also connected to conceptual orderings (the opposition between reason and madness). The anthropological insight of Douglas's work, though, has linked contemporary and Western practices to ideas of 'primitive' ritual, magic and symbolic thought. Her work has demonstrated that mental and spiritual phenomena are primarily social and institutional. Stephen Greenblatt's more recent work has also focused on the concept of hybridity, thus extending the enquiry into the ways in which cultures produce (and are produced by) borders and boundaries. When alien or foreign elements are encountered by a culture they are reorganised and assimilated through processes of symbolism and representation which are, then, characterised by a dynamic hybridity (Greenblatt 1988b: 4).

Ethnographic theory in the 1980s

While the anthropological work of writers like Geertz and Douglas still remains influential, recent literary criticism has also taken up many of

the concerns which stemmed from rethinking the possibility of anthropological study. Geertz had already, in 1973, argued that taking cultural
differences seriously would mean foregoing any general idea of 'man' or
the human subject. (And much new historicist work has focused on the
different ways in which individuals are produced in specific cultures.) At
the same time, Geertz's The Interpretation of Cultures does confidently put forward a general theory of culture and, with its emphasis on seeing things
from the participant's point of view, fails to problematise the position of
the observer. Geertz's more recent work takes up this problem. The
anthropologist, for Geertz, is a participant on the story he tells. His
ordered descriptions are, in this sense, after the fact (Geertz 1995). The
'found' order is achieved by an act of encounter and narration and then
percieved to be 'there', in the culture.

Both Douglas and Geertz had done much to correct the nineteenth-
century perception that other cultures were primitive and opaque (while
the observer's culture was seen as rational and free from ritual or superstition). Douglas had argued that symbolic thought pervaded all thinking,
while Geertz refused any concept of 'man' in general – thus relativising
the 'subject' of European culture and philosophy. Indeed, by showing that
all culture worked through boundaries – from taboo to spring cleaning –
Douglas at once gave a unified sense of culture at the same time as she
pointed out the West's cultural specificity. Both Douglas and Geertz, and
anthropology in general, worked with culture as a general notion. 'Culture' may have served to relativise nearly everything – human nature,
Western culture, logic and so on – but it still left the anthropological
enterprise in tact. The problem, for Geertz, was how to avoid being reductive in one's cultural analysis given the richness of cultural difference. But
the way out of this problem is to be more rather than less of an anthropologist, to describe more, to observe more, and to have an acute sense of
culture as such. If we do not have a theory of culture and a sense of difference, Geertz argued, then the perceived particulars will never be seen
in their meaningful specificity. We have to have a theory of culture, but the
theory must attend to the problem of difference:

> The problem with ... a no-nonsense approach to things, one which extracts
> the general from the particular and then sets the particular aside as detail,
> illustration, background or qualification, is that it leaves us helpless in the face
> of the very difference we need to explore. (Geertz 1995: 40)

Geertz criticises general notions such as 'power' – which must be an
implicit reference to Foucaultianism, if not Foucault – for 'blocking per-

ception' (Geertz 1995: 40). If we have a general account then we have already reduced the possibilities of observation and difference. The difficulty generated by any theory of culture lies in its status as theory. To criticise, as does Geertz, 'the dim banalities of theory' for being so general as to avoid particulars raises more questions than it solves. While 'power' certainly does look like a totalising term which determines any observation beforehand, how does an appeal to 'particulars' or 'difference' avoid being a claim to generality? Traditional anthropology was criticised in the 1960s for being too confident about what it was going to find. For Douglas there were certain narratives – about civilisation, primitivity and development – which precluded the observer from really observing. Other practices were seen as early, less developed or imperfect forms of Western culture. (Magic was a not-yet form of religion). For Geertz it was universalist notions, about mind, man or intention, which led to incoherent accounts of cultural events. The implication of these interventions and others, is that only with a sense of difference can we really be doing description at all. But as long as we are describing, and as long as we give some general requirement for these acts of description, we remain within the problem of traditional anthroplogy: the problem of interpretation. To some extent any encounter with an 'other' culture is determined beforehand by our (culturally specific) general understanding of what a culture is.

More recent reflections by writers such as James Clifford, (and Geertz's subsequent work) have extended this critique of traditional interpretation by examining anthropology itself as a cultural phenomenon. The anthropologist is no longer a detached or sympathetic 'observer'; he or she too must be reckoned into the picture. Consequently, anthropology (the study of 'man') shifts its emphasis and more scope is given to ethnography (the writing of specific cultures). By self-consciously recognising the position, desire and cultural specificity of the ethnographer, the possibility of a general representation of culture is foregone. Rather, quite specific and local pictures are created where the ethnographer is more like a character in a fiction than a detached and absent scientist. As James Clifford argues: 'Now ethnography encounters others in relation to itself, while seeing itself as other' (Clifford 1986a: 23). This ethnographic self-consciousness (like the historical self-consciousness which acknowledges that all history is an effective history of the present) marks and foregrounds the ethnographer's own interests and cultural position. Ethnography itself, as text, is also an act – which can mark divisions, perform a rapprochement or act as a performance (Clifford 1986b: 98).

The ethnographer no longer has the privileged role of faithfully 'representing' another culture. Cultures are not 'there' pre-textually in order to be faithfully inscribed. Not only are cultures already textual and marked by their own (and other's) acts of description; any act of inscription already works upon, affects and changes both the culture under consideration and the ethnographer. As a consequence, the authority of the ethnographer as author/describer is undermined. Not only is the ethnographer's work likened to a literary fiction rather than an act of description; the members of the culture described can also be granted a voice in the text. Cultural participants can be seen as co-authors rather than objects of description. The ethnographic text is then, ideally, polyphonic or dialogic rather than monophonic. That is, it is ideally produced as a multiplicity of voices or as an encounter between the author and an other, rather than being the author's 'own' representation.

The problematisation of the ethnographer's own position and the undermining of authorial power have marked Stephen Greenblatt's later work *Marvelous Possessions* (1986). Here, Greenblatt notes his own cultural complicity with the writers he is studying. His work can be seen as an ethnography of capitalism – a study of its symbolism, desires and images – as well as a self-reflexive meditation on the motivation of ethnography itself. Just as Geertz acknowledges that anthropology is a form of fiction, so Greenblatt shows that in his own work and the works he studies 'the principal faculty involved is not reason but imagination' (Greenblatt 1988b: 17). His work is a way of understanding the fictional and discursive acts which construct his own cultural position: 'it is in these early exchanges that we can glimpse most clearly some of the founding acts of practical imagination in the European apprehension of the New World' (Greenblatt 1988b: 95).

The attention new historicists and cultural materialists give to the texts of a specifically European culture is marked by this sense of irreducible difference and particularity. A typical example of considering the interpretant's own position can be seen in recent changes in Shakespeare criticism. Shakespeare is no longer seen as the bearer of timeless values, nor as a 'picture' of an Elizabethan age. What Shakespeare means is both historically specific and has to do with the plays as acts of cultural construction. The traditional study of *Othello* as an exploration into trans-historical universals such as evil or jealousy is replaced by a focus on the way in which a culture produces ideas of evil in order to deal with certain historical particulars (the encounter with the New World, the experience of other races, the phenomenon of travel, etc.). According to Jonathan Dollimore, Shakespeare's *Othello* is an instance of cultural distancing in which Elizabethan England constructed other cultures as internally threatening in order to create a sense of its own national identity (1990: 187). But this historical description of Shakespeare can not be seen in isolation from the circumstances of its reading. Seeing *Othello* as part of a Western discourse on racial otherness depends upon the post-colonial position of the critic and on our current cultural divisions. An encounter with a text as a historical other is, like an anthropologist's engagement, both a relation to an other and a form of self-description. The traditional idea of interpretation which involves finding or revealing a meaning (however rich or infinite such a meaning might be) is challenged through the emphasis on cultural encounter. Meaning is not revealed or discovered but created across (cultural and historical) boundaries.

Consequently, many forms of contemporary ethnography preclude the possibility of textual interpretation. There is no meaning to be discovered behind the culture which would be considered as a sort of text. Rather, the act of ethnography is the product of a specific cultural and historical relation. As such, an act of cultural description already introduces another voice, another culture, another act. There can be no revelation or explication of a text or culture which does not involve the cultural and historical position of the historian, critic or ethnographer. If history had traditionally been used to explain or understand, by way of context, the meaning of a text, the idea of cultural specificity undermines such a hermeneutic approach. Literary criticism would, then, no longer be interpretation so much as an engagement in which the critic's own historical and cultural position is foregrounded. This explains why, perhaps, some forms of new historicism can be dominated by personal anecdote, reflection and overt description of the author's own desires. Just as the ethnographer shifts from being a detached observer to produce forms of ironic self-portrait, so the new historicist becomes a specific and interested figure encountering another text as another voice.

With this notion of criticism as active engagement we can see an extension of Geertz's emphasis on the thick description of particulars rather than a focus on general narratives. Because any supposedly general understanding is already articulated within a specific context its generality will always be belied by its articulation. From this it follows that the enterprise of literary theory or cultural theory, in the strict sense, would be impossible. As long as we have a theory of culture, we have started to generalise and to anticipate the character of what we are about to encounter. And the same would follow, as Greenblatt has argued, from a theory of the literary or aesthetic. This might explain why movements like new historicism remain ostensibly untheorised. The movement is nothing other than a series of specific engagements with texts – recognisable as new historicist only by the absence of any foreunderstanding. But of course much of the foregoing argument, from Geertz and Douglas to Clifford and Greenblatt, has insisted that we do not just encounter other cultures but that we do already have a general understanding of what culture is. This general understanding – this implicit theory – cannot be circumvented by factoring it into the narrative or explained away by recognising its cultural specificity. A recognition of our situatedness still enables us to universalise whatever it is that we recognise as the medium within which we are situated. Cultural relativism still posits culture as an inevitable feature of human life. There are two ways to go once we recognise the inevitable generality of terms like culture or history. Anthropologists accept the inevitable compromise of their aim to recognise difference within the anthropological project. 'Culture', as Geertz's early essays in The Interpretation of Cultures implied, might be the most benign of general concepts; unlike 'man' or 'mind', 'culture' might already harbour a recognition of difference within its generality. For literary critics, understanding texts as aspects of culture might enable a recognition of their specificity. 'Tragedy', if seen as a cultural practice, would describe a specifically Western ritual of dealing with conflicts of values. Literary criticism would still have to work with general categories – of genre, period or style – but the even more general category of culture would enable these features to be seen in their contingency. The fact that 'culture' itself has its own textual history, use and construction should not trouble a literary critic whose practices have traditionally dealt with textually-specific phenomena. Stephen Greenblatt's work, for example, is in many ways a literary analysis of the texts which open the discourse of cultural otherness. Ethnography, as he demonstrates, has its own culturally-specific history.

The idea of culture, its specific use and its historical articulation are not problematic as long as we are able to accept that ethnographic and literary interpretation, while being specific to a certain moment of Western culture, still retain a validity. Anthropology, ethnography and new historicism proceed with a critical self-reflexiveness. Recognising that their projects are not context-free, the cultural project itself is seen as perhaps the most sophisticated way of thinking difference through sameness, specificity through generality. The difficulties encountered by Foucault's attempt to move beyond horizonal concepts – such as culture, Being or history – is not one encountered by those who accept culture as suffi-

ciently capable of recognising difference. For Foucault, however, the practices of anthropology and ethnography appear able to relativise everything
by acknowledging the specificity and finitude of culture. But the one act
that can not be delimited or relativised is the act of anthropological analysis itself. Concepts of culture, representation and history return as transcendental horizons. 'Man' may, as Clifford Geertz argued, no longer be
definable by pointing to a substantive feature; but man as a representational animal is retained as long as we retain some general horizon – such
as culture – which sustains anthropological analysis. Anthropologism,
Foucault concludes, is the culmination of modernity. Through the study
of man – even in his cultural difference – we are able to retain some notion
of the human subject. This returns us to the claims made by Geertz. While
the concept of 'culture' exploded many of the features which were seen to
universalise human life there is still some general background – symbolic
exchange, representation, narration – against which particularity is
defined. This may be unavoidable but the question that presents itself is
whether there can be a way of, as Foucault put it, awaking from the
anthropological sleep. And if there is not – if terms like discourse, power
and positivity are no better than culture for disrupting the notion of a general human subjectivity – then how might we best theorise culture to
avoid falling too deeply into a comfortable dream that we have escaped the
dogmas of humanism? The project of theorising culture in general, while
recognising the cultural determination of the observer is explicitly taken
up by Pierre Bourdieu whose work will be the focus of the next chapter.

4

Pierre Bourdieu: habitus, representation and symbolic exchange

The work of Pierre Bourdieu, like that of Clifford Geertz and other anthropological theorists, has provided new ways of thinking through the relationship between literary texts and other events. While Bourdieu began his intellectual career examining the study of culture in general, his more recent work has directed itself to a theory of cultural analysis which would include literary and philosophical texts. But this direction in Bourdieu's work is more than an act of inclusion. The suggestions, which were made in the previous chapter, as to how thinking anthropologically might affect literary criticism are made explicit in Bourdieu's theory of symbolic value. The driving force of Bourdieu's work is the extension of sociological questions to domains which are usually seen as autonomous. But Bourdieu does not just assume that we can analyse philosophical and literary texts as aspects of cultural exchange systems; much of his work is taken up by explaining how it is that certain texts and practices – theory, fine art, literature, philosophy – are constituted as separate from other systems of exchange. As was argued in the previous chapter, the idea of culture can be seen as yet one more form of totalising description amongst others: a way of returning the differences of events to a horizon of comprehension. What Bourdieu's project seeks to achieve is both a non-reductive understanding of events as cultural phenomena and a recognition of the specificity of different modes of symbolic exchange. Most importantly, 'culture' for Bourdieu is not so much a closed social whole as it is an interactive network. As we have seen in relation to anthropological theory, the idea of culture goes some way towards overcoming problems of relating texts to contexts precisely because it locates texts and practices within a single and dynamic domain. Bourdieu's work provides a similar benefit but differs in its mode of interpretation of the cultural domain.

Despite the differences among the various theories of culture which have inflected recent literary criticism, the mere decision to consider ideas from ethnography, anthropology and sociology, as well as the concept of culture in general, *already* reorients literary-historical enquiry away from the idea of considering texts in their isolation. And it is precisely the possibility of this decision to study works of art from a sociological perspective that concerns Bourdieu. For to study literary texts as objects of a specific culture is to forego the immediate 'universalism' which would interpret texts in terms of timeless metaphysical notions. Rather, texts are seen both as specifically located in history, while that history itself is seen as one particular representation of a particular culture. Just as new historicism has problematised the notion of a single and coherent linear history, the idea of culture has also become more plural and dynamic in order to account for the differences between texts (rather than culture providing their common background).

A consideration of culture as a field of production provides a form of reading which examines texts according to the role they play in the constitution of the social and aesthetic domains. Bourdieu's own work sought to show how specific literary texts created aesthetic boundaries and how these boundaries related to other forms of social power. From such a perspective, one would no longer read *The Tempest* as a meditation upon the pre-existing categories of art versus those of nature; nor would one accept the play's representation of royal order as a reflection of a feudalist moment in an unfolding historical trajectory. Instead, the text would be located within a network of texts, statements and practices which produce history and its representation. The idea of feudal harmony is not a given which the text reflects; it is a contested symbolic phenomenon made possible by the working of texts and practices. Furthermore, these texts are not just historically bound (that is, occurring earlier in time), they are also culturally bound (the consequence of a particular set of practices within national, social and political groupings). Perhaps texts from the English Renaissance have been so amenable to new historicist and cultural materialist practice precisely because they occur at a historical point of cultural encounter. Faced with other cultures, the symbolic practices of fifteenth- and sixteenth-century English societies are forced to work overtime. To use Bourdieu's terminology, all those cultural practices which are considered to be natural and unquestionable (the *doxa*) are forced to legitimate themselves, to explicitly *argue for* (rather than presuppose) their naturalness. They do this by becoming *orthodox* and so excluding the contrary beliefs of the heterodox.

As we have also seen in the case of Geertz, certain moves in cultural anthropology have attempted to move beyond the idea that a culture (or a historical moment) can be defined and interpreted as a set of limiting rules which participants obey and the observer can formalise. Bourdieu's work, in particular his theory of practice, provides an explicit and detailed critique of this interpretive model whereby participants are structured by rules or manipulated completely by systems. But at the same time, he also rejects the idea of arbitrary or entirely free human action. Systems are continually re-produced by participants who act according to their interests; but such interests are not arbitrary. They stem from a *habitus* – a highly complex and central notion in Bourdieu's theory. A habitus is a predisposition, an orientation and a methodology which interested participants actively use to take part in cultures. As Bourdieu's work on space and bodies makes clear, a habitus is not a set of limits imposed from without; a participant in practices is (for analytic purposes) nothing other than the various strategies and methods he or she uses to go about their work. Consequently, a habitus is both enabling and regulating. In order for an action to have meaning and effect, it must be recognised. A habitus, therefore, draws on a rationale of past actions, but the strategies which an agent uses are motivated fundamentally by interest. The habitus of agents enables the perpetuation and reconstruction of the symbolic order – what is recognised as meaningful or valuable.

> The conditionings associated with a particular class of conditions of existence produce habitus, systems of durable, transposable dispositions, structured structures predisposed to function as structuring structures, that is, as principles which generate and organize practices and representations that can be objectively adapted to their outcomes without presupposing a conscious aiming at ends or an express mastery of the operations necessary in order to attain them. Objectively 'regulated' and 'regular' without being in any way the product of obedience to rules, they can be collectively orchestrated without being the product of the organizing action of a conductor. (Bourdieu 1990: 53)

As an example of the ways in which social regularity can be considered as enabling practice we might consider the classic anthropological instance of kinship systems. Bourdieu, characteristically, rejects the idea that kinship is a static, timeless and external order imposed upon individuals. Rather, such systems are produced with every new marriage and affiliation. Agents act according to their own interests. Two brothers decide that their respective son and daughter should marry each other; in doing so they do not follow a rule but fulfil their own interests by gaining symbolic value. The girl's parents are not left with the shame of an unmarried daughter, while the boy's family are not threatened by too external a tie. Such actions *may* be expressed or explained according to a rule: 'It is good for patri-lineal cousins to marry'. But such rules are the consequence and not the cause of relations between symbolic value and agents' interests. Agents seek to 'do the right thing' because such actions are enabling; they grant the agent symbolic value (Bourdieu 1977: 46).

The habitus is the possessed rationale which enables agents to maximise symbolic value. But actions also draw upon interests apart from symbolic value – economic, aesthetic and sexual interests, for example – which can also be acted out within accepted forms of behaviour. Bourdieu, therefore, warns against accepting too readily a culture's official self-representation (its explicit rules and norms). Codes of conduct are also inflected with agents' interests which can introduce irregularities, extraneous factors and further maximisations of value. Bourdieu's habitus allows for a play of irregular, local or *ad hoc* interests within a system of regularities.

While Bourdieu acknowledges the limits of a particular culture's economy of values, he insists that such limits do not occur in the form of static, timeless and external rules. His notion of the habitus allows for irregularity within regularity – particular actions which are still only meaningful in relation to the whole but whose efficacy cannot be subsumed within some logical order. According to Bourdieu:

> Talk of rules, a euphemized form of legalism, is never more fallacious than when applied to the most homogeneous societies (or the least codified areas of differentiated societies) where most practices, including those seemingly most ritualized, can be abandoned to the orchestrated improvisation of common dispositions: the rule is never, in this case, more than a second-best intended to make good the occasional misfirings of the collective enterprise of inculcation tending to produce habitus that are capable of generating practices regulated without express regulation or any institutionalized call to order. (Bourdieu 1977: 17)

Because a habitus is an 'orchestrated improvisation' which responds strategically to particular situations while drawing upon its own methodology, Bourdieu's social theory is both dynamic and directed towards moments of unpredictability. Explicit rules or moments of domination are only necessary when the habitus 'misfires'.

Before exploring further Bourdieu's highly important theorisation of symbolic value, we might reflect upon the relevance of the foregoing for a study of literature. Literary texts can be seen to operate in both modes – as examples of habitus in which practices are acted out and have effect (one could think of the text as a successful act in an improvisation, as a successful move in a ritual), as well as being subject to rules when the habitus fails (moments of censorship and proscription would be the clearest examples of when external 'rules' have to be brought to bear). To see the habitus as an effective strategy enables a reading of a practice (such as the performance of a drama) as a calculated move in a game where the rules are immanent to the practice itself. As Bourdieu argues, societies which are highly ritualised are characterised by largely successful and unquestioned strategies which stem from interests coinciding with symbolic values. A ritual 'works' to the extent to which it remains untheorised, implicit and seemingly natural and acceptable. The performance of power which new historicist critics argue characterises the Renaissance can be seen as a successful enactment – not of rules or a representation of order – but of a social group's own disposition. If symbolic value is accorded to kingship, this is because those practices which confer such value – court masques, coronations, stately appearances – are modes of performance which agents 'recognise' as valuable. Shakespeare's history plays could be seen as rituals which both recognise, and work within, the symbolic value of kingship.

Only when these rituals are questioned does explicit enforcement of rules take place. Generally, it is not rules, but a system of continually renegotiated relations with appropriate forms of practice, which characterise cultural groups. A participant acts out of interest; recognising the efficacy of kingly ritual is a way of surviving and maintaining one's position in a system of power. But such systems of power are also nothing other than this recognition/misrecognition of interests. What holds the system together is not merely economic power but the intimate relations between symbolic and economic power.

What Bourdieu's more recent work on the notion of habitus enables is a specific reflection on the status of criticism and theory itself. Perhaps his most interesting example of the specificity of habitus concerns the character of contemporary French theory. As we will see when we look at post-structuralism directly in the final chapter, the work of Jacques Derrida gains much of its force by arguing for the necessity of rigorous philosophical questioning. Derrida rejects the idea that we can simply step outside the metaphysics of western philosophy. To see all events as, say, historically specific is, he argues, to already harbour a knowledge of 'history in general' (Derrida 1978a). Some universalist truth claim is entailed in any act of generalisation. The projects considered so far, such as ethnography and anthropology, appear to operate within a field of pure differences. As Geertz argues, there is no single unifying feature which characterises all cultures. But Geertz's argument depends upon a notion of culture as the horizon within which all differences are located, perceived and understood; culture is ultimately a metaphysical category. The dream of stepping outside metaphysical concepts and finding pure particulars is, for Derrida, the metaphysical enterprise. Historicism, ethnography and anthropology are just further moves in a history of western metaphysics which can only encounter its 'other' according to some conceptual ground within which that 'other' will be understood. For Derrida, the notion of the pure and isolated fact is itself the most general of concepts. Consequently, the transcendental manoeuvre – the understanding of all events within a single horizon – is unavoidable. There are two ways of coping with this. Derrida's own response is to demonstrate that while we always rely upon some general concept or meaning to refer to that which is non-conceptual or prior to meaning, the general concept also has to have a non-general or particular inscription. The Derridean emphasis on text, writing, metaphor and the trace is a strategic way of demonstrating that all concepts have both an unavoidable generality and a textual particularity.

Bourdieu's response, on the other hand, is to show that what Derrida sees as an unavoidable entailment (whereby all particulars are always already conceptually determined) stems from a particular habitus. The consideration of a text according to its conceptual or logical condition depends upon a certain way of reading. Here, the text is considered in itself and what lies outside the text is seen as metaphysically determined; for Derrida, any 'other' to metaphysics is already posited through metaphysical enquiry. If we attempt to avoid metaphysical generalisation and say that a text is culturally or sociologically conditioned, a Derridean response would point out that ideas of culture and society are already metaphysical; we have to have some general concept of what a culture is . However, the primacy of metaphysical questions can only be sustained, Bourdieu argues, if we have certain institutionalised practices of reading. The Derridean move has as its condition a culturally specific notion of what constitutes good reading and what defines a text. Derrida ultimately locates all questions within a metaphysical problematic, but what is not questioned is the specificity of metaphysics or theory itself (Bourdieu 1983). The establishment of the necessity to think particulars in terms of

95

some general question is, for Bourdieu, an effect of the 'transcendentalist project' which is located in a field of cultural production and value (Bourdieu 1993: 256). For Bourdieu, the necessity of metaphysics is not logical but depends upon a history of isolating the text and constructing a field (of the purely aesthetic) such that all sociological questions would be subordinated to the text itself. The idea that it is *textuality* which is the ultimate condition for all meaning or experience creates an *a priori* – a single horizon which determines how texts and events are understood. But, for Bourdieu, 'the *a priori* is history' (Bourdieu: 1993: 256). Theory is a habitus. We ask certain questions of a text, give certain texts a value and see certain cultural objects as being outside or beyond sociological determination. This is effected through position-takings whereby critics and artists adopt a position of relative autonomy. Their questions and practices are seen as aesthetic or theoretical and are thus not seen as determined by interests, power or values. This autonomy, Bourdieu argues, is only relative; to establish the aesthetic as autonomous depends upon relations to other domains. There is not only an economic underpinning in the narrow sense – works of art and criticism depend upon the funding of institutions – but there is a broader symbolic economy. The practice of pure theory depends upon granting texts a certain value. This is achieved through literary criticism, publishing decisions, media reviews, practices of reading, and recognition by educational institutions. But it is also achieved by the texts themselves.

Flaubert is a typical example, for Bourdieu, of the construction of a notion of the 'pure aesthetic'. In his novels Flaubert creates the value of 'art for art's sake' and does so by intervening and reorganising an already determined cultural field. The idea of pure art depends upon a break with an increasingly commodified world of bourgeois art. The notion of the aesthetic cannot be explained by referring to a monetary economy, for it defines itself in opposition to this economy. The fact that the artist is not commercially successful grants the work a symbolic value. So there are always two fields of value which define themselves in relation to each other. The 'heteronomous principle' values texts and practices according to their economic monetary value. This would apply not just to art but to all forms of text which are given a position of social economic power. Today, there are forms of art (popular cinema) and intellectual works (best-selling works of feminism or psychology) which are powerful because they are successful financially. But there is also an 'autonomous principle' which is no less culturally located. Works of art which do not sell are defined as being intrinsically valuable, while texts of 'high' or 'difficult' theory are granted a value in so far as they are seen as being resistant to market forces (Bourdieu 1993: 34).

Flaubert is an exemplary case, for Bourdieu, because his novels explicitly react against the bourgeois field of monetary value. Certain characters are seen as economically motivated, while the contrary alienation and disempowerment of the artist is defined as a form of authenticity. To consider Flaubert's novels from a purely aesthetic point of view would be to sustain the 'narcissistic relationship' (Bourdieu 1993: 192) whereby a text is criticised according to the very values it, in part, produces. The Derridean emphasis on textuality would be yet one more move in the establishment of a field of textuality whereby certain positions are taken and certain questions asked. To see sociological questions as secondary and reductive is already to assume certain values. Bourdieu does not deny these values; but he argues that they are effected through a specific economy of position-takings, cultural recognition and the distribution of value. He therefore disagrees with Derrida who argues that theoretical questions have a 'purely formal' necessity (Derrida 1994). Bourdieu would argue that this supposed necessity has to be established through a contestation of the social domain. He also differs from Foucault by arguing that the cultural field of contestation is not just a distribution of power effects but has a principle of hierarchisation which is determined by interests. Power is not just anonomously dispersed; it is organised and differentiated according to the specific economy of symbolic value (Bourdieu 1993: 38).

Like all the approaches to culture considered so far, Bourdieu's description of society and its practice enables the text to be seen as an active event in the world. For Bourdieu, practices such as ritual and representation invest certain forms with a value; agents act in accord with these rituals in order to benefit from this value. The ideas of habitus and symbolic value are ways of thinking about the specificity of certain cultural objects such as art, philosophy or theory. Bourdieu recognises that no event can be seen as purely autonomous, and thereby avoids the problem of relating a cultural object to its field of production. But he does not want to adopt a reductive approach whereby works of art would be explained according to a general and unchanging system of exchange.

The theorisation of the specificity of certain cultural events requires seeing aesthetic autonomy, not as an illusion, but as an achievement of certain practices. For Bourdieu, the realm of representation or the symbolic order does not sit 'above' the world as an expression or effect; representation and ritual are agents in the continual reproduction of the society and its habitus. Applied to literary criticism, this would mean that instead of arguing that Renaissance dramas reflect world-views or enforce ideologies, we might see these texts as productions of symbolic power through a certain habitus. The text does not 'show' that the kingly character in a masque is all powerful; the text enacts and produces this power. Bourdieu provides an explicit theorisation of this performance of power which he refers to as 'demonstrative expenditure' – an expenditure which can take place through both symbolic and economic outlay. The significance of demonstrative expenditure lies in the fact that the material or (narrowly economic) outlay is a 'loss' in a monetary economy, but a gain or profit of a different mode of value. The performance of power operates in a different (symbolic) system of value but also begins from expenditure or value in the economic (material) sense:

> What might be called demonstrative expenditure (as opposed to 'productive' expenditure, which is why it is called 'gratuitous' or 'symbolic') represents, like any other visible expenditure of the signs of wealth that are recognized in a given social formation, a kind of legitimizing self-affirmation through which power makes itself known and recognized. By asserting itself visibly and publicly, securing acceptance of its right to visibility, as opposed to all the occult, hidden, secret, shameful and therefore censored powers (such as those of malign magic) this power awards itself a rudimentary form of institutionalization by officializing itself. (Bourdieu 1990: 131)

Other agents engage in this 'orchestrated improvisation' in order to take part in the produced power. The lavish performance of a court masque could be understood as a form of display which produces power – not by presenting an ideology but through the force of the display itself. By granting the display a value – by attending performances, participating in the action or producing the spectacle – those that surround the court would also benefit from the production of the counter-economic economy of expenditure. In a broader sense the entire enterprise of literary production and criticism could be considered as an extended 'orchestrated improvisation'. Certain texts are continually performed, re-read and interpreted; while the texts have a certain symbolic power it is also the case that by *recognising* that power the reader or critic also benefits. The act of writing a book about Shakespeare continues the 'Shakespeare industry' and gains a benefit from that industry. But this 'industry', in addition to its financial features, also relies upon a continual demonstration of profitlessness: Shakespeare is valuable *because* the plays are more than commodities, not reducible to profit. There is no simple opposition between local interests and dominant power; all acts of interest at once take part in the system of power (or stem from the habitus) but they also 'use' that system strategically. The performance of a play, to have any effect, would have to take part in, or recognise, the system of symbolic value; but it would also play a role in either sustaining or reconfiguring that system. Every performance or reading would also be a use, a reconfiguration and a reiteration of the habitus. There is, therefore, no *essential* political meaning of any action or text. Subversion is not a quality residing in a text, agent or action. The political efficacy of a practice is defined in relation to a dynamic field of forces – forces which are organised by systemic regulations, while these regulations themselves rely upon the continuation of orchestrated improvisation.

Actions are therefore negotiations within a field of given possibilities. The 'Elizabethan world-picture' which Tillyard identified as the essence of sixteenth-century England would be, from this perspective, neither an essence nor an illusion, but a symbolic organisation reproduced in particular situations by interested participants. These interested participants take part in practices in which they recognise each other's actions as effective to the extent to which they conform, not to rules, but to a rationale. The idea of feudal order is a system of symbolism and actions produced by interested participants who work according to certain expectations. When a Shakespearean tragedy, such as *Macbeth*, represents the transgression of social ordering as the disruption of a divinely ordained equilibrium, it is not because the play accepts a pre-existing set of values. By performing such a play the company would both be taking part in constructing a certain symbolic value – the values of just rule, virtuous conduct and due reverence – at the same time as the performance would benefit from reinscribing these values. Supporting the dominant cultural values is not just a form of obedience; power is gained by 'doing the right thing'. Any contestatory effect the play might have would also depend upon its location within a recognised habitus.

The enabling power of habitus can also be understood by looking at how we categorise texts into genres. Using a genre may not be a matter of obeying rules, but conforming to a genre can be seen as a way of recognising certain established practices in order to gain recognition. Genres could be understood as regular ways of proceeding; authors write in certain forms in order to gain cultural recognition. But each act of literary production, while taking part in that regularity, also uses and reconfigures that genre. The standard definition of comedy as an assertion of harmony and order is an extrapolation from a large number of particular instances in which order is affirmed in several ways. But certain particularities and interests underlie every performance of comedy and the standard representation of order may also be used to other ends – the representation of competing interests, economic motives and heterogeneous disruptions. While comedy may, in general, affirm the order of the state and legitimate rule, it may also on occasion be used for other interests – to expose the standard uses of comedy itself, to express highly particular and local meanings, or to work against traditional comic expectations.

Louis Montrose, for example, has shown how *A Midsummer Night's Dream* produces a profoundly ambivalent response to Elizabeth's power. It at once asserts the naturalness of royal power in traditional comic forms at the same time as it demonstrates the particularly unnatural form of Elizabeth's female power. Montrose's reading is only made possible by considering the play in its historical specificity. By working upon the cultural figure of Elizabeth the virgin-queen, Shakespeare's comedy 'call[s] attention to itself, not only as an end but also as a source of cultural production' (Montrose 1988: 31). To ignore these particularities is to accept the genre of comedy as an essential given or rule, rather than seeing it as a phenomenon which needs to be worked out in particular situations. New historicist readings of comedy do, in fact, emphasise the competing interests and vicissitudes which are negotiated in order for the final sense of order to be affirmed. The genre is a habitus, a recognised way of proceeding. And every articulation of the comic genre both works with the established regularities and uses them to culturally specific ends. 'Obeying' the form is not just a question of adhering to certain criteria; genres enable a certain articulation and, because they have a symbolic power, grant what is said a certain force and value.

In so far as Bourdieu's theory of the habitus emphasises the dynamism of practices as effective action, his work can also illuminate the recent literary critical stress on the temporality of performance. In his early work on the ritual of gift-exchange, for example, Bourdieu argues that a static rule-oriented anthropology would objectify a simple act of giving, receiving and giving in return. Bourdieu, on the other hand, emphasises the ritual of time in this act. Between the giving of the gift and its expected return there is a sense of debt, a suspension, or a moment of uncertainty which the 'objective' or atemporal account fails to notice (Bourdieu 1977: 171). Similarly, new historicist accounts of comedy show that while all comedies 'must' end in order, the performance of any comedy is only meaningful if the generation of anxiety and disorder (which is eventually resolved and allayed) is taken into account. Just as gift-exchange is made meaningful by the delay taken before returning the debt (however inevitable this return may seem to be), so comedies are meaningful only because of the anxiety and disorder experienced prior to the final resolution. Cultural forms are temporal and dynamic and should not be confused with the static nature of their description in terms of external rules.

Like Bourdieu, new historicist critics have refused to posit any extraneous or objective system, world-picture, ideology or form which texts or cultures express or embody. Instead, they see a continual series of 'orchestrated improvisations' in which a sense of such systems is continually produced and performed. Representations (such as texts, artworks, documents and performances) are not signs which lead to some outside world. On the contrary, representations are productions with an effective value. They re-inscribe social relations by re-enacting social positions and dispositions. Acts of both art and interpretation reproduce and sustain social positions because they reinforce systems of symbolic value (Bourdieu 1977: 165). All practices, therefore, take place within a terrain of cultural values. It is not the case that a single economy (monetary, material) determines all other practices (as in Marxism or in the purely aesthetic notion of 'art for art's sake'). Rather, any act is motivated by interest, but interests only seek the values which a society, collectively, recognises. Forms of honour, prestige, aura and power are symbolic values which both enable and are enabled by 'economic' power in the narrower sense (Bourdieu 1977: 183).

It becomes possible, therefore, to understand such economically disastrous and misguided acts as Charles I's courtly masques (which led him to bankruptcy) as acts of symbolic power. Such acts are only meaningful and effective in so far as they recognise and work upon social values – the display of power, wealth or national unity. But such values become social only by their continued performance in practice. Bourdieu's notion of symbolic capital is still material; values can only occur in spatio-temporally specific practices. But symbolic value cannot be reduced to economics in the everyday sense (Bourdieu 1977: 183). It is the specifically modern form of symbolic value which has become Bourdieu's main focus. Whereas Renaissance aesthetic display and power are explicitly connected, modern symbolic value is achieved more often by defining itself in opposition to the recognised locus of political power. In fact, the Renaissance is regarded by Bourdieu as the historical moment when a value can be accorded to aesthetic affect which is no longer directly harnessed to 'demonstrative expenditure'. Outlay is no longer a sign of power, where expense evidences a certain status and achievement; the counter-economic gains its own form of value.

Symbolic value and the market of symbolic goods

Given that new historicist criticism and cultural materialism have been concerned with examining how the realm of aesthetic or 'high' culture is produced, and given the dominance of terms such as 'negotiation', 'exchange' and 'circulation' in new historicist rhetoric, Bourdieu's theory of symbolic exchange can provide an explicit theorisation of the ideas of culture which preoccupy recent literary enquiry. In contradistinction to Marxist aesthetics, Bourdieu's theory of art and exchange attributes a specific and autonomous cultural value to symbolic goods. Whereas even the most sophisticated Marxist theories of cultural production still see the economic sphere as determining works of art 'in the last instance', Bourdieu's work posits an economy which includes monetary or capital exchange alongside symbolic exchange. As a result, Bourdieu's work enables an assessment of cultural value which resists subordination to economics in the narrow sense at the same time as it sees the value of symbolic objects as determined by cultural or socially-defined criteria. Where this theory differs from traditional ideas of 'ideology' or 'world-picture' is in its refusal to see social or political meaning 'behind' the work of art. For Bourdieu, textual analysis demands locating the work within a field of cultural production – which includes other texts, readers, criticism and interpretive procedures. The text is a 'position-taking' which takes part in and establishes symbolic exchange.

In order to understand the motivation behind Bourdieu's positing of a specifically symbolic system of exchange it might be helpful to think of Marcel Mauss's theory of the gift. According to Mauss 'the gift' is the form of symbolic exchange par excellence. Later theorists, like Bourdieu, have focused on Mauss's notion of symbolic exchange as a way of overcoming both structuralist and Marxist theories of value. For Mauss (1970), when a member of a culture produces a gift which passes from, say, one tribe to another, a type of social ordering and structuration is produced. A tie or a bond is made active. Between the act of giving the gift and its return, one tribe is indebted to another. Of course, some return of the gift is expected; but, according to Bourdieu, it is the moment of delay between gift and return that is crucial to this act of symbolic exchange. As Bourdieu insists, any structural analysis would lose the sense of this temporal delay precisely because it would see the gift and its return in a static system of obligations and equivalences (Bourdieu 1977: 6). The social paths produced by this exchange are made in the suspension of immediate reciprocation. Furthermore, the economy of the gift disrupts a Marxist economy of value based on materialism and capital; for it is not the value of the gift itself in terms of labour or use which is significant, so much as the 'symbolic' value of giving and receiving. What is produced is an economy of obligations and social intercourse. A society or culture is not a structure or grid which exists once and for all; it is in a continual state of production. For Bourdieu, it is symbolic practices such as 'the gift' which continually reinscribe the pathways of a social economy in which representations, capital, aesthetic objects and words are circulated. And because such pathways are characterised by temporal phenomena (such as the delay between gift and return) these symbolic practices resist any form of 'static' analysis.

But while being critical of structuralist or 'static' approaches, Bourdieu is also critical of what he refers to as Mauss's 'phenomenological' approach. That is, Mauss concentrates on the ways in which participants themselves experience the practices of symbolic exchange, rather than seeing it as operating within a socially-defined system of expectations and strategies. At the same time, Bourdieu rejects any structuralist account which would reduce the act of exchange to an objective system. His answer is to situate himself between the structuralist and phenomenological models. In opposition to the structuralist, Bourdieu argues that exchange works not according to a system of objective rules, but along the lines of a number of possible strategies which can fulfil the agent's interests. These interests are defined by what is socially recognised as valuable, but improvisations on possible strategies have the power to transform what constitutes a valuable or possible act (although not all acts have this transformative power). In opposition to the phenomenological model, Bourdieu insists that the subject's own representations of their actions must be measured against their actual practices as observed. The observer must then account for any difference between the subjective representation and the efficacy of the action, where the action is observed as a social and not an individual phenomenon. The importance of symbolic exchanges, such as the gift, lies in the extent to which they are delimited by socially-defined values at the same time as they reproduce and transform those values with every practical strategy.

Cultural objects therefore operate for Bourdieu within their own economy of symbolic value. Because societies differ as to what they accord value, there can be no general description of symbolic exchange without considering its particular divisions (class, tribal, ethnic, political) and values (honour, display, power, aesthetics). Like new historicist critics, Bourdieu's work has been characterised by a certain self-reflexivity whereby he has reflected upon the theorist's own world with the gaze

103

of the anthropologist. Similarly, Stephen Greenblatt sees his own work as part of the very culture (capitalist) whose formations he studies. Rather than taking the autonomy of the aesthetic sphere for granted, Greenblatt has argued that we consider the way in which such domains are produced through systems of negotiation and exchange which are peculiar to capitalism. Bourdieu has also attempted to define the particular character of symbolic exchange which typifies modern Western notions of art.

In 'the market of symbolic goods' (1985), Bourdieu argues that symbolic goods have a specific cultural value and that this value is determined by the division of the cultural field into two domains: the field of restricted production (FRP) and the field of large-scale production (FLP). This division has both a historical and a dynamic dimension. Historically, this cultural field emerges with the modern turn away from external authorities; the Church no longer dictates what will constitute legitimate art; the patron will no longer commission works for his or her own ends. Such external sources of legitimacy give way to a process of autonomisation, whereby the values of cultural objects are defined within the cultural (rather than political or religious) field. The notion of art's autonomy is the result of institutional developments. The domain of pure theory, an attention to the text itself in formalism and the study of questions of pure truth – all of which characterise twentieth-century culture – are the most recent manifestations of a modern change in the field of cultural value. The possibility for the modern understanding of aesthetic autonomy, Bourdieu argues, is the post-Renaissance division between goods produced for profit and an economy of art production. A domain is initially established whereby art and knowledge are economically supported but no longer directly commissioned or ordered. Art gains a commercial value only when it is produced by the artist to be sold, and not when the artist is employed by a patron. In modernity, Bourdieu argues, paintings are bought and sold and authors start to receive income from their writing. The eventual institutionalisation of copyright and practices of publishing, criticism and consumption become increasingly market-directed. The subsequent reaction *against* this field of general market-oriented production occurs in the form of 'high' art or aesthetic autonomy. Works gain a value because they are not marketable, because they resist commodification. But this pure aesthetic could only occur once a domain of cultural production could be detached from the external control of the church, state or feudal patron. This shift of cultural production from the Church and court to public consumption is also accompanied by a growth in the body of potential consumers; this is enabled by a continual increase of education and availability (Bourdieu 1985: 15).

Once a market has been established through a break with the control of Church and state in the Renaissance, the process of 'autonomisation' develops by an increasing detachment from the demands of consumers. A particular field of restricted production sets itself against market-values and establishes for itself a network of cultural exchange which places a putatively 'purely aesthetic' value upon its objects. These objects are produced by artists, for artists, and become increasingly esoteric in order to set themselves against the market-driven field of large-scale production. Such élite works of art do still partake in an economic exchange (by being bought and sold) but they repress this dimension by producing 'another' economy of symbolic values. At this level, an object is valued precisely to the extent to which it remains rare, uncommodifiable and esoteric:

> The end of dependence on a patron or collector and, more generally, the ending of the dependence upon direct commissions, with the development of an impersonal market, tends to increase the liberty of writers and artists. They can hardly fail to notice, however, that this liberty is purely formal; it constitutes no more than the condition of their submission to the laws of the market of symbolic goods, that is, to a form of demand which necessarily lags behind the supply of the commodity (in this case, the work of art). They are reminded of this demand through the sales figures and other forms of pressure, explicit or diffuse, exercised by publishers, theatre managers, art dealers. It follows that those 'inventions' of Romanticism – the representation of culture as a kind of superior reality, irreducible to the vulgar demands of economics, and the ideology of free, disinterested 'creation' founded on the spontaneity of innate inspiration – appear to be just so many reactions to the pressures of an anonymous market. (Bourdieu 1985: 16)

In this realm of the field of restricted production, those features which draw attention to the cultural object as an aesthetic phenomenon (form, technique, style) are accorded the most value. But this development of 'a dynamic autonomy' is made possible by continual practices of differentiation between the field of restricted production and the field of large-scale production Those features most valued as 'intrinsic' and purely aesthetic receive that meaning only because of the strategic opposition to market demands. Thus, Bourdieu accounts for both the phenomenon and practice of the realm of the autonomously aesthetic and art's relation to a general economy of exchanges. From this perspective, the specificity of a work of art is determined by its value within an exchange system in the field of restricted production. Economic value can play a part in this exchange (think of how, in the world of fine art, the price of objects is a foregrounded aspect of their cultural achievement). But the values which dominate the field of restricted production are defined within its own economy. Intellectuals and artists define what constitutes legitimate art, while art itself continually takes as its subject this very legitimacy. The notorious bricks placed in the Tate Gallery in London are 'art' precisely because they question the limits and boundaries of the aesthetic.

If we accept Bourdieu's argument that the 'purely aesthetic' depends upon a *difference from* established or marketable goods then we can understand why a value is accorded to aesthetic transgession. Art is defined as valuable precisely to the the extent to which it challenges given values. Bourdieu's work challenges one of the dominant assumptions of contemporary French theory and Modernism which sees art, particularly literature, as essentially counter-economic. Because the work of art was seen to foreground form at the expense of meaning or content, many critics saw art or literature as inherently transgressive, as not reducible to *any* system of exchange. On this picture art is associated with nothingness because it exists outside any order or economy; it has no value and says nothing. Further, art is art only in so far as it can embody the nothingness of an absence of meaning, exchange, value or convention. This is an idea explicitly articulated by Maurice Blanchot who defines literature in general as a form of silence and a form of nothingness (Blanchot 1982: 48). But the idea is repeated in a number of ways by a number of critics. For Foucault, nineteenth-century literature is valuable because it is no longer representational: not a meaningful picture of the world, but a site where 'language shines once more on the frontiers of Western culture' (Foucault 1970: 44). For Deleuze and Guattari, artists define themselves by breaking with recognisable meaning and recording affect or sensation (Deleuze and Guattari 1994: 204). For Kristeva, poetic language harbours the possibility of revolution precisely because poetic texts are a form of negativity: their meaning is disrupted by purely textual or non-signfiying affects (Kristeva 1984). Bourdieu responds to this near cult-like celebration of the literary text by arguing that the very *absence* of value accorded to texts is precisely the effect of a symbolic economy. Certain texts are celebrated – typically those of Modernism or the avant-garde – because they have been consecrated. Their 'value' is achieved by certain ways of reading so that we do not read Joyce through questions of Irish national identity or the relation between Catholicism and metaphysics, nor do we read Kafka as concerned with the problem of the finite human self in the face of an alien law. In the cult of the purely aesthetic, texts are seen as formal breaks and ruptures with an economy of conventional art. Joyce's *Finnegan's Wake* (rather then the less 'transgressive' *Dubliners*) is read as pure text, a signifier with no signified or referent. Kafka is not interpreted as an existentialist facing the human condition, but as the creator of a nonsignifying language (Deleuze and Guattari 1986: 19). This economy of the purely aesthetic is, according to Bourdieu, based on a disavowal of the economic. Certain texts, and ways of reading those texts, do not have a monetary value. But they have a value in so far as they embody a principle of aesthetic autonomy which is no less culturally-determined or valued. It depends upon valorising certain authors (avante-garde rather than popular) certain ways of reading (formalism) as well as the positions of those who confer certain values (the institutional legitimation of critics and theorists).

The celebration of aesthetic autonomy can also be gained by looking at high modernism's own self-representation. Reacting against the commodification of culture enabled by modern technology, writers such as Woolf, Pound, Eliot and Joyce produced works which took the loss of high culture as their theme. In seeking to intensify the purely 'aesthetic' dimension of their work, Modernists foregrounded form and technique, and were avowedly esoteric in their attempts to resist simple consumption by distributing their work in small magazines and limited editions for other producers and academics. As a result, the meaning of such cultural objects is defined by their position in the economy of symbolic exchange. Produced by artists and consumed by other artists who define themselves explicitly against market-driven forms of culture, the work of high art gains its meaning from this specific pattern of negotiations and circulations:

> The public meaning of a work in relation to which the author must define himself, originates in the process of circulation and consumption, dominated by the objective relations between the institutions and agents implicated in the process. The social relations which produce this public meaning are determined by the relative position these agents occupy in the structure of the field of restricted production. (Bourdieu 1985: 21)

The process by which the field of restricted production attributes value to various cultural objects is referred to by Bourdieu as 'consecration', a term with significant religious resonances. Just as the Church had, in the Middle Ages, determined the spiritual value of objects such as relics and icons, so the practice of consecration is today located in specific institutions. Institutions, such as the university, produce a distinction between what Bourdieu refers to as 'intellectual' and 'scholastic' culture. That is, the cultural values disseminated to the public by educational institutions are resisted and worked against by the producers in the field of restricted production. But educational institutions also contain those very specialists involved in the act of consecration. There is thus an ambivalent relation between artists and the academy. The cultural values made available to the public must constantly be challenged by the artist who resists market forces. At the same time, however, the artist relies on a community of other artists and academics to 'consecrate' or legitimate his or her work of art. The sense of the autonomy of the work of art is therefore both a mis-recognition of the relational nature of the cultural field *and* a lived social fact which has to be taken into account in any consideration of the work's meaning. Both the artist and the intellectual 'occupy a subservient position in the field of power'. Not only are they determined by their reaction against market values and the field of mass-production, their work occurs within an economy also determined by material forces (subsidies, com-missions, promotion) and systematically-defined interests:

> The opposition between art-for-art's sake and middle-brow art which, on the ideological plane, becomes transmitted into an opposition between the ide-alism of devotion to art and the cynicism of submission to the market, should not hide the fact that the desire to oppose a specifically cultural legitimacy to the prerogatives of power and money, constitutes one more way of recogniz-ing that business is business. (Bourdieu 1985: 31)

This is not to say that art is solely determined by economic forces, but it is to stress that the 'autonomy' of art is a *relational* phenomenon – defined by the position of the artist and the value attributed to their work by a system of symbolic value. Concurrently, this system is itself enabled by its relation to a culture driven by consumer demand. The subjective representation of art as autonomous, possessing an 'aura' and being purely aesthetic is not to be dismissed. But the question of the production of this aura can only be answered by looking at the hierarchy of conse-crations:

> In short, the most personal judgments it is possible to make of a work, even of one's own work, are always collective judgments in the sense of position-takings referring to other position-takings through the intermediary of the objective relations between the positions of their authors within the field. Through the public meaning of the work, through the objective sanctions imposed by the symbolic market upon the producer's 'aspirations' and 'ambitions' and, in particular, through the degree of recognition and conse-

cration it accords him, the entire structure of the field interposes itself between the producer and his work. (Bourdieu 1985: 38)

Marxist aesthetics had continually troubled itself with the question of aesthetic value; but it did so only by seeing the valorisation of art as either a 'mystification' or as a reflection of economic forces in the narrow sense. Marxists have argued that a work is successful in so far as it accurately 'reflects' the relations of production. Lukacs, for example, favoured nineteenth-century realism over Modernism because the former was supposed to give an adequate picture of the social totality. A modified form of this argument is given by Fredric Jameson who criticises postmodernism for not adequately representing the conditions of its own history (Jameson 1984: 67). Such Marxist theories have been critical of any strong sense of the aesthetic field as 'autonomous'; all art must be related back to the unity of its historical context. But according to both Greenblatt and Bourdieu, the autonomous domain of the aesthetic is a cultural and historically relative fact which can be neither ignored nor merely accepted as given. On the contrary the production of the sense of aura (or as Greenblatt terms it, 'resonance and wonder') becomes the very object of enquiry. To see these forms of symbolic value as produced in systems of exchange is to account for their existence within a more general field of values (including the economic) while at the same time not seeing the cultural field as an epiphenomenon of some economic 'base' in need of interpretive relation.

In order to take the specificity of the aesthetic into account, the theory of symbolic exchange posits a system of producers and consumers involved in the active negotiation of symbolic values. Bourdieu's notions of culture and symbolic exchange emphasise the importance of the consumption and circulation of cultural goods. But the system of exchange is also seen as open to reconfiguration. By seeing participants as both enabled and delimited by their positions, Bourdieu's theory avoids any simple pre-determination of what will constitute a possible action or event. Of course, the emphasis in Bourdieu's work has been away from any idea that there exist practices or events, which are simply disruptive or transgressive. Any external event, any disruption of an economy of value, is still defined in relation or opposition to the field of value. This is not to say that all positions can be determined in advance, but difference always works within a 'space of possibles' (Bourdieu 1993: 177). For Bourdieu, practices of reading and consumption are part of a larger network of value, recognition, consecration and position-taking. While the field of cultural production is in a state of continual reconfiguration precisely because it is a site of struggle, Bourdieu's work still offers an account or explanation of events which are all seen as aspects of a field of value. While all events cannot be predicted; they can be explained. And while Bourdieu acknowledges that theory and analysis are themselves a specific habitus he goes on to argue that a recognition of his own position is sufficient to grant his method the status of science:

> And one's only hope of producing scientific knowledge – rather than weapons to advance a particular class of specific interests – is to make explicit to oneself one's position in the sub-field of the producers of discourse about art and the contribution of this field to the very existence of the object of study. (Bourdieu 1993: 36)

It is the exercise of self-analysis, then, which Bourdieu claims precludes his method from becoming yet one more interested totalisation of historical or cultural wholes. Or, in his own terms, while aesthetic autonomy may be a partial misrecognition (because it misperceives its relational status), scientific analysis is possible as long as one's position is recognised. Certainly, by thinking of theory itself as a habitus, Bourdieu conducted an effective critique of an anthropological analysis which left its own position out of consideration. But if it is the case that a specific theory is always an interested position-taking, what is the interest that sustains Bourdieu's sociological analysis? Bourdieu acknowledes that there is always more than one economy; there are competing sets of values which cannot be reduced to a single horizon of analysis. But to what extent does the focus on value and interest already determine that which it is about to encounter in terms of its own schema? Bourdieu's project can itself be delimited in so far as it understands all events within a field of production with a concomitant system of values and benefits. For Bourdieu, even the 'gift' which breaks with economic value has a symbolic value and efficacy. Everything can be explained, if only after the fact, through an economy of culture.

The possibility that there might be a non-profitable or valueless event is not admitted by Bourdieu. It is this possibility which occupies the attention of Michel de Certeau whose theory of consumption as an active practice attempts to locate an 'outside' to the conventional domain of cultural production. By seeing consumption in this way de Certeau enables ways of thinking about those marginal moments and acts which resist dominant systems of representation, production and circulation. To a certain extent we can see that Bourdieu's interpretive enterprise remains within the field which Foucault referred to as modern 'anthropologism'. Culture and cultural production act as ultimate horizons within which all particular events can be interpreted, explained and comprehended as forms of human self-constitution. What cannot be admitted is a meaningless, undetermined, valueless, arbitrary (or in Foucault's term) 'positive' event. For Bourdieu, it is precisely this difference between his own theory and Foucault which he wishes to emphasise. In terms of offering a theory of social analysis Bourdieu insists that the cultural field *ought* to be interpreted according to a general principle and ought to be a science. In terms of the specific problem of literature, Bourdieu's theory ultimately perceives aesthetic or literary values as determined by the interests of the symbolic economy. This approach has no doubt been valuable in showing that aesthetic autonomy serves certain interests and depends upon institutional boundaries. But can the aesthetic or literary be located entirely within an economy of interested position-takings? Can there be an event of production or consumption not exhausted by the consideration of interests and value? Foucault argued that any positing of the cultural field was itself a positive event and would have to admit the possibility and validity of other ways of thinking. But Foucault never located or defined a single locus where dominant strategies would be challenged. De Certeau reacted against both Bourdieu's and Foucault's use of a single principle – power or production – to account for culture. The idea that the consumption of cultural production involves, or can involve, a break with the dominant economy of interest is perhaps the main challenge of Michel de Certeau's theory of tactics. De Certeau's theories of practice, consumption and representation will be the subject of the next chapter.

5
Michel de Certeau: oppositional practices and heterologies

As we have seen in the first chapter of this work, two questions which have dominated recent literary and social theory have been the nature of a text's relation to its 'outside' and the problem of whether there can be any general theory regarding this relation. The very possibility of theory becomes questionable once all those theoretical terms which were put forward in order to cope with difference – culture, history, particulars – become further instances of establishing homogenous horizons. It is perhaps not surprising, then, that new historicism has, by and large, rejected the notion of any theoretically-defined relation in any general sense. The text is seen, rather, as having no pre-determined relation to an outside world; its position within the world is historically contingent and shifting. The text produces, rather than relates to, its context. A text's reception occurs differently in different historical moments. The reading or performance of a text is not extrinsic to its meaning; the text is nothing other than its various concrete and particular activations. It is here that de Certeau's emphasis on consumption as production becomes important.

For both new historicism and cultural materialism a text cannot be divorced from the processes of its reception, for such processes play an active role in the meaning and effect of the text. For Bourdieu, the ways in which texts are read is delimited by an already determined field of production. In his work on the politics and philosophy of Martin Heidegger, Bourdieu (1991) argues that the political meaning of a text cannot be isolated in the intentions of an author; for it is in the institutionalised ways of reading texts that certain meanings are legitimated and others excluded. In the case of Heidegger, questions of truth in general, and the history of metaphysics and ontology are regarded as appropriate issues. To refer Heidegger's discourse on 'dwelling' to the housing crisis in Germany would be regarded as a violation, reduction or vulgarisation of Heidegger's properly philosophical concerns. Bourdieu uses this example to argue that practices of consumption are both important and occur within a space of possible position-takings. For Bourdieu it is theorised critical reading, rather than everyday reading, which will reveal the political determinants of a given text. De Certeau, on the other hand, shares with the new historicists an emphasis on the critical potential of everyday reading. Consumption, for de Certeau, *can* be a part of dominant strategies, but it can also – particularly if it is untheorised, local and aberrant – mark a break with accepted practice. De Certeau's work explicitly deals with a growing trend in recent criticism. For many new historicists and cultural materialists it is the possibility of different forms of consumption which is the appropriate object of literary criticism, precisely because local readings can mark a break with the 'closure' of theory.

This is not to say that new historicism can be aligned with what has come to be known as 'reader response' theory. In that theory the idea of 'interpretive community' or 'horizon of expectation' is used to uncover the various possibilities for a text's meaning (Iser 1978; Jauss 1982). But reader response theory, as its label implies, concentrates on the relation between the reader (historically located in a community) and the meaning that reader can produce. While being attentive to reception, new historicism differs from this approach by looking, not at 'communities' of readers which have some form of coherence and identity, but at peripheral, perverse and highly-specific effects which the text can produce.

Again, it is here that de Certeau's work can help to theorise the ways in which power is resisted and co-opted by 'consumers'. An emphasis on consumption need not involve determining a general historical context, nor the character of the text's cultural field of production; on the contrary, the theory of consumption as a practice attends to the *atypical*, the specific and local event of the text. In order to focus on aberrant readings and forms of consumption, however, it seems that we would still need some way of recognising the dominant or culturally-sanctioned meaning. New historicism frequently describes central moments or standard performances of power (for example, the production of courtly masques) with the intent of showing the production, limits and specificity of this putatively all-encompassing power. By showing how dominant modes of consumption have been organised, new historicism can also show how texts might be read otherwise. To challenge the 'Elizabethan world-picture' reading of Shakespeare is not just to quibble over a historical issue; the way

113

Shakespeare is currently read has a lot to do with our notions of power and legitimation. To 'misread' Shakespeare, and to show that 'official' readings were established only by the continual exclusion and contestation of 'mis-readings', is already to expose the power of different modes of consumption. Reading *against* the foregrounded power structure of the past is also a way of resisting the present. So, instead of focusing on the dominant, competent or 'successful' readings which have been the concern of reader response theory, recent criticism has paid attention to multiple, aberrant and marginalised readings. In so doing, criticism can take canonical texts and open these texts to other possibilities. Such a task would be more than just a historical exercise; it would also provide an intervention in the present and a way of questioning the norms which have been constituted through dominant interpretations of the past.

The difference between dominant and resistant readings might appear to be simply an institutional division. The legitimate Shakespeare would be the one canonised in a history of performance and criticism and its legitimacy would be nothing other than its acceptance and production in dominant institutions (such as universities, theatre companies and arts councils). 'Misreadings' would not be essentially different and would only be characterised by their failure to gain institutional validity. De Certeau's theory of strategy and tactics, however, goes further than this. De Certeau argues for two types or modes of practice whereby dominant strategies have a certain character. Unearthing the resisting 'tactics' in the past both challenges dominant forms of rationality and demands that we think differently about certain forms of consumption:

> Our 'tactics' seem to be analyzable only indirectly, through another society … They return to us from afar, as though a different space were required in which to make visible and elucidate the tactics marginalized by the western form of rationality. (de Certeau 1984: 50)

Just as Foucault's work moved towards 'description' rather than interpretation or commentary, so de Certeau's model of unearthing tactics aims to describe a field of effects produced by readers rather than uncovering a text's meaning. Furthermore, whereas reader response theory focused on readers and the semantic content they produced in reading, the attention to tactics shows the concrete effects of specific acts of reading. This distinction can be made clearer by examining de Certeau's theory of strategy and tactics.

Strategy, tactics and oppositional practices

Setting itself explicitly alongside Foucault's theory of power, de Certeau's notion of tactics (de Certeau 1984: 29-42) sought to emphasise the powerful appropriation of discourses and texts by their consumers. It ought to be noted that de Certeau's work assumes a certain reading of Foucault which has also dominated American literary studies. For de Certeau, Foucault's emphasis upon dominant (or 'foregrounded') power structures, such as the panopticon in Discipline and Punish, took place at the expense of other multiple, disordered and peripheral forms of activity. For de Certeau, because Foucault's work was a genealogy it would always attempt to trace regularities in the present back to a past; in doing so it would have to ignore other acts of power. Foucault's genealogy of modernity, according to de Certeau, accepts too readily the foregrounded structures of modern power. In Discipline and Punish, for example, Foucault looks at the way Bentham's panopticon – an architectural structure in which a prison warden can survey prisoners without himself being seen – forms a grid of power. The panopticon exemplifies modern forms of discipline in which power is no longer located in a central and intervening authority (such as the king) but is organised in a network in which individuals become self-regulating. It was this notion of power as diffuse and systemic (rather than the 'top-down' model of Marxist ideology) which enabled new ways of thinking about political structures; and major literary critical texts such as Greenblatt's Renaissance Self-Fashioning and Orgel's The Illusion of Power clearly work with this Foucaultian notion of power. Many criticisms of new historicism and its re-reading of the Renaissance have accused writers like Greenblatt of working with an all-pervasive sense of power which offers no hope of resistance. While it could be argued that Foucault himself never saw power as monolithic or totalising, it is certainly the case that readings of Foucault which focused on Discipline and Punish and The History of Sexuality, Volume 1, rather than works such as, say, I, Pierre Riviere, interpreted power as an all-encompassing system. De Certeau offers his own work, in contrast to Foucault, as a theory of the tactics which can resist, subvert and make (illegitimate) use of foregrounded power structures:

> A society is thus composed of certain foregrounded practices organizing its normative institutions and of innumerable other practices that remain 'minor', always there but not organizing discourses and preserving the beginnings or remains of different (institutional, scientific) hypotheses for that society or for others. It is in this multifarious and silent 'reserve' of procedures that we should look for 'consumer' practices having the double char-

acteristic, pointed out by Foucault, of being able to organize both spaces and languages, whether on a minute or a vast scale. (de Certeau 1984: 48)

Whereas Marxist theory had located the political effects of a text in its meaning, de Certeau's theory of tactics shifts the politics of the text to the reader or consumer. If we accept the Marxist idea that a text is in some sense a form of ideology then the critic's task is to reveal or disclose that ideology. Even in highly sophisticated forms of Marxism, such as the structuralist Marxism of Althusser or the post-structuralist Marxism of Fredric Jameson, a text is assumed to have a political meaning. For Althusserian literary critics, the most well-known being Pierre Macherey, the critic's job is to reveal the ideological contradictions inherent in the text's structure. For Jameson (1981), the Marxist critic demonstrates the ideology of the text by locating it within history and by showing the ways in which it acts to mask or resolve intolerable social conditions. In both of these cases it is the text itself which is politicised; the work is assumed to have a political content which it is the critic's task to disclose. Of course, it is not only Marxist criticism which locates the political value of the text in the text's meaning. Various forms of feminist criticism have also argued that certain texts are either 'patriarchal' or revolutionary – either by virtue of their intrinsic meaning or by their, no less intrinsic, power to produce effects on the reader. Julia Kristeva (1980), for example, has argued for the 'revolutionary poetics' of certain Modernist works. In all cases where either ideology or revolutionary potential are located as aspects of the text's semantic or formal content, the reader is assumed to be either passive – in the case of ideology – or uniform across historical and social boundaries so that a text can be deemed to have a certain effect regardless of the position of the reader. Reader response theory, while shifting the burden back onto the reader, still seeks to produce a semantic content or a meaning (although this is now co-produced by the reader).

De Certeau's theory of practice, on the other hand, enables a focus both on the political effects of a text and on the specific position of the reader. Although de Certeau was concerned more with practices in general, rather than specifically literary theories, his opposition between strategy and tactics focuses on the possibility of opposition or resistance. When this theory is applied to the reading of texts, the idea of anything like a single interpretive community or a monolithic and totalising ideology collapses. Not only are texts capable of offering a number of readings, de Certeau explicitly valorises practices which do not repeat dominant or already given practices. If we followed this through in literary theory we would move away from the problem of interpretive validity, or finding a just account of the text. The idea of tactical reading defines the text as a site of play and use for an active and creative reading practice. The idea of a text as being accurately or authentically interpreted would not only no longer be an aim of criticism; a tactical approach actually seeks disruption, difference and non-coincidence.

One of the main features of cultural materialist and new historicist forms of criticism has been a refusal to accept a culture's foregrounded self-representation. While new historicism reads the Renaissance as the origin of the present (as the beginning of capitalism or modernity), it also takes a critical stance towards Renaissance self-representation. Such critique is itself a use of Renaissance ideology for the tactical, or 'effective', forces of the present. The politically hegemonic forces in Elizabethan society may have represented themselves as the natural and universal rulers in a divine and immutable order; but this representation was always subject to contestation. There was always a multiplicity of discursive domains such that dominant modes of representation which universalise themselves were always undercut by other voices. Rereading the hegemonic representations of the past with an attention to this discursive plurality opens the text to a number of uses. This ability to contest a dominant order of representation stems from the fact that a text's function cannot be controlled or delimited by context, interpretive community or the intention of its producer.

A focus on the tactical use of texts would give problems of intention and meaning a different inflection. An interesting example might be the long running debate over Milton's Satan. Almost as soon as *Paradise Lost* was printed readers raised the question as to whether Milton might have done too good a job in his representation of Satan. In order to give the epic dramatic force Satan's rebellion had to appear as more than a foregone defeat. But in making Satan's rhetoric at least ostensibly persuasive some readers argued that Milton had made Satan the hero of *Paradise Lost* and that the verse epic (possibly unwittingly) justified Satan's rejection of God's rule. The debate was rife in the eighteenth century and was made notorious by the claim, in Blake's 'The Marriage of Heaven and Hell' (1793), that Milton was 'of the Devils party without knowing it' (1975: xvii [1793]). Since Blake, there have been other arguments made regarding *Paradise Lost* and the legitimacy of God's rule. William Empson (1965) argued that *Paradise Lost* couldn't help but show God as a tyrant because any form of pseudo-monarchial rule could not possibly be justified. Empson's argument then became the focus for a lot of studies which 'proved' that, however convincing Satan might appear as a rebel, Milton couldn't possibly have been a Satan sympathiser (Danielson 1982). And similar debates occurred surrounding Milton's sexual politics. Feminist critics argued that *Paradise Lost* repeated a history of patriarchal metaphors and associations by showing Eve as Adam's passive mirror (Froula 1984). Others argued that Milton was one of the 'first' feminists and it was only misreadings of Milton which made him appear patriarchal (Wittreich 1987). Such interpretive approaches assume that we can take a line of literature – Satan's 'Evil be thou my good' – and determine its meaning according to context. But how do we understand context? Those defending Milton's Christian orthodoxy will say that we are meant to see Satan's statements as self-refuting. In this case the context, *Paradise Lost*, is determined by the broader context of Milton's Christianity and his status as an epic poet (with all the skills of rhetorical complexity such a position would demand). On the other hand, if we read 'Evil be thou my good' as a phrase which shows that good and evil are arbitrarily divided and that what is defined as good depends on power and will, we take *Paradise Lost* as a different sort of context: as a poem written in revolutionary England by a writer with radical Protestant tendencies. But the conflict over contexts shows that reading literature cannot just be a question of placing lines in their context. We have to determine those contexts. Reading is more than revealing or uncovering a meaning. Reading is a creative act, with its own uses and effects. However strongly we insist upon the legitimacy of certain readings – critics have clearly demonstrated that Milton was an orthodox Christian – it is always possible that the text might be used otherwise: the fact that Milton, as an orthodox Christian, could not but help make Satan's arguments convincing is a sign of how strong the revolutionary position is. However much we insist upon the dominant modes of meaning production, there is always the possibility that the text may be put to other uses. This argument is not one of semantic relativity. It is not that any reading is possible. On the contrary, a dominant reading is in place, and it is precisely because there are dominant readings that there can be tactical resistance or uses of dominant strategies. The possibilities of use are the main concern of de Certeau's notion of oppositional practice.

In *The Practice of Everyday Life* (1984) de Certeau focuses on the role of the consumer. Rather then being seen as the passive recipient of previously created works, the act of consumption requires a form of 'secondary production' (de Certeau 1984: xiii). While de Certeau argues that a consumer is always capable of 'poaching' or inventing 'ruses' which will alter the rules of consumption, his theory is not just a celebration of individual imagination. The consumer is always located within a field of social forces, but because such a field is dynamic and shifting the possibilities for consumption are multiple and incalculable. The consumer may have to rely on what is available; he or she cannot 'transcend' culture in an act of political will. But while the consumer can by no means 'escape' cultural or social forces, he or she can 'short-circuit' or pervert the conventional rules which regulate behaviour, consumption or interpretation. (We could even see new historicist and cultural materialist interpretations as examples of 'short-circuiting' – that is, as readings which refuse the dominant or fore-grounded modes of reading.) Interestingly, de Certeau argues that the usual notion of reading provides the archetype of consumer passivity: 'Reading (an image or a text), moreover, seems to constitute the maximal development of the passivity assumed to characterize the consumer, who is conceived of as a voyeur ... ' (de Certeau 1984: xxi). De Certeau's the-orisation of consumer activity, would therefore set itself against such a model. On de Certeau's revised model, readership involves using the text as a means of pleasure. The reader neither faithfully receives an author's intention, nor produces a coherent content in accord with an interpretive community. Reading is an act of 'silent production' in which the contin-gent social and historical forces which have produced the reader go on to recreate the text in highly-specific and incalculable ways. Such readings cannot, therefore, be reinvoked by referring to historically determinate communities, for the specific acts of reading will always produce other meanings which will then become 'silent histories':

> He [the reader] insinuates into another person's text the ruses of pleasure and appropriation: he poaches on it, is transported into it, pluralizes himself in it like the internal rumblings of one's body. Ruse, metaphor, arrangement, this production is also an 'invention' of the memory. Words become the outlet or product of silent histories. (de Certeau 1984: xxi)

De Certeau's invocation of 'silent histories' may seem like an almost mystical positing of individual readers' responses, but it is important to understand that such 'silent histories' are not the result of a reader's imag-ination or inspiration, or any other such psychological or interior faculty. In fact, the comparison with bodily 'rumblings' gives a highly corporeal and material sense of this irreducibility. By refusing to locate the act of lit-erary 'poaching' in a domain of present intention, de Certeau reiterates a theme which is important for his own work, and that of many other French theorists: the self-presence of meaning can always be disrupted by the non-present or the non-meaningful. Here, the 'memory' or 'silent history' which occupies the text is not a former present but is radically past. This is why it can neither be reduced to meaning nor be seen as present in the text. It is an event, a break or a disruption. If dominant forms of representation see time and history as a series of meaningful presents, de Certeau sees tactical invention as a temporal event which breaks with meaning. The invention is silent precisely because it disturbs conventional meaning, and is a tactical event because it fissures the present. What we see here is not personal or individual response but the singularity of a 'pre-personal' rumbling. These silent histories are defined oppositionally in relation to the culture's dominant strategies. As such, then, de Certeau aims to theorise the non-general, the specific and the singular. Unlike Bourdieu he does not see consumption as determined by position-taking and interests. Unlike Foucault he does not see the disruption of dominant strategy as another form of strategy, as counter-strategy. Rather than theorising a single field of cultural production or power, de Certeau posits the tactic as a specific mode of deviation. He offers, in many ways, a theory of the non-theorisable. This is why the tactic depends upon the strategy – which *can* be theorised and which is produced through acts of generalisation – and why the tactic is never given as such but is only seen as a detour from the dominant strategy.

Just as Foucault's genealogy sought to unearth other possibilities in order to open up the present, so de Certeau's 'silent histories' can be seen as ways of undermining any sense of naturalness or inevitability about the present, by showing that other readings were always possible. But whereas, for Foucault, the diffuse forces which could not be completely contained within the dominant grid of power were neither hidden nor radically opposed to power, de Certeau's 'silent histories' or tactical ruses posit a greater, almost inexplicable, distance from institutional norms. The ruse is a spontaneous, unpredictable and arbitrary deviation from the norm; as such, it is incalculable and can neither be explained nor predicted according to a pre-existing structure of interests, norms, rules or values.

Like the theorists of culture examined in previous chapters, de Certeau's theory of 'oppositional practice' seeks to show the ways in which societies operate by rules while at the same time refusing to locate those rules either in the mental space of something like conscience or in the external imposition of prohibitions. But de Certeau also challenges the notions of 'structure', system, control mechanism or exchange as it operates in traditional anthropology and ethnography. The ethnographer makes sense of a society by assuming an underlying system which, if it is not expressed in conscious rules, must lie at the unconscious level of structure – a structure the ethnographer goes on to reveal. The culture is then typified by its dominant form of organisation. Geertz had already challenged this illusion by arguing that the rules were never underlying; the patterns of a culture are determined after the fact of their production. Bourdieu, similarly, argued against the idea that societies followed lines of organisation and insisted on the agency of participants. But for both Geertz and Bourdieu the active role of the participant was at the same time culturally-inscribed and could be explained (albeit subsequently) according to a pre-given rationale. De Certeau, on the other hand, gives a far more *oppositonal* role to individual practice. He accepts that while societies are ordered by dominant strategies (clearly deployed sets of rules), these strategies are always resisted by tactics (irregular ruses which undermine those quite explicit structures). De Certeau's methodology focuses on a 'silent technology': a network of resisting practices which cannot be reduced to a meaning or an unconscious determination. Rather, it is the actions themselves which form part of a network of resistance. Resistances are defined by de Certeau as the use of strategies against themselves.

Strategies are movements whereby a space is appropriated and marked out, carved up according to a body of rules and regulated by a system of norms. Like Foucault's theorisation of 'disciplines' which shows the way bodies are ordered in spaces or technological grids, de Certeau's 'strategies' shows the way institutions delimit movement and practices by organising space. De Certeau's use of space as the defining characteristic of strategies is both literal and figural. At the literal level it can be argued that strategy achieves its ordering of behaviour by locating itself in a specific site. In de Certeau's famous example, the building of the factory defines a place where certain rules of practice delimit the movements of individuals. We could also see theatres, art galleries, cities and universities, for example, as sites which regulate certain forms of consumption. At the figural level strategies are spatial in so far as they are non-temporal: they seek to formalise and rigidify the necessarily disruptive movements of time. Strategies seek to apply the same rules and formal structures across time; they resist difference and alteration. In the writing of history or anthropology, for example, a strategy formalises the rules of a culture; it totalises all the specific, changing and individual acts into a single system. For de Certeau, history or everyday life is 'unreadable' precisely because it is plural, temporal, incalculable and non-systematic. Historiography is a strategy which takes the multiplicity of history and orders it into a 'readable form' (de Certeau 1984: 35).

The traditional sociological method of describing societies which uses statistics and generalisations from statistics has a similar strategic effect. It takes the contingent multiplicity of everyday life and transcribes it according to an overarching logic. De Certeau's theory therefore assumes that a culture is formed according to strategic boundaries, but that there is also an essentially unbounded or plural life which the boundary delimits. It is only because of de Certeau's commitment to the pre-strategic chaos of everyday life, that forms of order are seen as 'missing' the fullness of existence. As such, the act of strategy is a form of power. Like Foucault, de Certeau does not relate power to knowledge; he sees power as the condition for knowledge. But, unlike Foucault, de Certeau posits an 'other' to power's productive divisions; this 'otherness' is given or known in its disruptive effects on strategies. By spatialising temporally shifting forms of life, knowledge is a form of power which appropriates and orders that which it describes. As a strategy, knowledge colonises time by spatialising and freezing its differential effects. A strategy is also the point at which the metaphorical and literal aspects of space intersect. By taking over actual spaces (institutional sites), a strategy is able to constitute a form of knowledge which will produce formal and regulative rules – or, at least, generalities which will systematise and order the multiplicity of events:

> It would be legitimate to define the *power of knowledge* by this ability to transform the uncertainties of history into readable spaces. But it would be more correct to recognize in these 'strategies' a specific type of knowledge, one sustained and determined by the power to provide oneself with one's own place. Thus military or scientific strategies have always been inaugurated through the constitution of their 'own' areas (autonomous cities, 'neutral' or 'independent' institutions, laboratories pursuing 'disinterested' research, etc.). In other words, *a certain power is the precondition of this knowledge* and not merely its effect or its attribute. It makes this knowledge possible and at the same time determines its characteristics. It produces itself in and through this knowledge. (de Certeau 1984: 36)

Setting his work against those forms of description which both produce and focus upon strategies, de Certeau posits a theory of tactical description which concentrates on specific and individual practices and their *differing* forms:

> Statistical investigation grasps the material of these practices, but not their form; it determines the elements used, but not the 'phrasing' produced by the bricolage (the artisan-like inventiveness) and the discursiveness that com-

bine these elements, which are all in general circulation and rather drab. Statistical enquiry, in breaking down these 'efficacious meanderings' into units that it defines itself, in reorganizing the results of its analyses according to its own codes, 'finds' only the homogeneous. The power of its calculations lies in its ability to divide, but it is precisely through this analytic fragmentation that it loses sight of what it claims to seek and represent. (de Certeau 1984: xviii)

What statistical or ordered knowledge misses, then, is the *act* of ordering itself, the production or creation of the statistics. This production, or forming, would be prior to any created order; and to concentrate on this *bricolage* or collecting would be to undermine order's naturalness. A certain primacy might be granted to literary texts or works of art in so far as they present themselves *as artifice*, by foregrounding their production. Works of science or standard history, on the other hand, miss the reality which they seek to represent precisely because the very act of ordering is antithetical to the character of the real.

Representation is, for de Certeau, a hardening of the meanderings and arbitrary inventiveness of everyday life. How, then, can representation avoid this 'losing sight' of reality? A representation which did not present itself as an adequate ordering of the real would not be a re-presentation at all. It might be more like an invention itself – not a 'finding' of order, but an active and creative production. In short, it would be a tactic: a local and contingent, rather than overarching and adequate, inscription or mapping. Writing, considered *as writing*, as an inscription and delimitation rather than a passive and transparent representation would be tactical. There would be less focus on meaning, content or conceptual generality – this would be the effect of strategic ordering – and an attention to the singular act of inscription which is necessarily repressed in the acceptance of strategy. De Certeau's work seems to favour an aesthetic view of representation. As long as we see representation as the production, rather than reflection, of meaning then we will be aware of the strategies which belie the singularity of the real. By foregrounding their representational processes literary texts show strategies in action. A text is not an expression or reflection of its world. The very experience of a world as a general, meaningful and identifiable order is the effect of a textual strategy or organisation.

The acceptance that representation is both a production and a form of powerful (or strategic) ordering has underpinned much contemporary criticism. De Certeau's focus upon strategies as a form of power/knowledge circumvents the problem of relating a text to its context. The text, as

an act of writing and formalisation, is already a strategy. It fixes and delimits by creating a distribution of relations. As such it can be related to Foucault's notion of discursive practice; the text is part of a field of forces
which it both draws upon and reorganises. But unlike Foucault, who
posits resistance or freedom as the limit condition of power (there is no
power, for Foucault, unless it has a force which it also works upon and
produces), de Certeau stresses the qualitative differences made by the tactical use of strategies. In the case of reading, the strategy of a text can always
be 'poached' or consumed for the reader's own ends; reading can become
a tactic, *a different mode of power.*

A strategy, according to de Certeau, is the means by which dominant
rules and norms form themselves. Tactics, on the other hand, are practices
which pervert or use those rules in opposition to the strategy. Such resistance is therefore defined oppositionally. So while Foucault, as we have
seen, argues for general description of a single field rather than an interpretation which would reveal some depth or uncover a meaning, de
Certeau argues that there is a 'silence' of tactical ruses opposed to the
dominant field of power. De Certeau therefore tries to emphasise those
practices which acts of statistical description miss: the 'efficacious meanderings' which have an entirely contingent and unpredictable quality. Foucault's notion of 'event' (as that which disrupts a discursive formation),
like the notion of tactics, suggested that resistance could only be defined
in relation to the already given system of relations. But while Foucault
relies on notions of reconfiguration, redistribution and rearrangement to
describe discursive events (and thus still retains the primacy of systemic
relations or power) de Certeau argues for tactics as highly particular and
counter-systemic ruses.

De Certeau's famous analogy for such acts of 'antidiscipline' is *la perruque* (De Certeau 1984: 24–8), translated literally as 'wigging' or 'ripping
off'. A factory employee, for example, while working for (and being
exploited by) a large company may decide to use the site of the factory for
his or her own ends. Using the company's time and materials, the worker
may make a coffee table to take home; a secretary could type personal letters on company stationery in office hours; or a builder's labourer could
use his truck to undertake removals for a friend. In all cases these tactics
take place on the site of the strategy but introduce an 'efficacious mean-
dering' which wanders away from the purpose and function of strategic
ordering. More importantly, these tactics may break with any possible
economy or predetermined horizon of understanding. A *perruque* might be
an utterly profitless and useless act. A worker might simply waste time.

This would not be explicable in terms of intention, production or interests but would just mark a loss or deviation as such. If strategies are identified with space and the creation of systemic rules imposed upon a field
of differences, then tactics are aligned with time. Occupying the gaps or
interstices of the strategic grid, tactics produce a *difference* or unpredictable
event which can corrupt or pervert the strategy's system.

De Certeau also historicises the practice of tactics in everyday life.
While some critics, particularly Marxists, look back on times when there
was a strong folk culture which is now lost in the totalising age of corpo-
rate capitalism, de Certeau argues that *la perruque* sustains a contemporary
form of folk know-how. Tactics introduce into the ordered space of the
capitalist system other times (of home life and leisure). The spatial site of
the factory serves to order and discipline bodies but it cannot totally control the capacity for those bodies to occupy that site for other ends. Instead
of being geared to a logic of maximum profit, workers can use the site of
the company to create useless, profitless and inventive products which create other organisations (lines of gift exchange) which cannot be controlled by the strategy of production. And these other forms of production
would be enabled through the disruption of the space of the factory by
another time: the worker no longer devotes all hours to profit but either
wastes time or produces for 'another time' (when he or she returns
home).

Because tactics are characterised by temporality – by disrupting the
'freezing' of time by the dominant strategy – they are linked powerfully
to memory. According to de Certeau the art of memory, again revealed in
the folk-tale traditions of recounting and retelling, introduces into the
ordered space of the present other times and other forms of know-how.
The act of memory can become a type of *la perruque* by invoking excluded
practices, actions and narratives. Memory resists the detemporalising
moves of strategies by looking back to a past of popular culture and
retrieving a 'repertory of tactics for future use' (de Certeau 1984: 23).
Memory is therefore set against the strategic practice of history writing
which, by constructing narratives of the past as authoritative knowledge
geared towards a predictable future, has to dominate the historical contingencies and specificities of the past. It 'spatialises' time by seeing the
past as yet another aspect of the present. Memory, anecdote or folk-tale is
a fragment of the past as such, not determined completely by the ordering strategies of the present.

De Certeau therefore argues that the critic should try to resist the
strategic totalisation that enables conventional forms of sociology, history

writing and interpretation. Like Foucault, de Certeau sets his work against the hermeneutic tradition which seeks to reveal a general meaning behind other cultures or texts. This tradition of interpretation assumes that there is a form of knowledge hidden behind the practices of everyday life, a form of knowledge which the practitioners themselves do not know, a form of knowledge made available only to the critical and distanced eye of the observer. In fact the metaphor of visual and distanced observation is essential to a strategy's belief in the possibility of detached and impartial knowledge. But de Certeau argues for a form of enquiry which would not distance itself from its object but become a participant. Rather than seeing the logic of social forms in hidden or unconscious meaning, de Certeau suggests that practices themselves are a form of know-how. Like Foucault, de Certeau posits that there must be certain extra-linguistic moves which make discourse possible. But, again like Foucault, he does not see that such conditions for discourse can be revealed and made transparent by the interpreter. The foreign observer is not in a privileged position; analysis is itself a form of involved participation occupying yet another position alongside the practice. Interpretation of a culture's deep rules is neither possible nor desirable. Practices and tactics are themselves a form of logic and do not require the interpreter to posit a hidden level of meaning which would explain their ordering. Narratives are not texts which need to be interpreted; they are efficacious actions, storehouses of practices. The telling of a folk-tale can be itself a form of practice. De Certeau there-fore agrees with Pierre Bourdieu's criticisms of the opposition between theory and practice. Theory itself is a form of activity; it is a 'labour of sep-aration' which produces the material it seeks to know as both 'other' and subordinate (de Certeau 1988). At the same time, practices are themselves a form of theory. The opposition between narrative or mythic logic and scientific or theoretical knowledge is produced by science itself; but such a separation cannot be sustained. Theory or speaking of any form is a way of operating. Both scientific and narrative modes are part of a network of practices and actions. The practice of narration or storytelling is not some-thing 'added on' to the putative 'pure' truth of science; it is not just a remainder. On the contrary, the production or narration of truth or sci-ence is constitutive and necessary. Legitimate discourses are, like folk-tales, already forms of practice:

> Narrativity haunts such [scientific] discourse. Shouldn't we recognize its sci-entific legitimacy by assuming that instead of being a remainder that cannot be, or has not yet been, eliminated from discourse, narrativity has a neces-

sary function in it, and that *a theory of narration is indissociable from a theory of practices, as its condition as well as its production?* To do that would be to recognize the theoretical value of the novel, which has become the zoo of everyday practices since the establishment of modern science. It would also be to return 'scientific' significance to the traditional act which has always *recounted* practices (this act, *ce geste*, is also *une geste*, a tale of high deeds). In this way, the folktale provides scientific discourse with a model, and not merely with textual objects to be dealt with. It no longer has the status of a document that does not know what it says, cited (summoned and quoted) before and by the analysis that knows it. On the contrary, it is a know-how-to-say (*'savoir-dire'*) exactly adjusted to its object, and, as such, no longer the Other of knowledge; rather it is a variant of the discourse that knows and an authority in what concerns theory. One can then understand the alternations and complicities, the procedural homologies and social imbrications that link the 'arts of speaking' to the 'arts of operating': the same practices appear now in a verbal field, now in a field of non-linguistic actions; they move from one field to the other, being equally tactical and subtle in both; they keep the ball moving between them – from the workday to evening, from cooking to legends and gossip, from the devices of lived history to those of history retold. (de Certeau 1984: 78)

Criticism can therefore become a form of *la perruque* by focusing upon everyday practices and their own know-how, by revealing the strategic function of theoretical and scientific knowledges and by demonstrating the continuity between forms of narrative and science: 'To deal with everyday tactics in this way would be to practice an "ordinary" art, to find oneself in the common situation, and to make a kind of *perruque* of writing itself'. (de Certeau 1984: 28)

One can see the effects of writing as a type of *la perruque* in a number of recent literary critical methods. Firstly, peripheral, mundane or 'folk' knowledges are not only presented by the new historicist critic; they are also set alongside works of high art, gynecology, physics and theology. Stephen Greenblatt's famous essay, 'Invisible Bullets' reads Shakespeare through a belief held by the native American population. Struck by European-introduced viral infection, the locals believed they were being killed by 'invisible bullets'. The truth or relevance of this belief is beside the point. The 'scientific' explanation is less authoritative in this instance precisely because the explanation of 'invisible bullets' had more effect in the relation between the invaders and the local Americans. Further, the 'anecdote' may ostensibly bear no relation to Shakespeare's history plays and may have had nothing to do with Shakespeare's intent. But the motif – that the English possessed a way of killing which had no physical weapon – is used to link the text to questions of power. The fact that such minor nar-rative forms as anecdote, folk-tale and opinion are often presented with-out interpretation, introduction or explanation demonstrates a resistance to hermeneutic approaches (such as those criticised by Foucault and de Certeau) but it also reveals an attempt to form a critical tactic, whereby dominant discourses are disrupted by the 'ordinary' level of discourse. Just as de Certeau refuses to legitimise a privileged theoretical position, so many new historicist critics are content to rely on anecdote, folklore and reportage without positing a hierarchy, truth or legitimacy which could order such discourses. In addition, de Certeau's focus on the individual act of utterance rather than the system of discourse itself, shifts the emphasis away from discursive limits (as in Foucault's work) towards discursive dis-ruption. In fact, de Certeau's emphasis upon the 'other' of dominant strategies (either mystical, cultural or fictive otherness) is both where he differs most from Foucault and where his work has been most influential. An attention to the local, marginal and particular, while resisting its expla-nation through some interpretive framework has characterised much recent literary criticism. Rather than seeing texts as exemplars of a domi-nant ideology they are often figured as perverse, peripheral and potentially oppositional. By retrieving such forms of popular knowledge criticism forms a *perruque* of memory; it unearths the 'other' of a strategic Western rationality.

Heterology, historiography and New World encounters

Related to the theory of strategies and tactics is de Certeau's idea of a 'heterology' or science of the other. In various ways – through an analysis of travel-writing, historiography and scientific theory – de Certeau sought to demonstrate the ways in which the 'other' shadowed Western rational-ity. Alongside an interest in everyday culture, de Certeau also concerned himself with the 'discovery' of the New World from the sixteenth to eigh-teenth centuries, the writing of history throughout the same period and varieties of religious mysticism. Trained initially as a Jesuit, it could be argued that de Certeau always retained a 'theological' bent; for a concern with the 'other' was granted a primacy in all his work. For de Certeau the 'other' of strategic rationality occurs in the form of a tactic. If the individ-ual subject is created through learning the rules of space and practices, then the subject can also offer resistance by remembering and re-ordering that learning. For the obedient subject, then, the 'other' is memory – other times which can disrupt the logic of the present. For historiography, the

'other' is the past; for reason the 'other' is narrative or metaphor; for theology the 'other' is mysticism; while for travel-writing the 'other' is figured through different cultures. Such forms of otherness provide tactical
material whereby the totality of the strategic present can be disturbed
through various acts of recognition, remembering, representation or revelation.

According to de Certeau, the idea of travel, or the voyage, was a central myth of Western culture. One need only think of Homer's *Odyssey* as a
central text in the epic tradition to see the importance of the voyage – in
which a culture encounters and comes to terms with its others. But this
mythic voyage also occurs in the key texts of the English epic tradition,
though less obviously. In *Paradise Lost* a number of worlds are presented:
Adam and Eve in Eden, Satan's pandemonium, the angels in heaven and
the Old Testament world described to Adam in the vision of world history
which concludes Milton's epic. This traditional mythic or literary interest
in travel, the voyage and other worlds has been of central importance to
the re-interpretation of the Renaissance, where travel writings have been
set alongside ostensibly more fictional works. According to de Certeau, in
the encounter with other cultures in the sixteenth century knowledge had
to go through a process of exchange and confrontation. Not only did the
presentation of new material provide the travel writer with challenges to
disciplines of knowledge and their boundaries (the travel writer was at
once scientist, anthropologist and story-teller); travel-writing had to
include in its corpus new modes of representation which could deal with
the new world. Like Greenblatt's idea of negotiation and exchange, in
which a culture orders its 'other' by providing signs and representations
which can be circulated as part of a system of knowledge, de Certeau's
'exchange and confrontation' focuses on both the challenge which 'otherness' presents to Western science as well as the West's strategic capacity
to organise that 'otherness' in forms of knowledge.

The literature of travel is, therefore, typical of the link between scientific discourse and narrative. Writing the culture of the 'other' both produces that culture as an object of knowledge – by enacting a distance – and
orders that object in scientific discourse. Such writing represents science
itself as powerful and effective while creating those very powerful effects
of science, the production of a body of knowledge and a space of order:
'At once a staging (fiction, in the English sense of the term) and an ordering (discourse), travel narratives offer to analysis various combinations
between the practices of scientific investigation ... and their figurations in
literary space-time' (de Certeau 1991: 222). The writing of science's

129

encounter with the New World enables the reinforcing of the difference both between science and myth and the West and its others.

De Certeau seeks to demonstrate the ways in which the literature of travel supports and produces the 'imaginary' of reason. The 'imaginary' of reason is the store of images, metaphors, fictions and divisions which makes reason, as an ordering strategy, possible but which reason also represses or denies. Travel literature, through its separation which produces the other as irrational, non-Western, mythic and superstitious, provides the West with the image of itself as an ordering strategy:

> The successive definitions of ethnic difference or of 'superstition', the progressive elaboration of concepts of 'fable' or of 'myth', the distinctions between writing and orality will require special attention. Indeed, these distinctions involve strategic elements of Western culture, enact classifications that refer back to the social divisions that organize knowledge, and, conversely, are divisions that have structured the social agency of science. (de Certeau 1991: 222–3)

Like Foucault, de Certeau shows here the identification of knowledge with power. The act of description or writing is not just *used* for political ends; the process of writing itself produces and reinforces the divisions which are at once conceptual and social. It is from this type of perspective that Louis Montrose, writing of Ralegh's New World narratives, declares: 'the text is also an event, and the event, a text. ... The performance of Ralegh's discovery becomes socially accessible and meaningful only as a writing performance, as *ethnography* – only, that is, when it has been textualized as his *Discoverie*' (Montrose 1991: 14). Montrose's essay works through the idea that writing *is* power and that ethnography, as the production of the other *as* other, is a mode of power peculiar to a specific historic moment of Western culture. The relation between literary criticism and ethnography here is complex. Because theories of cultural analysis, such as de Certeau's, acknowledge their own status as texts (and texts with a certain mode of power) literary criticism does more than *use* ethnographic insights to illuminate texts. The category of writing has shifted the terrain of the relation between texts, contexts and theory. It is now writing, textuality or representation which is seen as foundational. Only through the writing of the other does the other appear as other. Any theory of the relation between textuality and world would , itself, still be textual. De Certeau's 'heterology' recognises that otherness is never purely given; it is always encountered through a written imaginary. Nevertheless, the writing of the other, the ethnographic project is always haunted by that which writing cannot contain. The reading of a text and its limits is no longer a purely literary critical form of enquiry. If we want to avoid including all cultures, historical periods and experience within a single horizon, such as history or culture, then we have to recognise the limits of any single horizon. The recognition of the limits of conceptual strategy is enabled by attending to the writing of that strategy. Only in re-reading a text is the text's other given. 'Heterology' is, in this sense, an attention to writing. History, ethnography and anthropology become, in part at least, forms of textual criticism.

At the same time, however, and in keeping with the spirit of his previous work, de Certeau's description of travel literature will focus on the particular and specific resistances those 'other' cultures presented to the ordering power of the West. Once again, Louis Montrose's work on the discourse of discovery also stresses the local resistance that can be set against the dominant narrative. For Montrose, like de Certeau, the critic's task is not to interpret but 'to reveal, beneath the apparent stability and consistency of collective structures, myriad local and individual sites of social reproduction, variation and change' (Montrose 1991: 2). According to de Certeau such resistance is attended to by showing:

> how, in the text of the ethnographic project, oriented initially toward reduction and preservation, are irreducible details (sounds, 'words', singularities) insinuated as faults in the discourse of comprehension, so that the travel narrative presented the kind of organization that Freud posited in ordinary language: a system in which indices of an unconscious, that Other of the conscience, emerge in lapsus or witticisms. The history of voyages would especially lend itself to this analysis by tolerating or privileging as an 'event' that which makes an exception to interpretive codes. (de Certeau 1991: 223)

In the introduction to his own study of travel narratives Stephen Greenblatt argues that his use of anecdote stems from an attempt to seize the local disorder and specificity which are lost in 'grand' historical narratives. Like de Certeau he, too, places an emphasis on the power of retelling:

> Anecdotes then are among the principal products of a culture's representational technology, mediators between the undifferentiated succession of local moments and a larger strategy toward which they can only gesture. They are seized in passing from the swirl of experiences and given some shape, a shape whose provisionality still marks them as contingent – otherwise, we would give them the larger, grander name of history – but also makes them available for telling and retelling. (Greenblatt 1988b: 3)

An anecdote occurs at the level of folk or popular culture; it is neither a pure and immediate saying nor a coherent and strategic order: lying between experience and form, it provides an opening into the ideological closure of imperialist discourse. If history, as de Certeau argues in The Writing of History (1988), is enabled by a 'labour of separation', then its strategic fixing of time and events can always be challenged by a counter-labour. Such a labour would recognise that all acts of knowledge are acts which take place in a network of other acts and procedures. A tactical history would reveal all those events, anecdotes, acts of memory and resistances which occur in the interstices of the historical text as indications of the 'other' which historiography has had to silence in order to be itself.

The awareness that history writing is a heterology, or science of an 'other', enables de Certeau to chart the conditions for modern historiography in The Writing of History. According to de Certeau, the writing of history, as a practice, occurs alongside the beginnings of modern anatomy. The idea of a 'body of knowledge', detached and available for observation, is the common precondition for both modern historiography and medicine; both discourses are 'heterologies' in that they posit an other as a silent object which they will enable to speak: 'Modern medicine and historiography are born almost simultaneously from the rift between a subject that is supposedly literate, and an object that is supposedly written in an unknown language' (de Certeau 1988: 3). The division between self and other, past and present has to take place continually: 'historiography separates its present from a past. But everywhere it repeats the initial act of division' (de Certeau 1988: 3). Just as the insights of anthropological theorists, such as Mary Douglas, have sought to show that Western society also has its rituals and symbolic practices, de Certeau argues that the division between past and present which enables history writing is itself a ritual. Writing on Michelet's History of French Revolution (1967), de Certeau argues that the events of the past are created as 'other' in order to establish the order of the present. Speaking of the 'voices' silenced by historiography he argues: 'Discourse drives them back into the dark. It is a deposition. It turns them into severed souls. It honors them with a ritual of which they had been deprived' (de Certeau 1988: 1). The ritual of history writing is an act of both silence and retrieval; the specificity of the past is made quiet while a form and order are given to the events of the past. Historiography becomes a performative act of exorcism in which the loss of the past (its silence and mystery) are made present and reified in historical discourse:

> Historiography tends to prove that the site of its production can encompass the past: it is an odd procedure that posits death, a breakage everywhere reiterated in discourse, and that yet denies loss by appropriating to the present the privilege of recapitulating the past as a form of knowledge. A labor of death and a labor against death.

> This paradoxical procedure is symbolized and performed in a gesture which has at once the value of myth and of ritual: *writing*. (de Certeau 1988: 5)

If history is, as de Certeau argues, an act of ritual which holds the threat of the 'other' at a distance; if modern Western knowledge is, like earlier forms of discourse, both religious and efficacious, then encounters between the West and the New World can no longer be figured as encounters between reason and savagery, science and superstition, or enlightenment and myth. Works of literature can no longer be seen as radically divided from texts of knowledge (or ideas) by which they are influenced. There is no longer a division between knowledge and myth; for knowledge itself is a form of ritual and a way of dealing with those forms of 'otherness' which haunt the West and upon which Western thought depends.

As a result, the once problematic relation between texts and their historical contexts is radically reformulated. A text cannot be *related* to history; not only is 'history' itself only known discursively, the very act of writing history is itself a modern and, to some extent, 'fictional' phenomenon. Historiography bears all those marks of myth and ritual which are supposedly the objects of reason; but reason itself can only be if it ritualistically (through historiography) distances itself from its 'other'. The critical implications of this insight are more than apparent in the work of new historicist criticism. When dealing with the colonisation of other territories, the literature of travel can be seen as a form of ritual which must compete discursively with those 'native' rituals it seeks to dominate. The process of such confrontation and exchange can never give us some pure historical origin, prior to the act of writing. But the texts of such a history can reveal the competing acts of ritual which have gone into their making. The phenomenon of 'exchange' is evidenced in the way images of the New World are circulated to produce an order and system of representation which can contain the other. But the act of confrontation – the conflict between acts of ritual – is also evidenced in those same representations. In fact, as Greenblatt has argued, the acts of both historiography and writing were powerful weapons in the conquering of the New World. Like de Certeau, Greenblatt argues that 'history' can only be achieved through a labour of writing: 'those who possess writing have a past, a history, that those without access to letters necessarily lack' (Greenblatt 1988b: 10). Those who did not possess the representational power of script were forced to use their own modes of symbolisation to communicate. Consequently, as Greenblatt makes clear, writing for the conquistadores was less an act of communication than it was a form of symbolic exchange in which the technology of representation that characterised Western logic was made to reveal its dependence upon ritual. In the face of the incomprehension of writing the *conquistadores* were forced to take the materials of writing (books, statutes, writing instruments) at the same level as the ritualistic objects of the culture they encountered: 'The absence of writing determined the predominance of ritual over improvisation and cyclical time over linear time, characteristics that in turn led to disastrous misperceptions and miscalculations in the face of the conquistadores' (Greenblatt 1988b: 11).

This point is demonstrated clearly in a reading of *The Tempest* where Prospero's books are deemed by Caliban to possess a magic or supernatural force which enables Prospero's power. At one level, we could see Caliban's belief as a primitive misrecognition of the rational power of texts. Caliban regards the texts as objects capable of physical effects and not as tokens or signs of meaning. Prospero's rhetorical power – his ability to impose narrative, order and meaning – is understood by Caliban as a form of magic. The distinction between Caliban's magical/physicalist understanding of Prospero's books and the rational definition of texts as signs of an ideal meaning, repeats the division between ritual and metaphysics which underpinned nineteenth-century anthropology. Only a 'primitive' culture not versed with the ordered and ideal phenomenon of writing could grant texts such a direct power. However, de Certeau's work on the ritualistic character of knowledge and Greenblatt's examination of the power of writing in New World encounters both demonstrate that, in a certain sense, texts are objects of physical power. Indeed, the sacredness of texts has been central to the industry of literary criticism which focuses on authoritative readings, editions, performances and grants certain texts (literary, scientific, juridical and spiritual) a great cultural significance. The writing of history is a ritual, then, in at least two senses. Following de Certeau we can see that the production of the text of history is a labour that produces the past as 'other' in order to organise a separate present. Secondly, through the concrete productions of historical texts in the form of writing the West maintains a strategic form of representation – which would be set against the more fluid representational forms of memory, folk-tale and anecdote. Writing is an act and not just an ideal meaning; its effects include the lived strategies which organise and produce cultures.

How, though, would we recognise those (tactical) forms of meaning, time and representational which were 'other' than the written forms of the West? Greenblatt's description of a division between (native) ritual and (conquering) textual history creates more of an opposition between representation and its other than does de Certeau's strategy and tactics. But de Certeau's references to silent histories, folk-tale, anecdote and myth also suggest that the processes of writing, conceptual ordering and history can be *delimited* within modern Western culture. De Certeau, no less than Greenblatt, suggests that reason and history might have an identifiable other. This other would resist the spatial, ordering and linear-historical strategies of Western power. The temporality of tactics may be parasitic on writing and may only be glimpsed as an other to strategic ordering, but de Certeau nevertheless provides a theory – as Greenblatt will later do – of those events and forms of meaning which escape the conceptual ordering of the West. In fact, this is de Certeau's main point of disagreement with Foucault and Bourdieu. Against the *theoretical* determination of all forms of otherness, de Certeau sets the efficacy of *practices*. The theory of practice provides theory with an other. Practice – unlike culture or power – is a 'heterology', a way of thinking about otherness without *knowing the other in advance*. In this sense, practice is defined as a break with the closure of consciousness, humanity and meaning:

> These practices present in fact a curious analogy, and a sort of immemorial link, to the simulations, tricks, and disguises that certain fishes or plants execute with extraordinary virtuosity. The procedures of this art can be found in the farthest reaches of the domain of the living, as if they managed to surmount not only the strategic distributions of historical institutions but also the break established by the very institution of consciousness. They maintain formal continuities and the permanence of a memory without language, from the depths of the oceans to the streets of our great cities. (de Certeau 1988: 40)

De Certeau's theory of practices is an attempt to think the other of theory. But by identifying the other of reason and theory in the form of the folk-tale, anecdote, legend or local practice, de Certeau already disrupts the division he is trying to create. It is not just that we would only know about these practices from the domain of theory. De Certeau's very description of the alterity of practices seems to already grant practices a form of meaning which could not place them in an order different from that of writing or history. How is formal continuity and memory possible if what is continued or remembered does not have some order or conceptualisation? Greenblatt's gesture to native ritual and de Certeau's invocation of folk-tale still grants these practices a meaning; they are still repeatable and recognisable. To this extent they must already have partaken of those features (of writing) which de Certeau wants to locate in strategic ordering alone; they must have a certain order or identity and cannot be purely singular. Foucault's theory of discursive practice already recognised this problem: in so far as actions possessed a certain regularity they were already 'discursive'. And this is no doubt why Foucault departed from his early position of seeing madness as some prior form of otherness which reason would subsequently contain and delimit. But de Certeau recognises a problem with the reduction of all forms of otherness to a single domain – such as writing, power or representation; and this is why he turns to the mute 'efficacy' of practices. It seems that the problem of the event and radical historicity is sustained rather than solved by de Certeau's heterology. If historical writing incorporates all forms of otherness into a meaningful present, how can we think of a truly historical past? Can we think a pre-representational event of the past? For de Certeau this problem is answered by a division between strategic and tactical forms of knowledge, whereby the tactic is only known through its silent disruption of the strategy. But it is questionable whether this distinction can be sustained. The work of new historicism has done much to show that those putatively 'other' forms of knowledge such as folk-tale, art and myth take part in the same discursive complex as legitimised knowledge. (This is why, perhaps, Greenblatt will turn to 'wonder' rather than literature to signal theory's other.)

Institutionalised knowledges, such as science, theology, anthropology and history are, for de Certeau, strategic practices in so far as they organise and objectify everyday life. Such acts of knowledge are also acts of power in their ordering or 'taming' of the contingencies and singularities of everyday life. Whereas for Foucault the power/knowledge identification precluded the possibility of seeking any pure 'other' or outside to the system of power, de Certeau's theory of tactics posits two quite distinct modes of power. The resisting tactics which short-circuit the ordering power of strategies are not just competing strategies: they are 'other' because they operate by a different logic (of singularities, difference and dis-order). When considered in relation to the question of other cultures, de Certeau's emphasis on a different mode of power enables the reader of historical or anthropological texts to attend to the possibility of an otherness which resists the dominant text. This otherness can be seen in the form of marginal practices (*la perruque*), other rituals (non-text-based cultures), other forms of temporality (in memory or myth) and other forms of knowledge. What de Certeau shares with Foucault and Bourdieu is, however, a disinclination to see any single phenomenon as a primary explanation. In this sense all these theorists offer a challenge to the Marxist account of power which posits economic forces as a privileged determinant. But while rejecting Marxism and economism there is also an attempt, particularly evident in de Certeau, to provide a theory of resistance. The paradox on which de Certeau's theory seems to depend – the representation of a 'silence' which disrupts representation – indicates a theoretical need to think the other of theory. De Certeau locates this otherness in the pre-semantic status of the tactic. But if the tactic is to be theorised or conceptualised it cannot remain purely other. To this extent, any *heterology* – any theory of the other – is already a reinclusion of otherness. Perhaps the question which needs to be directed to de Certeau's theory is why theory needs to posit practice as a radical otherness. As a theory of resistance de Certeau's oppositional account of practices can be defined against Marxism – which had always sought to unite, rather than divide, theory and praxis. It may well be argued that even though de Certeau's theorisation of theory's other sustains a paradox this is a paradox well worth having. But it might also be argued that resistance still finds its best theorisation in the Marxist tradition which sees theory itself as the possibility of oppositional intervention.

Despite the clear emphasis in Foucault and de Certeau to move beyond traditional accounts of power, freedom and resistance, one of the most common criticisms which has been directed towards both Foucault and new historicism has been that these theories are inadequate to deal with the political struggles inherent in the operation of power. Arguing against new historicism's supposed failure to posit resistance outside the system of power relations, cultural materialism has sustained a more Marxist notion of the character and location of power. Cultural materialism's definition of both culture and ideology has – while drawing upon Foucault, new historicism and recent theories of culture – concerned itself more directly with the possibility of resistance and subversion. And it does so, not by positing an ineffable 'other' to power, but by acknowledging that what resists dominant modes of power takes the form of conscious and meaningful interests. It is this reinvigoration of the Marxist tradition of criticism which will be the subject of the next chapter.

137

6

Raymond Williams
and cultural materialism

The term 'cultural materialism' is borrowed from its recent use by Raymond
Williams; its practice grows from an eclectic body of work in Britain in the
post-war period which can be broadly characterised as cultural analysis. That
work includes the considerable output of Williams himself, and, more generally, the convergence of history, sociology and English in cultural studies,
some of the major developments in feminism, as well as continental Marxist-
structuralist and post-structuralist theory, especially that of Althusser,
Macherey, Gramsci and Foucault. (Dollimore 1985a: 2–3)

This account of cultural materialism by one of its main exponents,
Jonathan Dollimore, clearly describes the breadth, eclecticism and flexi-
bility of a movement which, like new historicism, challenges traditional
theories of the relation between texts and historical contexts. The following chapters explore the complex phenomenon of cultural materialism:
writers who explicitly include themselves within the movement
(Williams, Dollimore and Sinfield), the work which provided the
theoretical ground for cultural materialism (Gramsci, Althusser and
Macherey), and writers whose work shares many of the features and concerns of cultural materialism but who also disagree with some of the
tenets of cultural materialist criticism.

It is by now a commonplace in criticism to distinguish British cultural
materialism from American new historicism by referring to the former's
more politically self-aware, or avowedly Marxist, character. While new
historicism is frequently attacked for its supposed political quietism, cultural materialism is far more integrated within, and indebted to, a tradition of Marxist theory with which it is still actively engaged.

Before going on to explore some of the specific features of cultural
materialism two problems of definition need to be noted. Firstly, like new

historicism, cultural materialism is by no means a unified theory identifiable with any single theorist or position (although Williams is a key figure). Secondly, cultural materialism and new historicism themselves cannot be clearly separated from each other. Cultural materialism is not just the British name for new historicism; there are differences of tradition and emphasis, but many examples of contemporary critical practice draw upon both cultural materialist and new historicist insights. New historicist work is frequently included in British cultural materialist anthologies (and vice versa). Both movements are indebted to the work of Foucault and some of the theoretical developments of post-structuralism (although in different ways). Alan Sinfield's recent work (1994), which is clearly located in the tradition of cultural materialism, also reflects on the relation between English literature in Britain and the United States; and this reflection is typical of a sense of the differences and common concerns of both movements. But while new historicism can be seen as a 'return' to history following a seemingly dehistoricised post-structuralism, cultural materialism's relation to post-structuralism is quite different. Cultural materialism pre-existed the advent of post-structuralism in Britain and its post-structuralist influences have been far more eclectic; cultural materialism drew upon the work of Althusser, Macherey, Foucault and (to a much lesser extent) Lacan and Derrida. Post-structuralism in the United States, on the other hand, was localised and more clearly identified with the Derridean Yale School. New historicism can be perceived, in some ways, as a 'break' with the formalist post-structuralism of de Man, Hillis Miller, Johnson and Hartman, while British criticism had more often already accommodated its post-structuralism within a Marxist or political framework.

Despite these divergences, it is difficult, and somewhat artificial, to consider new historicism and cultural materialism as two clearly defined movements. Today, it is perhaps best to consider cultural materialism as a theoretical trajectory which has intersected with what is now known as new historicism. The nature of this intersection is such that while British and North American literary criticism have quite different genealogies, the differences are becoming less marked. In a later chapter we will examine the ways in which new historicism can be understood in relation to its American new critical past. This chapter and the following two chapters will consider the various theoretical currents which have contributed to contemporary cultural materialism.

Raymond Williams

While new historicism emerged as a self-conscious critical practice in the 1980s, cultural materialism has a far longer history extending back at least to the 1950s with the publication of Raymond Williams's *Culture and Society* (1963). Williams himself adopted the term 'cultural materialism' to describe his own critical practice which directly engaged with the central problem of Marxist aesthetics: the relation between the economic base and the superstructure. The very term, cultural materialism, encompasses both sides of this equation: the materiality of the economic base and the sense that there is also a specifically cultural dimension of human life. But Williams broadened both terms. 'Materialism' no longer referred to the strictly economic in the Marxist sense (the mode of production); it also included the materiality of artistic production (printing, performance, distribution) and the physicality of human practices. Similarly, 'culture' signified more than it had in the earlier criticism of Matthew Arnold and F. R. Leavis; culture was not just art and tradition but included practices, expectations, ways of seeing and everyday communication. Williams's idea of culture also expanded the traditional Marxist problematic; culture was more than a mere reflection or expression of the economic base. In order to understand how Williams effectively problematised the Marxist question of the relation between the base and superstructure, it is necessary to understand a key word in Williams's theoretical corpus: 'experience'.

The concept of experience was a key term in the Leavisite literary criticism which was dominant prior to Williams's theorisation of literature and society. While Williams self-consciously placed himself within the Marxist tradition (Williams 1976; 1977), it was his radicalisation of Leavisism which enabled a subsequent tradition of British Marxist criticism to move beyond the reductive base-superstructure relations which saw literature as an effect of a prior economic reality.

While a certain form of English literary criticism can be located as early as the eighteenth century, the establishing of criticism as a university discipline with defined modes of practice and purpose really takes place with F. R. Leavis, the publication of the journal *Scrutiny* and the focus upon texts themselves (in contradistinction to the earlier philological emphasis on tracing sources, influences and allusions). The idea of experience was crucial to Leavis's grounding of definite criteria for literary value and purpose. According to Leavis, the value of a literary text (indeed the specific value of literature *as such*) lay in its ability to embody experience. And experience was seen as valuable literary content precisely because the reinvigoration of experience enabled the reader to get in touch with those eternal human feelings which are the foundation of human life and morality. The emphasis upon literature's privileged relation to experience was not confined to Leavis alone. According to T. S. Eliot and his notion of the 'dissociation of sensibility' (Eliot 1934: 287), the seventeenth century marked a historical point at which literature no longer faithfully accorded with possible human experience. Milton, as far as Eliot was concerned, had developed literary and rhetorical style at the expense of poetry's ability to reveal actual experience or, in Eliot's terms, an 'objective correlative' (Eliot 1934: 145). For this reason, Eliot valued that literature which preceded or overcame this dissociation between words and experience. Leavis repeated, approvingly, Eliot's condemnation of Milton precisely because he too saw Milton's style as only rarely achieving 'unusual life'; when Leavis did approve of Milton it was when the 'hollowness' of Milton's mere style gave way to the evocation of a sensible experience:

> To say that Milton's verse is magniloquent is to say that it is not doing as much as its impressive pomp and volume seem to be asserting; that mere orotundity is a disproportionate part of the whole effect; and that it demands more deference than it merits. It is to call attention to a lack of something in the stuff of the verse, to a certain sensuous poverty. (Leavis 1936: 45)

For Leavis poets from the 'line of wit', on the other hand, such as Marvell, produced a far more 'rich' poetry in which a fuller range of experience was engaged. Compared to Milton, Leavis argued that Marvell's poetry displayed 'the finer wisdom of a ripe civilization' where the values of the text are also 'present implicitly in the wit' (1936: 31). Whereas Milton's poetry revealed a divorce between language and feeling, Marvell's choice of words enabled feeling and experience to be conveyed directly through word and image. It was this sort of use and definition of 'experience', 'life' or 'feeling' which, according to later cultural materialists, rendered traditional humanist criticism 'idealist' (Dollimore 1984: 190).

The charge of idealism – still used as a critical term in cultural materialism – refers to a refusal or denial of material and historically specific conditions. (In a similar manner Catherine Belsey (1984) has used the term 'metaphysical' to refer to any dehistoricised theory or truth claim). The central tenet of Marxist materialism – that economic or material conditions are in some way determinant – sets itself against any positing of a timeless or eternal human value or reality. To posit pity, life, sensibility, tragedy, human nature or any phenomenon as universal is an act of idealism: a blindness to the specific economic and historical (material) features of human life. To see literary value and literary practice as centred on the notion of experience is, therefore, 'idealist' precisely because for idealism 'experience' is conceived as universal and located within the private space of a dehistoricised individual subject.

While traditional criticism's use of 'experience' may have had a de-politicising and dehistoricisisng effect, the centrality of this term in the work of Williams should not be used to dismiss his work as similarly guilty of idealism (Eagleton 1976a: 5). It is precisely because of Williams's redefinition of culture as 'a whole way of life' that the concept of experience can no longer be seen in an ideal or non-material sense. To the contrary, because culture is defined by Williams as the entire complex of practices, significations, institutions, material forces and personal responses, the problem of relating lived experience to a politico-economic reality is circumvented (Williams 1977: 94). Experience itself is already part of a larger cultural unity. At the same time, the notion of the economic or material is no longer seen as some pre-cultural, ultra-real determinant; any understanding of the economic must, for Williams, be understood through experience. Reacting against crude and mechanistic uses of materialism, Williams argued that the validity of Marxist theory could only be sustained with a constant attention to the specificity of culture as it is lived:

> As for Marx, one accepted the emphases on history, on change, on the inevitably close relationships between class and culture, but the way this came through was, at another level, unacceptable. There was, in this position, a polarisation and abstraction of economic life on the one hand and culture on the other, which did not seem to me to correspond to the social experience of culture as others had lived it, and as one was trying to live it oneself. (Williams 1968: 28)

Any explanatory or interpretive practice cannot simply assert, in a quasi-scientific manner, the economy as a simple cause. For the 'economy' is already within culture, is already understood in a certain way; and as an interpretive or explanatory concept it must be considered in relation to the entire range of cultural phenomena. Williams had, early on, perceived a key problem which was to concern many literary and social theorists. How could 'history' or 'economy' be used critically to challenge generalist or 'idealist' claims about society? Wasn't the notion of 'economy' itself an ultimate explanation? And wasn't the Marxist concept of history, in some ways, ahistorical in its reduction of all events to a single determining force? Because theories of history and economy had their own historical specificity, they could not be invoked without an attention to the differences within history. History itself was a cultural phenomenon; not so much an explanation for events as the way events are lived.

This is, of course, where Williams's 'culturalism', as it has come to be known, marks a shift away from a strongly Marxist notion of economic determinism (Williams 1976; 1977: 88). It is also where Williams's work as a whole has met with the most criticism (mainly from more 'faithfully' Marxist critics). It has been argued that there is an essential vagueness or lack of clarity in Williams's work on culture (Eagleton 1976a), an inability to distinguish clearly, or rigorously, relate economic causes to cultural life. But the lack of a general theoretically or 'scientifically' grounded concept of the relation between economic reality and culture in its narrow sense, can also be seen as highly enabling. The vagueness of the precise nature of how economic forces influence cultural production precludes any single overarching theory of causality for culture in general.

Recent cultural materialist criticism has been most fruitful in its refusal to see the economic as a single or consistent explanation; a work of art may have a multiple and contradictory relation to the mode of production in which it is produced or consumed. A work may reflect *and* contest *and* effect *and* disrupt *and* reinforce economic conditions. To assume a single or general relation between economic causes and art is to grant artworks a certain unity and essence. Reacting against such a stable notion of relating art to economic determinants, cultural materialist readings have shown the ways in which the political force of Shakespeare's plays, for example, has differed in the history of performance (Sinfield 1985), while any given play may have a number of conflicting conservative and disruptive impulses.

Henry V, for example, works at one level to establish a sense of national order, and had to do so at a historical moment when the move from religious to secular social norms threatened the idea of divine rule. Whereas traditional Christian doctrine promoted a sense of resignation to God's ordered world, the Elizabethan period saw the emergence of a conflicting ideology: the Protestant sense of active engagement. Dollimore and Sinfield define these two ideologies as 'static' and 'activist' respectively. In *Henry V*, they argue, both ideologies are at play. Human actions are seen as essential but they also reinforce a natural and divine order (Dollimore and Sinfield 1985: 213). There is, they conclude, at any historical moment a number of ideological forces as well as a multiplicity of ways in which such forces can operate in a work of art.

It was Williams's argument that at any moment in a culture there are dominant, residual and emergent elements which provided a way of understanding the presence of conflicting ideologies in a single work. The ideological forces of a text are never simply unified into a single and coherent 'vision' or meaning; a work bears the marks of its historical conflict and dissension. Furthermore, as Dollimore and Sinfield go on to argue, ideology itself only works by articulating the very voices it seeks to deny or contain. Not only does any text represent the contradictory emergence of dominant, residual and emergent cultural forces (Williams 1961), ideological dominance is only ever achieved by the negation and marginalisation of conflicting representations. According to Dollimore and Sinfield, the achievement of order in *Henry V* works by constantly invoking the characters, actions and utterances of insurrection in order that these disruptive factors can be controlled and delimited. Written and performed at a time when foreign wars were a vexing taxational burden for the English populace, *Henry V* has to legitimise and perform (rather than represent) a pre-given national order. Such order is achieved through the play's 'strategies of containment'. Through acts of confession, punishment and the characterisation of the monarch himself, the play takes the socially disparate forces of the Elizabethan polity and stabilises power in the single figure of Henry (Dollimore and Sinfield 1985: 221). The disruption and misrule which were in actual fact threatening the state from within are accordingly displaced and refigured onto a foreign 'other'. But in so far as these forces are *represented* in order to be contained, the play bears the marks of its act of ordering. There is always the possibility that the King's rhetoric of order may not convincingly contain those other forces against which it is defined. This is where a cultural materialist criticism recognises its intervention:

> If we attend to the play's different levels of signification rather than its implied containments, it becomes apparent that the question of conviction is finally a question about the diverse conditions of reception. How far the King's argument is to be credited is a standard question for conventional criticism, but a materialist analysis takes several steps back and reads real historical conflict on and through his ambiguities. (Dollimore and Sinfield 1985: 225)

The assumption throughout cultural materialist criticism that both ideology and works of literature are neither coherent unities nor trans-historically identical owes a great deal to Williams's retheorisation of culture. In fact, as Williams's work makes clear, the very notion of culture as a 'whole way of life' (Williams 1963: 311), while appearing to be unified or organicist, resists positing any single factor as causal; any dominant feature of a culture is also accompanied by residual and emergent forces. The very rich tradition of cultural materialism which has debated, explored and multiplied the political and economic meanings of literary production and consumption would not be possible if a single and general base-superstructure relation were sustained. Economic, political or material factors are not related to, or discovered behind, a text which is seen as an instance of ideology. Williams's notion of culture rejects both determinism and dualism. A text is part of a network and history of practices; and the network of relations may well vary from text to text, or culture to culture. Once overarching Marxist historical epochs are inflected by Williams's emphasis upon cultural specificity, then a text needs to be explored for the quite particular ways in which it negotiates its cultural locale.

Williams's work on the novel, for example, regards the early novel as occurring within a particular configuration in which bourgeois power begins to contest the mannered and rarefied classicism of the aristocracy. So much is standard Marxist criticism. However, while other Marxist critics have granted the novel in general a particular ideological character, Williams examines the particular conditions of emergence and production of specific novelists and their culture. Most importantly, the novel itself negotiates the problem of cultural wholes. Literature, here, is not regarded as a mute mirror which the theoretically informed critic then demystifies. The literary work – in this case the novel – is already engaged with the problem of representation and cultural understanding. As Williams argues in The English Novel (1970), novels are more than just reflections of a social whole. On the contrary, in the tradition of novel writing cultural unity was the novel's problematic. What novelists tried to achieve, in various ways, was a sense of cultural coherence – a way of relating social and moral elements into a coherent community. The novel becomes, then, more than a representation. As a cultural practice it seeks to provide a way of relating elements or of actively achieving a sense of cultural totality. The novel is neither an organicist masking of capitalist individualism; nor is it a revelation of a real social totality. The value of the novel lies in its attempt to achieve a social coherence which Williams, as a humanist, also regards as valuable. The particular 'structure of feeling' which informs the tradition of the novel is, according to Williams, a sense of the disconnection between individual experience and cultural meaning, as well as a striving for reunification. Furthermore, this structure of feeling is specific to the cultural production of the novel; it is a specific feature of this literary form (Williams 1970: 64).

George Eliot's novels, according to Williams, have the virtue of being the first works of literature to present the dialect of the rural poor. At the same time, Eliot's represented resolutions of social conflict can only take place in the highly individual consciousness of a few isolated characters; the rural poor remain as 'background' or landscape. Consequently, the sense of community so desired by the humanist tradition of the novel (and by Williams himself) meets with an increasingly intensified sense of failure. The problem of the novel, for Williams, is also the problem of his own project of cultural materialism: the possibility of an authentic community and the coherence of experience. By studying a novel's structures of feeling the connections that are seemingly no longer possible – the connections between individual experience and social worlds – can once again be recognised. To understand how individual experience is structured by forms of life is to regain the cultural totality that the novel's history mourns. Williams's cultural materialism, then, recognises the aim of the novelistic tradition – cultural unity – at the same time as it perceives the increasing failure of novels to achieve this social objective at an aesthetic level. Here, Williams's work sustains the Marxist tradition of critique. A text is taken as a 'false' or ideal resolution of a problem (social dislocation) which can really only be dealt with at an actual social level. Wlliams also works with a desire for cultural totality and coherence. Unlike Foucault or de Certeau, the problem is not how to deal with the 'event' that lies outside discursive ordering. For Williams, unity, comprehension and the ordering of difference are goals, rather than obstacles, of criticism. The novel's literary worth lies in its making of connections, its sense of the value, and the residual presence and eventual loss, of community. Like other Marxist critics (notably Lukacs) Williams is also critical of Modernism's increased isolation of individual experience at the expense of the novel's traditional focus on cultural wholes. Writing against Virginia Woolf's sense of the isolation of consciousness Williams argues:

> And we have to say in any case that 'the ordinary mind on an ordinary day' is social, that it relates us necessarily to others, and that consciousness, real consciousness, does not come passively like that, a receiving of impressions, but is what we learn, what we make, in our real relationships including with fathers and mothers and shops. ... All I'd go on to say is that the disjunction itself – where the two worlds seem to break but where in regular experience they of course interact, and more than interact: combine, fuse – needs our direct and very serious attention. (Williams 1970: 154)

If subsequent cultural materialist criticism has rejected Williams's humanist desire for a retrieved sense of community, it has nevertheless sustained the sense that the most individual and personal phenomena of human life are thoroughly social. Rather than positing the radical or potentially revolutionary value of singularity – as does de Certeau – cultural materialism tends to regard integration and comprehension as the starting point for political criticism. In fact, cultural materialism's intensified scrutiny of the social subject can be regarded as a radicalisation of Williams's politicisation of the domain of consciousness or experience. While Williams's clear agreement with the communitarian and organicist aim of the novel has been challenged by a sense of the politically liberating effects of disunity, Williams's idea that novels do not reflect but try to achieve a sense of social totality anticipates later cultural materialism's emphasis upon literature as an active cultural event rather than as a representation or reflection.

Because culture is not the reflection of an economic base but is a dynamic whole which includes practices, economic conditions and, most importantly, forms of communication, the nature of culture must itself be historically varied. Each culture will have its specific structures of feeling and its particular configuration of dominant, emergent and residual features. Not only does Williams's 'culturalism' have a malleability which enables the interpretation of cultural phenomena without presupposing a culture's economico-political character, his insistence upon experience avoids the monolithic or totalising emphases of notions like world-view or class-consciousness. Culture, in Williams's sense, is not just a way of seeing or the collection of meaningful practices which enable a society; as a whole way of life culture includes both material conditions and the way in which those conditions are lived. This idea of unity represents a nostalgic desire for a more integrated sense of community at the same time as it enforces Williams's rejection of any pre-cultural or external cause. For Williams, culture is dynamic and this dynamism is revealed in the historical complexity of any given culture which contains dominant, residual and emergent elements. But the differing elements and the presence of historical change are, for Williams, ultimately made to cohere within the novel's sense of a cultural whole.

In the case of George Eliot, for example, the dislocation evident in the novel between the speech of the rural poor and the moral analysis of the narrator is resolved by Williams's explanation of Eliot's specific historical position. Like Williams, Eliot recognises the loss of individual freedom which has followed from the industrialisation of England but, unlike Williams, she has not yet seen that the individual can be reintegrated in a

147

new sense of community. Eliot's ambivalent 'web' metaphors characterise the structure of feeling of modern consciousness, a sense in which inter-dependence is recognised at the same time as it is seen to impede individual life. Williams's analysis of this sense of frustration is enabled by his own sense of a more authentic unity of social coherence which Eliot's revealed structures of feeling have failed to grasp:

> to discover a web or tangle is to see human relationships as not only involv-ing but compromising, limiting, mutually frustrating. And this is of course a radically different consciousness: what is still called a modern consciousness; in fact the first phase of a post-liberal world: a period between cultures, in which the old confidence of individual liberation has gone and the new com-mitment to social liberation has not yet been made. (Williams 1970: 73)

The novel's represented unity has, for Williams, a utopian dimension. By recognising the striving for unity which is ultimately frustrated, the novel points to a social liberation not yet realised.

To analyse cultural phenomena in terms of 'structures of feeling' was, for Williams, a way of overcoming the economism and determinism of Marxist aesthetics. If Leavisite criticism's focus on sensibility and experi-ence had universalised and dehistoricised the meaning of a text, Williams's use of experience had precisely the opposite effect. With his notion of structures of feeling Williams effected an inclusion of the sub-jective dimension of human life within the socio-historical dynamic of culture. In so doing Williams was at once undertaking a traditionally Marxist manoeuvre: taking a supposedly apolitical or universal human phenomenon (experience) and demonstrating its historical specificity and contingency. At the same time, however, Williams's use of experience also reacted against traditional Marxism which had interpreted an emphasis on individual experience or feeling as bourgeois or mystificatory. Williams's theory of 'structures of feeling' engages, then, in a debate which is crucial for both conventional Marxist literary theory and the subsequent trajec-tory of cultural materialism: the politicisation of everyday life and the question of the individual or subject.

Traditionally, Marxist theory had set itself against individualism, pre-cisely because the ethos of individualism – notions of freedom, autonomy, choice and the sanctity of private life – were seen as so many manifesta-tions of capitalist ideology. If feudal societies relied upon ideologies of divine right and natural order in order to sustain their modes of produc-tion, the market economies of capitalism required the notion of the self-contained and pre-social individual in order to provide an illusion of equality. The idea of the individual as an inherently rational, self-determining and essentially equal pre-social unit was argued to be ideological in so far as this seeming autonomy belied the market forces of capital which determined that individual's existence. Against the public life of market society, capitalist ideology posited a private sphere: a domestic realm where emotions, morality, reason and autonomy could be cultivated. To this extent ideas of the individual, feeling and private experience were 'bourgeois' and represented a shift in value away from feudal society's emphasis on social order, duty, obedience and just hierarchy. But this supposedly liberated site of individual bourgeois freedom was – Marxist critics argued – actually political. The realm of privacy and individual experience had its own economic determinants – the very notions of freedom and self-development being the central tenets of capitalist ideology (Dumont 1988; MacPherson 1964).

Accordingly, Marxist literary theory has sought to demystify the realm of private experience by showing its historical and political character. The realist novel, for example, has been criticised as a form of bourgeois humanism, precisely because its form and thematics have underpinned liberal individualist ideology (Belsey 1980). Not only does the novel focus from its very beginning on questions of marriage (Richardson), individual projects (Defoe), domestic harmony (Austen), and on property and wealth (Dickens); the novel also becomes increasingly psychological – focusing more and more on individual consciousness in isolation from its social world. This, in fact, was Lukacs's criticism of Modernism. Where Williams's history of the novel's increasing focus on consciousness differs from Lukacs's anti-modernist critique, is in Williams's recognition that even the modernist novel sustains a structure of feeling which poses the problem of lost community. In fact, this sense of loss, for Williams, accounts for the greatness of *Women in Love*; the way experience is described by Lawrence reveals its very social conditions (Williams 1970: 147). According to Lukacs, on the other hand, the modernist novel, by becoming so psychological, had lost any of its social realism. In this criticism Lukacs drew upon a broader Marxist criticism of Modernism; while Lukacs's prescriptive promotion of realism has subsequently been criticised, it remains the case that Marxism, and cultural materialist criticism after Williams, has sustained an attack on capitalist individualism and its concomitant notions of privacy, experience and feeling.

Instead of dismissing the private sphere as an illusion of ideology, Williams's idea of structures of feeling accepted the experience of privacy and sought to understand this experience as culturally significant. In so doing his work can be compared to Foucault's later work on the subject and sexuality. Individuals, privacy, psychological interiority and the modern phenomenon of subjectivity are not illusions to be swept away by a demystifying critique. To the contrary, the modern realm of private experience has a crucial function. For Foucault this function lies in the positing of an ethical substance which in certain modern practices – such as confession, psychoanalysis and the human sciences – enables a 'subject' to be constituted. This subject is an effect of practices and the network of power within which these practices are formed. Williams has a similar focus on the constitutive nature of practices, on the thoroughly social and political character of feeling and a rejection of any single and autonomous notion of subjectivity: subjects or individuals are specific phenomena characterised by their place in an entire culture. Unlike Foucault, however, Williams never questioned the political value of subjectivity; to reflect upon structures of feeling and experience was, for Williams, politically efficacious. Foucault, on the other hand, directed his critical project against the modern positing of the self as a subject and object of knowledge.

Nevertheless, some of the most recent cultural materialist criticism which politicises and historicises the seemingly most private and presocial phenomena of subjectivity and desire can be seen as an extension of Williams's theorisation of feeling as culturally structured. While subsequent cultural materialism has been less sanguine about the utopian or redemptive quality of feeling, Williams's work can be seen as effecting a move away from a vulgar Marxist economic determinism in which all non-economic perspectives would be seen as ideological illusions.

The examples of structures of feeling given by Williams in his study of the novel do, however, demonstrate a residual humanism which grants the domain of human feeling or sentiment an inherently liberating role. His work on Romantic pastoral, for example, was valuable in so far as it demonstrated that the long-standing nostalgia and valorisation of the landscape in English literature relied upon the exclusion of the experience of those who actually lived and worked in rural England; the rural labourers are represented as a 'Nature' which is set against the ravages of an increasingly mercantilist city. Examining Wordsworth's The Prelude, for example, Williams argues that Romantic poetry provides an imaginary resolution to a quite real social problem:

> The spirit of community, that is to say, has been dispossessed and isolated to a wandering, challenging if passive, embodiment in the beggar. It is no

longer from the practice of community, or from the spirit of protest at its inadequacy, but from

> this solitary being,
> This helpless wanderer

that the instinct of fellow-feeling is derived. Thus an essential isolation and silence and loneliness have become the only carriers of nature and community against the rigours, the cold abstinence, the selfish ease of ordinary society. (Williams 1973: 131)

Romantic poetry's value for Williams lies in the articulation of this structure of feeling which intimates, however covertly, a representation and understanding of the cultural whole. Like Lukacs, then, Williams is led to support a form of realism or organicism which produces an awareness of social totalities. Unlike Lukacs, Williams's notion of culture is not economically determined. Consequently, again unlike Lukacs, his notion of structures of feeling enables a more sympathetic reading of modernist literature, as well as a sense of the liberatory power of new technologies and popular culture. Cultural materialism's subsequent emphasis on cultural studies – readings of popular culture and everyday life – recognises the extent to which experience is not just a misrecognition of some economic real; popular culture and everyday life can be read as quite adequate articulations of structures of feeling. What cultural production achieves (in novels and plays but also in the new media of film and television) is not the concealment of a reality more properly considered as economic, but the articulation and active formulation of the way quite specific realities are lived.

Culture is not, then, a re-presentation of the economic 'real', nor are cultural wholes entirely explicable according to overarching Marxist epochs, such as capitalism. Cultural production is also the effect of quite specific ways of living. The idea of 'structures of feeling' plays a central role in recognising the peculiarity of particular cultural forms. Stream of consciousness in the modernist novel, for example, would not be considered under the *general* rubric of capitalist individualism but could be seen as part of a quite specific set of practices and forms of life. Virginia Woolf's *The Waves* (1931), with its focus on the private experience of colour, form, affect and sense-perception would be understood within the culture of Bloomsbury. As a group of privileged intellectuals and artists living in London in the early twentieth century, Bloomsbury's structure of feeling – its intense subjectivism and aestheticism – could be read, not as ideological distortion, but as the way Woolf and those around her lived their lives. The works of Bloomsbury articulate a particular structure of feeling: divorced from an increasingly technological world, experiencing the demise of high art's centrality in the face of commodification and popular culture, concerned with art's seeming irrelevance for anything other than pure feeling, the members of Bloomsbury turned to the site of the subject as pure affect. Woolf's attention to privacy, aestheticism and sensibility could also be seen as a structure of feeling which was culturally 'residual'. In the face of developing monopoly capitalism, technology and popular culture, Bloomsbury articulated those earlier English upper-class values of inherent individual worth and the sanctity of the private sphere – values which were being threatened by the War, urbanisation and workers' movements ('emergent' cultural factors). Woolf's modernism and its structure of feeling are not merely ideological (in the sense of being illusory or repressive); they are cultural – part of a network of relations and practices defined against other cultural forms and practices.

The value of Williams's definition of culture lies precisely in its recognition of the diversity within social wholes, where different structures of feeling are understood as different modes of life and practice. It is here too that Williams's work takes on a materialist edge. Williams's understanding of culture is communication-based and is, in some ways, similar to the Geertzian idea of culture as 'traffic in significant symbols'. Culture is not a mental state, a picture in the mind, nor a set of rules. Rather, it is a dynamic and, for Williams, *materially embodied* network of interactions. It is because these interactions are forms of communication that they need to be understood materially; for communication must always occur through a medium. Williams's work – both on traditional literature and popular culture – has consistently focused on the material forces of cultural production: printing, distribution, the new technologies of film and television and the availability of these media. Williams's materialism departs, therefore, from the Marxist notion of materialism – which sees economic factors in the mode of production as the primary material determinant of human life. Williams, on the other hand, sees materiality, not as an underlying cause or explanation of otherwise 'ideal' phenomena such as art or experience. Culture is material because as the circulation of meaning it must always take on some specific material form: print, film, performance or embodied human practice.

The traditional Marxist practice – of relating the aesthetic production of culture to economic materiality – is replaced by seeing aesthetic production as already social and thoroughly material. Cultural materialism understands the modern notion of aesthetic autonomy as part of a specific technological development in which art forms are no longer embedded in traditional cultural practices (religions or community ritual) but can be circulated freely through printing and ever-increasing audiences. Such early insights in Williams's *The Long Revolution* (1961) problematised any general definition of art or experience: his historical and social understanding of culture demonstrated the specificity of art's (perceived) specific autonomy. According to Williams the idea of art as a privileged mode of creation and experience was culturally and historically specific; from this he concluded (in contradistinction to many Marxist theories of art as ideology) that the relations between art and society varied historically and were also varied within any particular culture (Williams 1961: 241). In the late eighteenth century, for example, a variety of literatures emerged; the period is marked by a diversity of social groups and literary forms contributing to the production and consumption of literature. Even the dominant form, English Romantic poetry, was 'a movement in which all social classes, educational patterns and methods of life are represented, often with marked individual variations from inherited social norms' (Williams 1961: 240). Against a general theory of ideology or even of a general cultural world-view, Williams's work suggested the value of specific investigations into a text's emergence and distribution.

However, Williams did grant a certain political efficacy to those structures of feeling (such as his own) which represented emergent class experiences; and Williams also valorised cultural productions (such as realism) which articulated these structures. To this extent his work sustained a humanist emancipationism: he could locate, within a culture, a more authentic experience of life which could be liberated and appealed to in order to criticise the cultural dominant. The idea of culture as such granted the unity of interpretation and understanding a moral value. Williams's theory depended upon a particular definition of human life. A life lived through understanding and a sense of integration was unquestionably more valuable than the alienated, fragmented and dislocated individual whose lament Williams read in the modern novel. To this extent, Williams's theory did not have the conflicting problems of validity and cultural relativism which have troubled the approaches considered in previous chapters. Williams had a clear and unquestioned value – integrated experience – from which to begin his theoretical enterprise. It was not a question of 'getting outside' one's theoretical prison; nor of validating or defining this problematic outside. For Williams, as long as an understanding of culture was sufficiently inclusive, as long as it considered the variety of factors which produced a cultural whole, it would achieve both theoretical validity and emancipatory value. The theoretical enterprise of inter-preting and reincluding phenomena within cultural understanding was ethical itself; interpretation was not a violence done to the singularity of 'otherness'. Williams had a sense of the 'human' – as integrated experi-ence – which both enabled his interpretive endeavours but which was subsequently seen as the limit of his work. In order to understand how later cultural materialism developed a critique of such forms of humanism we need to understand the attack on both realism and subjectivity which followed the uptake of Althusserian Marxism.

7
Ideology and hegemony: Althusser, Macherey and Gramsci

Althusser

Althusser's Marxism should in no way be seen as eclipsing or surpassing Williams's work. While Williams's work was severely criticised from an Althusserian perspective (Eagleton 1976a), his definition of cultural materialism and its anti-economism remained as a sustained influence on British literary criticism and tempered the structuralism of Althusser's Marxism. What Althusser's work did enable was a critical examination of the notion of the subject and a structuralist retheorisation of the concept of ideology. In his highly influential essay, 'Ideology and ideological state apparatuses' (1971), Althusser achieved two significant critical manoeuvres. The first was his definition of ideology which granted ideology a positive (and not a merely reflective or expressive) role; ideology was itself a structural determinant in the mode of production. Secondly, following from the positive role attributed to ideology, the subject was regarded as a political and ideological effect.

Althusser's work is perhaps best understood as a reaction against both Marxist economism and Hegelian humanist historicism. Hegel regarded history as the progressive understanding and development of human spirit or *Geist*. Forms of Marxism which emphasised Marx's Hegelian heritage therefore privileged the role of consciousness as an agent of history. In literary criticism Lukacs's emphasis on class-consciousness as the catalyst for revolutionary transformation provides an example of the humanism against which Althusser reacted. For Lukacs, literature was valuable precisely in so far as it enabled a recognition of class-consciousness. Novels with a strong sense of realism which made the connection between individual experience and social forces were applauded. This is perhaps why Lukacs preferred the nineteenth-century historical novel over twentieth-century modernism. Whereas Walter Scott located individual pursuit and

endeavours against a background of historically-specific values, movements and shifting political boundaries, Joyce filtered experience through
the consciousness of individual characters. Leopold Bloom could never be
seen as a 'typical' individual precisely because all those historical and
social forces which produced him were displaced; the world we see in
Ulysses is within consciousness and language. Reading *Ulysses* is unlikely to
give us a sense of the economic and historical determinants of a bourgeois
life, for the novel itself is a series of individual points of view. Only by
overcoming the isolation of the individual can literature produce a recognition of those larger forces which constitute individual life. This traditional Marxist critique of modernist individualism was still a humanism.
There was still a value placed on consciousness; individualism and Modernism were criticised for their impoverishment and limiting of experience. In reading a realist novel, on the other hand, the reader can
recognise herself or himself as part of a larger social whole and can see her
or his circumstances connected to a broader range of human concerns.
Despite a long history of being critical of bourgeois individualism, traditional Marxism was an intensified humanism. The bourgeois individual
was criticised as a form of alienated consciousness deprived of a sense of
potential historical agency. A critical representation of the social totality in
realist art, it was argued, would overcome this alienating modernist illusion of isolation.

Against humanist forms of Marxism which relied upon the historical
self-understanding and progression of oppressed consciousness, Althusser
posited the anti-Hegelian notion of 'history without a subject'. His model
for critique worked within ideology's own contradiction and did not posit
a critical or normative subject outside ideology as a critical lever.
Althusser's Marxism was not only opposed to the inevitable movement of
Hegelian History as Absolute Spirit but was also critical of economic
determinism. If one accepted the simple Marxist explanation that the economic mode of production determined human existence, then non-economic or social phenomena would be seen as effects (or insignificant
illusions) of an economic base. The major problem of this explanation for
twentieth-century Western Marxists was provided by the example of
Stalin's Soviet Union; here an economic revolution had taken place but, as
was becoming increasingly apparent, no communist utopia had followed
in its wake. As was already argued in the first chapter, economism also presented a number of theoretical problems. For literary critics the most significant difficulty lay in reducing aesthetic production to economic causes.
Althusser's concept of ideology and structural causality provided a far less

reductive approach to non-economic phenomena which could neverthe-less still be interpreted politically.

According to Althusser, a mode of production required the repro-duction of the *relations of production*. Workers needed to continue to sell their labour for the profit of the owner of capital. Economic factors could account for the reproduction of the mode of production: capitalists owned the means of production (technology and raw capital) and therefore had a certain power. But to sustain this relation of power there needed to be a submission to power relations. For Hegelian Marxist theory, once histori-cal consciousness had developed to the point of a *recognition* of exploitation then the conditions of oppression would be overthrown and conscious-ness would be emancipated. A theory of such recognition relied upon the idea of a subject who would eventually perceive its alienation and then overcome the distorted representation of itself and its world. Althusser, on the other hand, argued that the relations of power could not be removed in order to reveal an essential subject; on the contrary, *the subject was nothing other than an effect of these relations*. The subject's recognition of itself, as a sub-ject, was not emancipatory but ideological. Ideology was not just a mask or illusion concealing economic forces; rather, ideology played an active or causal role in the structure of capitalist relations. This argument is what enables Althusser's idea that while the economy may be determining, it is determining in the last instance. There are other determining, or struc-turally essential, factors. Ideology is such a factor, for ideology is necessary for the reproduction of the relations which enable the mode of capitalist production to continue.

For Althusser, the State is divided into two functions: the repressive State apparatus (police, prisons, armed forces) which manifestly coerce subjects into obedience; and Ideological State Apparatuses (ISAs) which work through the ideological production of individuals as subjects. Here, the process of 'interpellation', or hailing, *produces* subjects. There is no humanist subject, then, which is repressed or imposed upon by ideology; rather, the subject is an effect of ideological interpellation. When a police officer hails a subject with the call, 'Hey you!' and that subject recognises himself in the call, then the subject is produced as a subject for ideology. At a more complex level, it could be argued that when a text addresses a reader either overtly or indirectly through empathy, then the reader is ide-ologically interpellated. George Eliot's *The Mill on the Floss* (1860) provides a classic example of literary interpellation. Here, the narrator addresses the reader and in so doing constitutes a reading subject as morally sympa-thetic. Commenting on rural superstition, the narrator assumes a common feeling: 'I share with you this sense of oppressive narrowness; but it is necessary that we should feel it' (Eliot 1903: 289 [1860]). Such narratorial devices, according to a theory of interpellation, produce the character of the reading subject by positing their addressee in a certain way.

The subject, then, does not pre-exist the act of recognition; but is produced through recognition. By educating individuals as moral subjects with private integrity, duties and inviolable rights or feelings, capitalist ideology produces subjects who then recognise themselves as natural, pre-social or universal.

Using Althusser's notion of ideology as productive, critics have attempted to demonstrate the ways in which texts produce the positions of their readers. If subjects are ideological effects, it follows that the modern individualist subject of capitalism would have to be actively produced in the superstructure. The novel, on this argument, would not *represent* the individual who 'emerged' with modernity or capitalism. Rather, novels could be seen as ideologically productive in their 'hailing' of individuals: both explicitly (in their addresses to individual readers) and implicitly (in their representation of subjects who are putatively 'just like us'). In Romance novels, for example, a certain female subject is produced: a subject who has certain desires (marriage, love), certain duties (mothering, domesticity) as well as certain virtues (sensitivity, care). From an Althusserian perspective these novels would not be read as mystifications (inaccurate or stereotyped representations of women), nor as structures of feeling (articulations of real women's values and experiences); nor would such novels be seen as ideology in the traditional sense (as distorted representations of actual economic conditions). As ideology, such literary forms produce those individuals they seem to represent. 'Femininity' would be read as a discursive production, the effect of readers recognising themselves as a certain form of subject.

The value of Althusserian criticism lay in its ability to see texts as active and productive forces, as events in themselves, rather than as expressions or reflections of prior contexts. To this extent the problem of relating texts to contexts gave way to seeing texts as already within a social whole that was itself structured like a text. Nevertheless, there was still some sense of a social whole or structure with a unifying character – an idea that was to be challenged in later cultural materialist and new historicist work. Texts were often seen as ideology and were consequently given a specifically political character and were located within a general economico-historical formation and explanation. Furthermore, the Althusserian notion of the subject as the product of ideology precluded traditional criticism's notions of intention, experience, authorship, desire or feeling; for such notions were all referred back to the ideological structure. While this exclusion did have a liberating effect on literary criticism it did lead to some seemingly absurd ways of dealing with conventional literary problems. While there was a general theoretical agreement that subjects were the effect of ideological discourses, when it came to literary practice critics often still found themselves referring to authorship. A case in point is Terry Eagleton's Criticism and Ideology (1976b). Whereas Williams had seen Eliot's novels as an articulation of her particular experience of a culture, Eagleton still needed to retain her particular authorship as a site of political intent but used Althusserian theory to locate this intent in a discursive structure rather than individual experience:

> The phrase 'George Eliot' signifies nothing more than the insertion of certain specifically ideological determinations – Evangelical Christianity, rural organicism, incipient feminism, petty bourgeois moralism – into a hegemonic ideological formation. (Eagleton 1976b: 113)

By accepting Althusser's stringent anti-humanism, subjectivity was seen as nothing more than the production of discourse; all analysis of ideology was to take place immanently, from within the structure of ideology. As Althusser argues, 'ideology *has no outside* (for itself), but at the same time … it is *nothing but outside* (for science and reality)' (Althusser 1971: 175). That is, ideology presents itself as nothing other than the real, as what is obvious, already there – a pure and pre-given outside; as such, then, ideology is an immanent system in which its ground – the subject – is already one of its effects. Any references to seemingly non-discursive factors, such as bodies, desire or experience, are seen from this point of view as further essentialising manoeuvres of bourgeois ideology. In this sense Althusser's Marxism was structuralist. While early Marxist Althusserian criticism and cultural materialism drew upon Althusserian and structuralist rejections of the subject, later work took a more Foucaultian and post-structuralist approach to subjectivity.

For Foucault, the subject was still the effect of discourse and discursive practices. However, it was also argued that while the subject was discursively constituted, discourse did not *exhaust* subjectivity. There would always be some remainder or exteriority: the articulated subject could never fully account for the *process* of articulation. While discourse and subjectivity were productions, the process of production could always be revealed as an absence which resisted the closure of discourse. The event of the subject's production could never, itself, be experienced, expressed

159

or made meaningful by the subject. From within any structure there was always the absence of that structure's production. Althusser, as a structuralist, had accounted for the totality of an ideological structure by referring to the 'last instance' of the economic. Foucaultian criticism, on the other hand, resisted the closure of structuralism by arguing that no single pre-discursive ground (such as the economy) could be appealed to as an explanatory horizon. As a consequence discursive practices could never be fully or exhaustively accounted for from within discourse.

Althusser's structuralism is an instance of, rather than an answer to, the vexing problem of cultural and historical closure. Because Althusser accounts for stucture within a general understanding of economic modes of production, he does not have to question how one can know what a structure is. For Althusser there is a perspective – economic determination – from which structure can be analysed; and this position is epistemologically or 'scientifically' privileged in relation to those positions that remain within structure. The historical and economic specificity of Althusser's own position becomes problematic if we question the supposed scientific objectivity of his own structuralist Marxism. To argue that the narrative of economic history might be situated within its own ideology would preclude the possibility of a Marxist science. Furthermore, if, as Althusser argued, subjectivity is an *effect* of ideological structures then the subject would be a purely discursive or representational phenomenon; the body of the subject would be nothing other than the site for discursive constitution. Not surprisingly, one of the main ways in which Althusser's theory of ideology was seen to be limited was in its failure to take into account the specifically corporeal or embodied character of power in discursive practices. In so far as Althusser's 'science' of ideological interpretation had already decided upon the character of the subject – as discursive interpellation – his theory was enabled to account for other factors such as the body.

Whereas Althusser's work was vigorously anti-humanist and argued that subjectivity as such was ideological, Williams's concept of structures of feeling had the opposite failing of arguing for domains of authentic subjective experience which could somehow provide critical levers to be used against the cultural dominant. Current cultural materialist work locates itself somewhere between these two alternatives. The subject is a site of power but this power is always multiple, diffuse and contested. There is neither a single structure which can account for all events (such as ideological interpellation) nor is there an event which can be seen as absolutely outside any structure (such as experience). There are a number

160

of modes of determination (including economic determination); and no determining factor determines an event completely. No event, text or phenomena is given once and for all; its meaning and effects are always open to contestation and reconfiguration.

In terms of literary criticism this means that a text's politics has a dynamic and ambiguous status. Writing on sexual dissidence, Dollimore has shown how certain forms of desire could be both socially transgressive and reactionary. The literature of Gide, for example, demonstrates how homosexual desire threatened cultural norms; at the same time other structures of power (such as racism, colonialism and traditional humanism) informed Gide's expression of homosexuality (Dollimore 1991: 338). What such examinations reveal, as do most cultural materialist writings, is that literary texts have no single or determinate political effect or meaning — either of transgression or repression. Dollimore's earlier work on Renaissance tragedy which argued, against traditional views, that tragedy was 'radical' had already qualified the text's political efficacy by arguing for the text's multiple effects (Dollimore 1984: 7).

The Marxist notion of ideology, then, as a structure of power with a dominant economic determinant was of less use in examining literature than other notions which enabled a consideration of literature's multiple political relations and possibilities. Foucault's concept of power as differential (rather than repressive or monolithic) and Williams's idea of culture as having residual, emergent and dominant features provided other ways of thinking texts and politics than through a strict sense of ideology. Texts would have to be considered both in their specific material production, media and consumption (Williams) and in terms of a whole field of power and practices (Foucault).

The use of Williams's definition of culture and Foucault's theory of power in cultural materialism can be seen as responses to the problem that arises with any strict adherence to Althusser's theory of ideology in relation to literature. If literature is part of an Ideological State Apparatus — although Althusser himself never claimed it was — then its effect is inherently tied to sustaining capitalist production. If earlier notions of art, such as those of Lukcacs or even Williams, were naively humanist in granting novelistic expression a certain emancipatory role, Althusserian literary criticism often went to the other extreme in seeing literature as part of an all-pervasive mode of ideological production. The question of criticism or transgression of ideology could not be located in individual resistance, for individuals were the constructs of ideology. As Alan Sinfield has argued, 'if our subjectivities are constituted within a language and social system

161

that is already imbued with oppressive constructs of class, race, gender and sexuality, then how can we expect to see past that, to the idea of a fairer society, let alone struggle to achieve it? How, indeed, could Althusser see what he did?' (Sinfield 1994: 24).

Whereas Althusser's theory of Marxism as a 'science' which could criticise ideology did have some literary-critical currency (Eagleton 1976b), the idea that literary discourse was purely ideological posed the problem of how criticism could position itself outside the closure of the text's ideology. In addition to Foucault's theory of power, which attacked the notion of any external critique of ideology, cultural materialism also drew upon the earlier work of Macherey in order to establish both the possibilities of literary criticism as well as a relation between literature and ideology. Pierre Macherey's theory of the immanently contradictory character of literary ideology was more capable of seeing the specific character of literary texts and the possibility of a 'scientific' or 'theoretical' criticism.

Macherey and literary production

According to Macherey, ideology cannot be criticised from some non-ideological space of individual freedom. But ideology is contradictory, and its contradictory character can be seen in a text's construction. If ideology proceeds, as Althusser argued, by producing subject positions, then the *process of production* can be read in the moments where a text betrays the 'gaps' or determined absences of its construction. The text is still seen as thoroughly ideological but certain reading practices which attend to textual production can reveal ideology *as* ideology.

For Macherey criticism could establish itself as scientific only by rejecting the traditional fallacies of conventional interpretation. To begin with, the critic would have to recognise that the text had its own logic and autonomy. It would not do for a critic simply to reveal some supposedly inherent, unified and essential meaning; to do so would assume that criticism merely explicated the act of readership or consumption. On the contrary, truly theoretical criticism attended to the text's *production*. Literary texts for Macherey were characterised by their peculiar autonomy; because such texts are fictive and establish their own world and logic they have to be examined according to their unique structure. A literary text is autonomous in so far as it should be seen as an independent structure and not referred back to an author's intention or a general historical context. But this autonomy does not mean that a text is a unified totality; on the contrary, a text is made up of a number of conflicting and contradictory elements. It is precisely by examining these immanent contradictions that the critic is able to reveal the text's production. Literary criticism's proper task is not, then, to reveal some inner meaning, nor to assess the text according to some ideal aesthetic model, nor to refer the work back to an individual author and their single intention. Macherey argues that literary texts work on ideology. Because texts are made up of language or discourse, they take the very material of ideology and enable it to be viewed as ideology. By giving the language of ideology a form, literary texts show ideology in its working; they reveal its contradictions and demonstrate its production:

> This enables us to say that the autonomy of the writer's discourse is established from its relationship with the other uses of language: everyday speech, scientific propositions. By its rehearsing but never actually performing its script. But in that evocative power, by which it denotes a specific reality, it also imitates the everyday language which is the language of ideology. We could offer a provisional definition of literature as being characterised by this power of parody. Mingling the real uses of language in an endless confrontation, it concludes by revealing their truth. Experimenting with language rather than inventing it, the literary work is both the analogy of a knowledge and a caricature of customary ideology. (Macherey 1978: 59)

Macherey goes on to say that literary discourse, as parody, can be seen as a 'contestation of language' (1978: 61). The critic should not, then, accept the text as a pre-given unity but should ask how the text comes to be according to determinate conditions. As a Marxist, Macherey sees literature not as the free and spontaneous creation of individual authors but as determined by the specific ideological materials upon which it works. Texts are conditioned not by direct economic forces but by the ideological motifs upon which they conduct 'secondary work' (1978: 62). Literature is not directly equated with ideology; literary texts, precisely because they are manifestly not true, enable ideological illusion to be revealed as produced, constructed and 'confronted with its own unreality' (1978: 60). Macherey's theory does depend, however, on granting literary language a specific autonomy. He sidesteps the question of how a text relates to an outside world. For Macherey the value of literary texts is that they do not relate to intention, context or reality. Texts are autonomous; criticism does not read a text for its meaning or content. Criticism attends to the text's form. In the explicit foregrounding of form the text reveals the repressed form of ideology. Here, the 'real' world is derealised; the 'naturalness' of ideology is demystified: not by appealing to a more authentic reality but by revealing ideology's ideological status from within. Not only does Macherey's form of criticism accept that there is a specific literary language which, unlike conventional representation, is non-referential and rhetorically self-foregrounding, he also takes a single feature – ideology – and uses this structure to account for literature in general. In this sense his theory – like Althusser's – depends upon a confident division between a 'scientific' theory and the structure of ideology.

Macherey's argument that texts should not be seen as bearers of some intrinsic meaning but as specific and determined productions enabled several effective critical manoeuvres. Firstly, the text viewed *as production* was no longer accepted as a pre-given and unified whole. By attending to the gaps, silences and absences of a text a critic could reveal its unconscious: what it *could not* say. Secondly, by accepting the *literary* status of texts a critic would not reduce the text to ideology or reflection but would see the way the text worked upon ideology. Thirdly, by accepting that a text was the effect of specific conditions, criticism would no longer refer the text to an author or intention but would investigate the text according to its own logic. Finally, the critic's focus was the text's production as a 'parody' or 'reworking' of given ideological motifs and materials. If a text inscribes a certain ideology it can also be read in such a way that the discursive production of this power can be made manifest. An instance of this type of reading is given by Dollimore who argues that Renaissance tragedies 'provide the bases for a materialist understanding of the interrelations between the social, the political and subjective' (Dollimore 1984: 174) precisely because they reveal power and ideology in its actual working and production (1984: 161).

Macherey's own reading of *Robinson Crusoe* (1719) saw the determinate gap in Defoe's novel in the circularity of the narrative (Macherey 1978). The novel is meant to show the emergence of society from the individual enterprise of a single individual on an island. But, Macherey argues, the narrative presupposes the very society it was meant to explain. The text's silence lies in its inability to recognise that the individual is not an entirely free, autonomous and isolated unit but is already the product of certain (capitalist) forces. Crusoe's production of 'society' assumes certain desires on the part of its central character – the desire to accumulate goods for example – and certain abilities – the production of certain tools and an understanding of their use. The individual does not arrive on the island and then demonstrate the natural inevitability of capitalist society; on the contrary, Crusoe's adventure shows just how illusory capitalism's natural individual is. The text's silence – its refusal to address how Robinson Crusoe's island actually becomes a proto-capitalist society – shows the limits of capitalist ideology. Defoe's text works on ideological motifs: the idea that nature is raw material, the concept of the free and autonomous individual, the spontaneity of the production of goods for exchange. But in order to give these motifs form it reveals a contradiction; Robinson Crusoe's individual adventure succeeds only by introducing the character of Man Friday. In so doing the island is no longer there as so much raw material to be produced – it has to be appropriated; and Crusoe's paradigmatic individualism is shown as being premised upon a (power) relation with others. But this supposedly immanent reading of a text's own structure depends upon Macherey's own theory regarding human life. In order to see certain gaps in the text – the absence of Crusoe's real economic conditions – the critic has already decided upon some other (Marxist/economic) explanatory narrative. This form of reading is not, then, a purely formal or immanent science of the text but relies upon the Marxist theory of ideological production. Macherey's claim that such criticism is immanent depends upon regarding the Marxist narrative as epistemologically privileged; Marxism is a scientific theory of textual production and is therefore exempt from Macherey's ideological critique.

While Macherey's emphasis upon literary theory as a science was never really carried over into cultural materialism, the critical force of his work enabled new ways of overcoming traditional interpretation's humanism. The idea that a literary work is not a pre-given unity but the effect of production has been extremely influential. However, if we accept Macherey's theory completely we are forced to accept that all literature is inherently, or potentially, transgressive. By its very nature – the encapsulation and distantiation of ideology – literature marks a critical break with ideology. Literature in general, then, is potentially transgressive. If what neither Althusserian ideology nor Foucaultian power could offer was a more traditional Marxist sense of the specific location of power and the possibility of resistance, then Macherey's theory of literary production seems to go to the other extreme. If all literature 'works' upon ideology then it is not clear how the different effects of texts, the various modes of power within a culture or throughout history or the specific distribution of power can be theorised. It is here that recent cultural materialism has intervened: by questioning the class-based interests of power and its cultural manifestations. Consequently, in addition to Macherey, Foucault and Williams, cultural materialism has also employed the Italian Marxist Antonio Gramsci's theory of hegemony.

Gramsci and hegemony

Like Althusser, although writing considerably earlier and in quite different intellectual and institutional circumstances, Gramsci sought to theorise a Marxism which would take account of the specificity of cultural formations. Gramsci's concept of hegemony provided the later tradition of cultural materialism with ways of thinking about culture in a historical and political manner while avoiding the reductivism, economism and historical determinism which had also been anathema to Williams and Althusser. Gramsci's idea of hegemony was never formulated in a single, unified or programmatic manner. In fact, the term was articulated in a shifting series of relations throughout Gramsci's work (Anderson 1977). This can be partly explained by Gramsci's particular situation; his most fertile writing is contained in the extensive notebooks written in the 1920s and 1930s while Gramsci was imprisoned under Italian Fascist rule. The intellectual isolation suffered by Gramsci and the very genre of the 'notebook' (rather than the essay or manifesto) accounts for a lack of structural unity in his work. At the same time, the absence of a strict theoretical delimitation of the idea of hegemony can also be explained by the very nature of the problem of hegemony itself.

Because Gramsci set himself the task of inquiring into the relations between intellectual and economic production, and because the idea of hegemony was deployed to this end, the very concept of hegemony was bound to have a dynamic quality, differing according to the specific historical and social conditions in question. Consequently, part of the value of the idea of hegemony was that, unlike simple notions of ideology, it was formulated to account for the specific power and cultural relations under bourgeois capitalism. Like Althusser's theory of ideology, the concept was also located within the question of recognition and consent. Given that economic conditions are exploitative for the majority of society (workers), how is it that this relation of power is sustained? For Gramsci, the answer to this question would have to pay quite particular attention to the specific nature of bourgeois power and capitalist relations.

Whereas pre-capitalist societies were dominated by the State and its directly coercive institutions, modern bourgeois or capitalist culture secured its power through civil society — the domain of cultural life, intellectual production and social relations. Gramsci's theorisation of hegemony as the form of power within civil society can in some ways be likened to Althusser's function of ideology in ideological state apparatuses. In both cases, cultural production is not a mere distortion or reflection of economic conditions; rather, intellectual production plays an active role in producing and sustaining political relations and the distribution of power. However, the value of Gramsci's idea of hegemony, in contradistinction to Althusser's concept of ideology, lies in the contestatory character of Gramsci's defini-tion of culture and the position of hegemony within civil society.

Althusser saw ideology as a structural condition for the production of individuals as subjects; the only opposition to ideological state apparatuses would have to come from a non-ideological 'science' of Marxist theory. As such, the position of a critic in relation to a literary text would be spelled out beforehand: to examine its ideologically constitutive production. Gramsci's theory of intellectual production, on the other hand, saw the domain of intellectual production as a site of contestation. This is partly due to the fact that Gramsci still adhered to the validity of certain class interests; opposition to dominant powers could be sought by appealing to the interests and legitimate perspectives of the dominated. (Althusser's ideology, on the other hand, could make no such appeal; all subjects, by definition, were ideologically interpellated.) But Gramsci's theory did problematise the idea of class-consciousness. The idea of hegemony sought to explain how the interests of a particular dominant group – in capitalism, the bourgeoisie – had come to be accepted as the interests of society as a whole. To overcome this acceptance Gramsci appealed to an oppressed class – the workers – and the problem of the adequate articula-tion of their real interests through intellectual production. Hegemony was therefore a fact of cultural production; through cultural practices certain forms of life were presented as natural and valuable in general. Hegemony was always, then, more than a question of false consciousness. It was not just a misrecognition of economic circumstances but the positive accep-tance of certain social conditions and values.

From an idea of hegemony it could be argued that the early novel's promulgation of certain values – individual endeavour, financial enter-prise, the securing of a stable domestic sphere – were not just representa-tions of the interests of a particular class. Rather, novelistic production disseminated these values and ways of seeing to the point where they were recognised by society as a whole. Whereas Lukacs could criticise a novel's individualism because it precluded reflection on the social totality, Gram-sci's idea of hegemony could accord a positive (and not just mystificatory) role to cultural manifestations. In the domain of civil society power is attained not through coercion or delusion but through a production of interests (Gramsci 1971: 349). In so far as these interests are economically to the benefit of the bourgeoisie they are class-based, but once these interests are culturally disseminated and accepted by all they become hegemonic.

To challenge bourgeois hegemony, then, it would not be sufficient to appeal to an already-formulated proletariat class-consciousness. Whereas Lukacs believed that a properly realistic representation of social relations would develop class-consciousness, Gramsci's idea of hegemony problematised a demystificatory criticism that would merely reveal or uncover a pre-existing consciousness. It was not just a question of exposing the ideological concealment of economic reality. The hegemonic character of bourgeois power had secured the general assent to class-based economic relations. The problem, as Gramsci saw it, was not to reveal or liberate proletarian class-consciousness; to the contrary, such a consciousness would have to be actively produced. This meant that the site of hegemony – civil society and its modes of intellectual and cultural production – would be a site of cultural struggle. Gramsci acknowledged that the oppressed of a society did not possess a privileged and already revolutionary consciousness which merely needed to come to sufficient self-awareness in order to achieve power. But, unlike Althusser, for whom ideology was the structural condition for experience, Gramsci did see the possibility of contesting bourgeois hegemony through the development and production of other (contestatory) forms of cultural and intellectual production. Central to such contestation would be the role and function of the intellectual.

The traditional intellectual, according to Gramsci, is not identified with any specific social or political group and works within a certain transhistorical tradition (Gramsci 1971: 7). For Gramsci, idealist philosophy – with its seeming disconnection from political or worldly issues – presents itself as independent or autonomous and therefore provides a typical example of traditional intellectual production. But this independence of the traditional intellectual is the effect of quite specific historical and economic relations; the very idea of the 'disengaged' intellectual has political ramifications. Only with other relations of intellectual production, Gramsci argues, can radical social change be achieved. Gramsci's Marxism foregrounds the importance of the re-engagement of the intellectual domain with political struggle as well as the institutional relation of intellectuals to political life. Whereas intellectuals in bourgeois capitalism are located in spheres of 'specialisation' (Gramsci 1971: 12), Gramsci argues that a new division of intellectual labour would be required if the capitalist state were to be contested. He therefore argues that modernity is characterised by an institutionalisation of intellectual labour that secures an increasing importance and dominance. The reconfiguration of capitalist relations demands a securing of the means of intellectual production through the development of new types of intellectuals (Gramsci 1971: 9).

According to Gramsci, in addition to traditional intellectuals there are organic intellectuals who represent and articulate the specific interests of a class. Gramsci's idea of the 'organic intellectual', like his theory of hegemony, was directed towards overcoming economic determinism and recognising the power and political character of non-economic forces. Because hegemony was secured through cultural production and was concerned with interests, bourgeois domination in capitalism could be explained by examining the function of intellectuals.

To take a quite specific example from literature, it could be argued that D. H. Lawrence's entire novelistic aesthetic is interpretable as an articulation of his specific class interests. In Lady Chatterley's Lover Clifford Chatterley is a figure of the traditional English aristocracy. Paralysed from the waist down, traumatised by the First World War, pale, impotent, ineffectual and driven by intellect rather than physical passion, Clifford's physiognomy appears as a metaphor for traditional English humanist values. Here, Lawrence refigures English humanism as weak, sterile, oppressive, outworn and in decline. The gamekeeper, Mellors, with whom Lady Chatterley conducts her affair is dark, swarthy and driven by 'life', physicality and passion. In establishing this type of dichotomy throughout his fiction, Lawrence valorises those features associated with working-class life. His very aesthetic – which marks the physical body with psychological attributes – emphasises the importance of a physicality which traditional humanism had expelled from its rational self-image. Physical labour is represented in the novel as bearing a more authentic relation to nature than the exploitative industrialism of England's ruling élite. The dominance of sexuality in Lawrence's fiction underlines the significance of the body which provides the basis for a revaluation of conventional definitions of what it means to be human. Lawrence's fiction does not just articulate a particular interest, it presents that (hitherto denigrated) sphere of values as desirable in general. His Modernist critique of a culture which had become increasingly divorced from its productive or fecund origins is expressed quite particularly in terms of an agonistics of social forces. To a certain extent, then, Lawrence's fiction can be seen as an act of hegemonic contestation – where the traditionally accepted interests of liberal humanism are presented as otiose, class-based, illegitimately dominant and ultimately stifling. At the same time, however, any reading of Lawrence's work which championed him as a working-class writer would have to ignore the extent to which those aristocratic values of natural supremacy which

Lawrence attacks are not done away with but displaced onto a new form of sexual/physical hierarchisation. The shift in analysis from class-interests to the idea of hegemonic contestation would enable a way of considering writers like Lawrence in their political complexity.

From a Gramscian perspective the value of Lawrence's work would lie in its hegemonic *contestation* which exposed the particularity of previously universalised values. Lawrence's work can be seen, in part, as the production of a counter-aesthetic. To this extent, Lawrence could be considered as an organic intellectual – emerging from a dominated class and reacting against the interests of a hegemonic humanism. But a truly or successfully organic intellectual would also have to articulate and disseminate the politically liberatory values of the dominated class. Lawrence's residual sense of aristocracy (now shifted to another social group) would fail in this regard. This example also represents the limits of the idea of hegemony and its contestation by the organic intellectual. Like Williams, Gramsci's Marxist heritage allowed him to appeal to a particular group whose interests supposedly did have a general validity. The problem with bourgeois hegemony was not that it universalised a specific set of values, but that it universalised the wrong set of values. The interests of the proletariat, on the other hand, are for Marxism the interests of historical liberation. What the example of Lawrence might lead us to question is whether the representation of previously marginalised interests as more authentic is, in fact, liberatory. Lawrence establishes his revaluation of values – his representation of the interests of his own social position – through processes of exclusion and hierarchisation. One might question whether Lawrence is a working-class writer; and there are far more 'authentic' examples of literature which do champion class interests without displacing those interests onto a pseudo-aristocratic rhetoric in the manner of Lawrence. But how a critic might decide as to what constitutes the writing of an organic intellectual would depend upon some idea of what constituted authentic working-class interests. The category of the organic intellectual demands an already determined understanding of class interests and is in itself hegemonic. As such, Gramsci's theory of the organic intellectual has a prescriptive dimension. Because hegemony is a site of struggle, political emancipation demands an intellectual production faithful to workers' actual (economic) interests. Whether such production would be aesthetically valuable or politically possible is, however, highly questionable. But if we set aside the possibility of some pure counter-hegemonic positon, what Gramsci's theorisation of the intellectual has enabled is a thorough politicisation of the aesthetic, intellectual or cultural sphere.

If it is the case that hegemony is secured through intellectual production, then all aspects of cultural life – including literary criticism itself – can be seen as forms of political contestation. If one looks at cultural materialism and its history, Gramsci's notion of the role of the intellectual has a great deal of pertinence. Not only can literary production be seen as invested with class interest, literary criticism can also be seen as a site of hegemonic contestation. Criticism would not be an act of objective scrutiny or demystification; rather, critical acts themselves would be interested manoeuvres which established positions of hegemonic contestation. Furthermore, art can then be seen as having a dynamic relation to hegemonic structures; the political intent of a work is not secured by referring to a particular author's biography but is understood within a schema of class relations. At a positive level, Gramsci's prescriptive procedures, while possessing a utopian dimension directed towards the ultimate expression of workers' interests, also harbour a more practical aspect. The task of political change cannot be left to the forces of economic development but must also be secured from within intellectual and cultural life. Cultural production is not merely reflective or critical but operates productively and actively with quite specific interests.

Subsequent theorisations of power, such as those of Foucault, have problematised the location of emancipatory potential in a single oppressed group or historical agent. Gramsci's goal of the seizure of intellectual power by workers shares the Marxist assumptions that political liberation in general must be concerned with the proletariat and that properly defined proletarian interests are emancipatory in general. This single focus on class struggle has been challenged by cultural materialism and other theoretical and practical movements. The recognition of other forms of domination – sexual, racial, cultural and gendered – has led to a proliferation of critical procedures. However, what Gramsci's notion of hegemony provided was an active politicisation of the cultural sphere – an insight that could be used to explain other forms of continued domination (such as the position of women in patriarchal culture). On the theory of hegemony, art and cultural life are not just reflections or concealments of an economic reality; artistic forms are productive of assent and interests. Acts of intellectual endeavour – such as criticism – occur in a field of political relations and can themselves actively refigure such relations. While Gramsci's ideal of the proletariat's organic intellectual may be tied to traditional Marxist delimitations of political struggle as class-based, Gramsci's work at least recognised the intellectual's political function as well as an awareness of the possible contestation of this function. If Althusser's theory of ideology saw ideological state apparatuses (such as the institution of literary criticism) as forces for the reproduction of relations of exploitation, Gramsci's work provided the possibility for contestation within cultural and intellectual production.

Cultural materialism, which has drawn upon Gramsci's theorisation of hegemony, has been most fertile in locating political struggle within cultural institutions as well as seeing acts of criticism themselves as political interventions. To examine a work in the light of hegemony is to examine its peculiar socio-historical location; it is also to see the work (and its reproduction) as productive of cultural relations. At this level, Leavis's criticism of D. H. Lawrence can be seen as a hegemonic act. Leavis's argument that the value of Lawrence's novels lies in their articulation of the rich experience of 'life' recuperates the work for traditional humanist institutional interests. Leavisite criticism's concern to sustain a moral sensibility within the ravages of an increasingly commodified world reinforced that very humanism against which Lawrence's fiction had been directed. Raymond Williams's focus on Lawrence's use of language would, on the other hand, be seen as a way of stressing Lawrence's cultural specificity. What Lawrence's fiction articulates, according to Williams, is not some timeless human vision but the structure of feeling of his own quite localised community: 'He is writing like that because he is feeling with his people, not of them or about them, but within a particular flow' (Williams 1970: 140). On a theory of hegemony, then, Williams's stress on local particularity and Leavis's emphasis upon a universal sensibility both contest the meaning of humanism. Both argue for a generally shared value which they see achieved in Lawrence's fiction. For both critics Lawrence's novels harbour a validity which transcends their particular circumstances: for Williams, the sense of a 'knowable community'; for Leavis, a sense of 'life'. While it is possible to argue that both Williams and Leavis share humanist assumptions regarding the worth of experience and its expression, it is also possible to see their different brands of humanism (Leavis's stress on the cultivation of sensibility and Williams's valorisation of spontaneous local communities) as forms of hegemonic contestation. Both seek to give some general legitimation to the values which underpin their critical procedures. On a theory of hegemony these values are class-specific but become hegemonic only through presentation as universally or generally valid. Leavis, for example, argues for a certain 'vitality' in Lawrence's work. While Leavis in no way denies Lawrence's social background, it is the sense of 'life' which demonstrates a 'superlative fineness' in his writings. For Leavis, Lawrence 'has an unfailingly sure sense of the difference between that which makes for life and that which makes against it' (Leavis 1964: 324–25).

Williams's argument, against Leavis, that Lawrence's fiction is valuable for its presentation of the culturally-specific character of life would not represent a more correct reading so much as an act of intellectual struggle. Accordingly, subsequent readings could challenge the inclusiveness which Williams finds in Lawrence's feeling of community. A feminist reading might argue that Lawrence's sexual metaphorics – which use the image of the male body to signify cultural paralysis (in Clifford) or fertility (in Mellors) – establish a masculine hegemony. Those values associated with the male body – phallic power, physical strength, vigorous and active self-projection – are used to signify cultural value in general. A feminist use of hegemony might begin by showing how other values – of passivity, other-directedness and care – are excluded from Lawrence's supposed 'humanism'. To use hegemony in this way would be to extend Gramsci's original analytics beyond its original focus on class. But the critical power of the idea of hegemony lends itself to precisely this end. In so far as hegemony describes the way in which specific interests are articulated as general values it suggests a continual contestation of any form of general legitimation.

The hegemonic constitution of culture and subjectivity

Stuart Hall has taken this lead to argue that ideas of culture, community or the 'popular' are constituted through hegemonic contestation. There is no pre-given, naturally delimited object of community or culture; rather, what is considered to be a culture's character is produced through acts of description, ascription and definition. The normativity of culture – its generally shared assumptions – is not something to be taken for granted. On the contrary, a theory of hegemony focuses on how such normativity is established. Arguing against the idea that cultures are unities which then express their meanings or structures of feeling, Hall argues that culture is

> composed of antagonistic and unstable elements. The meaning of a cultural form and its place or position in the cultural field is not inscribed inside its form. Nor is its position fixed once and forever. ... The meaning of a cultural symbol is given in part by the social field into which it is incorporated, the practices with which it articulates and is made to resonate. (Hall 1981: 235)

According to John Frow (who extends Hall's use of culture as a site of

173

hegemonic contestation), ideas of what constitutes both a culture and its cultural values are not objects to be examined by the critic; the critic's own practice of analysis is crucial to the production of cultural legitimation (Frow 1995: 65). The very existence of cultural value is an achievement of a whole range of conflicting and institutionally located practices (including the critic's own procedures). If culture is a form of unity, then this unity is only ever the effect of culturally-specific practices of legitimation:

> the primary business of culture is distinction, the stratification of tastes in such a way as to construct and reinforce differentiations of social status which correspond, in historically variable and often highly mediated ways, to achieved or aspired values – to class position – with the aim of naturalizing one's own set of values, distinguishing them from the values of others, and attempting more or less forcefully to impose one's values on others. It is thus not just a matter of self-definition but also of struggle for social legitimation. (Frow 1995: 85)

What the concept of hegemony enables is not a final definition of culture and its relations so much as a way of thinking these relations as dynamic, historically contingent and open to dispute. At the same time, as it is articulated in Gramsci's Marxism, hegemony is still located within a theory of class and the focus on the emancipatory character of a specific class's role in history. Cultural materialist criticism – differing from the tradition of Marxist literary criticism – has proceeded to problematise the unity and location of political struggle within class conflict. In fact, it is the negotiation of the contradictory and multiple character of power which has provided the impetus for many recent cultural materialist readings.

8
Contemporary cultural materialism: subjectivity, desire and transgression

Central to cultural materialism's post-Marxist theorisation of criticism has been the problematisation of political identity. Questions of gender, race and sexuality have meant that classes can no longer be seen as coherent groups united by a general consciousness or world-view; for differences cut across these already differentiated groups in a number of ways. In addition to the multiplication of differences among individuals, subjects themselves, it has been argued, are also non-self-identical, 'split' or divided. The theorisation of the split subject and the politicisation of this divide has been undertaken within cultural materialism primarily by questioning the production of sexuality and desire.

We have already seen how Marxist theory was characterised by a changing but critical relation to traditional individualism. Althusserian Marxism intensified the critique of bourgeois individualism by regarding any subject position (and not just the individual of capitalist societies) as an effect of ideology. In addition to Althusser's anti-humanism, which saw the subject as an effect of its discursive construction, cultural materialism has also drawn upon theories of the sexual construction of the subject to criticise traditional theories of humanism. The idea that sexual desire is not a natural, pre-social or primal instinct has been challenged in different ways by both Lacanian psychoanalysis and Foucault's theory of discourse and power. Although Foucault regarded psychoanalysis as an institution which produced sexual subjects as objects of knowledge and normalisation, both Foucault and Lacan have been deployed in cultural materialist investigations of the desiring subject. In many ways this amalgamation of theories of discourse and psychoanalysis is achieved by seeing psychoanalysis itself as a textual production. Lacan's theory of desire, as interpreted within the cultural materialist tradition, does not describe subjectivity in general; on the contrary, it is argued that psychoanalysis occurs alongside other specifically modern discourses which produce modern forms of subjectivity.

What the specifically psychoanalytic account of the subject leads to is a problematisation of the traditional interpretive lexicon in cultural theory. The idea that societies might be examined according to interests, interested position-takings, values, or enabling procedures is questioned by positing the complex character of desire and investment. Within the historicist, Marxist and Hegelian traditions of theory social wholes may have possessed a hidden meaning which could be interpreted; but this latent content was both meaningful and presentable. Psychoanalysis concerns itself with the origin of meaning and value and to this extent posits, however problematically, latent material which is *essentially repressed* and which may be radically anterior to any possible comprehension. The psychoanalytic project, therefore, opens the possibility for interpreting culture and historical periods without assuming that the object of such an interpretation would be a world-view or a structure of pre-consciously obeyed rules or norms. Psychoanalysis, at least ostensibly, differs from the previously considered approaches which seek to think cultural difference and events in their otherness. Like Marxism, psychoanalysis begins by positing a privileged domain – desire rather than the economy – from which all other phenomena are to be interpreted.

Lacan, desire and the divided subject

In the case of Lacan the task of interpretation is not that of finding the authentic or hidden meaning behind a statement. Desire is not a 'content' which reveals itself in a coded form in dreams or texts. The analytic enterprise, for Lacan, entails coming to terms with one's closure within symbolic systems and a recognition that desire will never be revealed in its presence, that analysis or interpretation is interminable. This is because desire is *essentially* not present. Lacan's structuralist 'return to Freud' proceeded by demonstrating that the subject was produced through social signification. Desire was the *effect* of the subject's symbolic structuration. Because subjectivity is achieved by the recognition of the self *as a signifier* ('I'), the subject is always dependent upon a system of differences which it cannot master. Those differences (as language) which exceed the subject produce an originary lack or absence which constitutes the subject as such. Desire, the search for a pre-significatory unity, or the overcoming of lack, must therefore always fail within the structure of signification.

Unlike Althusser's strict structuralism, however, Lacan emphasised that what was outside symbolic structuration – the real – was always felt as an absence, gap or tear in the symbolic order. We may have no unmediated access to what lies outside structure but it is precisely this lack or distance which constitutes us as desiring subjects. The object of desire can, therefore, never be fully presented. As a consequence, the subject is forever distanced from the fulfilment of desire. Interpretation or the analysis of desire is infinite. Lacanian criticism, accordingly, shows the way in which any representation of the self as unified proceeds by masking or misrecognising its desire – a desire which, by definition, can never meet with adequate representation – precisely because the self or subject is always in excess of any representation.

A schematic description of Lacan's theory of the subject is probably best conducted through the allegory of the child's psychogenesis. The difficulty of Lacan's theory lies in the status of this allegory. The theory of the subject is not a brute fact. Lacan does not describe the biological origin of the human subject and its passage to culture. Rather, he argues that the subject is the effect of positing its origin. That is, it is through representing our origin as, say, biological that we become 'other' than biological, we become social/cultural. Any 'theory' of the subject is also what creates the subject. The subject produces itself in representing the non-subjective otherness from which it emerges; but the subject and the other are also effects of this representation. Because the subject is an effect of this self-representation, the process of this representation can, itself, never be rendered present.

In schematic terms the allegory of the Lacanian subject takes up the classic Freudian picture of the emergence of the subject from the maternal origin. Here, the child at the breast exists in a state of complete plenitude and fulfilment – and, therefore, has no self-consciousness. Only when the child feels a break with maternal plenitude can it have a sense of its own self. This sense of self would, then, be founded on separation, lack or negation. This initial division – which is the first stage of subjectivity – produces a being who is disorganised, lacking, incapable, dependent and incomplete. In a moment of recognition – seeing oneself in a mirror – this incomplete being sees its body and (mis)recognises this objective wholeness as a form of self-unity or integration. This body-image is taken up or introjected as a desired form of identity; the ego forms as the result of this imaginary identification. The desire for the original wholeness, plenitude and integrity from which the child has been divided leads to a desire for the unity which the body-image *represents*. This represented unity, as a desired object, is introjected as the ego and constitutes the identity of the subject as embodied.

But this imaginary identification is, Lacan insists, a misrecognition – and it is this aspect which sets Lacan against humanism and ego psychology (Lacan 1977: 71). The subject, properly speaking, is not what is recognised in representation, but is always other than any represented presence The unity and integrity of the ego constituted through the imaginary belies the very character of a subjectivity which is constituted through lack, negation and desire. Any description of the subject as a type of thing, with representable interests and motives or patterns of behaviour (such as the anthropological account of human life) is a misrecognition. Subjectivity can never be recognised in a system or order, because the subject always posits itself as an *excess* of any represented system. In order to understand this dimension of subjectivity it is important to consider Lacan's further stage – the symbolic.

While the ego of the imaginary phase is an introjected *object* produced through identification, subjectivity proper always exceeds the ego. In the symbolic stage the 'I' is a signifier which, as part of an entire system of signifiers, constitutes the subject – not as an objectified ego but as part of an intersubjective network which has definitively broken away from the originary plenitude of the maternal body. Unlike the ego which is formed by identification with a thing (Lacan 1977: 132), the 'I' is formed through the symbolic network of language and is, therefore, never self-present (Lacan 1977: 90). For within a system of signs, meaning and presence must always be deferred, elsewhere or 'other'. The wholeness, plenitude and integrity which has been (mis)recognised in imaginary identification is still desired. But this desire for plenitude at the symbolic level must now work within an entire network of signs; for the difference or negation which constitutes the 'I' is systemic and relational. Accordingly, the unconscious – the anterior realm of difference of which the 'I' is an effect – is structured like a language.

The misrecognition which characterises the imaginary is a consequence of seeing the self as a unified ego image, rather than the differing, temporal and divided character of the subject. To take up the 'I' within a system of signifiers necessitates foregoing the illusory integrity of the ego. The symbolic position, then, shatters the dyadic identification of the imaginary by situating the subject within the systemic order of language. Language must, then, be the other in a radical sense – an other that promises full recognition but that can only ever reveal the subject's lack (Lacan 1977: 86). In psychoanalytic terms this lack is represented as an originary or constitutive castration. The subject, once divided from the maternal or Oedipal origin, can only ever figure that origin through signification. The phallus is the privileged sign which promises to restore that originary lack; to 'have' the phallus would be to arrive at an overcoming of lack – a full restitution of the pre-Oedipal plenitude through the self-presence of the phallus.

According to Catherine Belsey (1986), who historicises and criticises Lacan's theory of the subject, Lacan's recognition of the role of signification in the construction of the subject enables a critique of his own 'patriarchal' premises. Psychoanalytic discourse (and, for Belsey, the discourse of Romanticism in general) constructs the unconscious. Freud's own works are part of the German Romantic tradition and should, therefore, be referred to their particular historical conditions of emergence. Belsey's reading of psychoanalysis is typical of the historicising impulse we have seen in the approaches examined in previous chapters. The generality of Lacan's description – his positing of desire and representation as explanations of subjectivity in general – is undermined, Belsey argues, by locating psychoanalysis within history. Why 'history' is more accommodating to specificity than 'desire' is not something Belsey seems to think requires justification. For her, historical explanations simply are less universalist than those which deal with different modes of desire. What makes Belsey's reading of the modern unconscious materialist is, she argues, her attention to the ways in which subject positions are the effect of discursive practices which are historically located; there is no unconscious or desire prior to the divisions enabled by specific textual procedures. For Belsey, the value of Lacanian psychoanalysis lies in its disruption of the unified subject of humanism, a subject whose function is inherently political: 'The capitalist valorization of consumer freedom depends on the notion of a unitary and autonomous subject, ultimate origin of its own choices' (Belsey 1986: 58–9). What psychoanalysis's theory of the unconscious provides is a way of understanding a subject constructed by processes beyond its immediate self-understanding. But Belsey sees these processes as political, rather than existential or to do with desire. If subjectivity is only possible because subjects have an 'I' or discursive position, then subjects will never be able to grasp fully the construction of this discourse. Drawing upon structuralism, Belsey argues that because language is a system of differences, signs are always effects of an entire system. But this system can never be made self-present within a single sign. The subject, produced through a signifier ('I') is an effect of an entire system of signifiers. For Belsey, the subject's self-presence, as described by Lacan, actually

179

refers to the autonomy of the bourgeois individual and is, therefore, an effect of the repression of the historical system of differences which has produced it. By locating the subject within a particular ideological formation – 'bourgeois humanism' – Belsey suggests that there might be other ways that subjectivity could be constructed (although she does not give instances of what these might be). Belsey seems to accept some form of the general argument that the subject is an effect of difference and is produced through a loss of presence; at the same time she wishes to limit this explanation to the particular cultural moment of Western liberal humanism.

For Belsey, then, the modern subject conceived as autonomous, self-present and unified is produced by excluding or repressing the systemic division of which it is an effect. By arguing that the unconscious is not a timeless pre-discursive given but the effect of the construction of a culturally specific notion of the subject, Belsey can at once use Lacan's theory of the subject while at the same time arguing for its specifically patriarchal character. In her reading of Wordsworth, for example, Belsey argues that the speaking subject of The Prelude continually seeks to overcome division and difference. Traditional readings of Romanticism, she argues, have recognised Romanticism's attempt to create a sense of unity, an overcoming of the division between subject and object. But, for Belsey, this attempt to arrive at some final unity always fails precisely because the very possibility of speech, of subjectivity, of poetry lies in the inherent division of the subject. The Prelude's very attempt to achieve unity, order and the overcoming of loss actually reveals a constitutive difference and division:

> The project of The Prelude is both to sustain and finally to eliminate difference, and by doing so to contain desire, to define a reciprocity between subject and object which 'consecrates' the mind till it breaks free of objects. ... What The Prelude achieves is the constant demonstration of difference in episodes which dramatize the experience of the subject as alternately source and effect of meaning. Its subversive potential lies precisely in its inability to achieve its own project, and in its consequent refusal of a single position of intelligibility for the reader. (Belsey 1986: 73)

The problem with Belsey's approach, which is also what makes cultural materialism a difficult and hybrid movement to assess, is the status of its theoretical claims. Belsey wants to use Lacan's theory of the subject – and all its perceived radical potential – at the same time as she resists granting the theory any general validity. The unconscious, she argues, is at once the effect of a particular textual movement (of which Romanticism would be an instance) and a theoretical tool for reading texts. Belsey argues that there is a repressed at work: what the subject cannot acknowledge is its textual production as a subject. This is put forward as a fact about subjectivity and signification in general. And Belsey's argument does seem to grant this claim logical validity. Although Belsey cannot be seen as exemplary of cultural materialism, her position typifies a more general problem of theory. Her chosen theoretical authority (Lacan) is no longer seen as offering a general explanatory set of claims regarding the process of meaning and interpretation. Belsey argues that Lacan, like Wordsworth, is open to interpretation in terms of historical and political specificity. But it is also the case that Belsey's argument – for the way signifiers work, for the character of desire, for the repression of certain processes and, most importantly, for the primacy of history – makes a general theoretical claim which is at odds with her insistence that ultimately no theory can possess a general validity. Unlike other literary critical movements which explicitly accept the truth claims of a certain theory, cultural materialism will always be haunted by the staus of its claims. Whereas deconstruction or formalism had fewer qualms about saying that they could account for the way language and meaning worked (and then interpreted accordingly), the attempt at radical cultural and historical specificity is continually troubled by its appropriations of general theoretical endeavours, such as psychoanalysis. Not surprisingly, therefore, cultural materialism's use of psychoanalysis is amalgamated with a Foucaultian recognition of the historical particularity of the psychoanalytic paradigm. Indeed, many cultural materialists have employed both Lacan and Foucault within the same work of criticism.

Francis Barker's account of the modern subject, for example, is largely Foucaultian in the way it charts the modern subject's construction through discourse, practices and power. However, Barker also argues that the peculiarly modern, or bourgeois, character of the subject – its sense of itself as a disembodied and autonomous mind – is also the effect of the repression of its body. Where Barker's analysis is Lacanian is in its recognition that the subject is formed through its non-signification; any textual articulation of the subject fails to achieve adequate self-presence. The subject is always other than any thing. This is what leads to the modern subject's continual denial of its embodied or objectified self (Barker 1984: 25). But Barker uses Foucault's historical method to argue that the 'I' of the subject which sets itself against a bodily ego is particularly modern. Lacan's theory of the subject – as that absence which exceeds any representation – is on Barker's account a description of the modern subject, a

181

subject constructed discursively and privately as a disembodied individual. In his reading of Descartes's *Discourse on Method*, for example, Barker argues that the textual production of the 'I' is what produces the modern subject and that this very material production is what must be repressed in order for the subject to emerge: 'For the subject to apprehend itself as Other, which is the gesture of the Cartesian subject as it recounts the fable of its own subjection, to construct the legend, the readability of its own life, is not an accidental feature of this situation: not least because of the precision of its difference from what preceded its event' (Barker 1984: 56). Descartes's 'I think therefore I am' produces a subject, a subject which distances itself from the materiality of its textual production. What makes this subject modern, according to Barker, is this difference from itself, the sense of a disembodied and private individual. But Barker's account, like Belsey's, is strangely poised between two types of description: the subject of signification is both specifically modern *and* produced through a general logic of difference. Foucault's objection to psychoanalysis – that it is the question of the subject as such which constitutes the modern *episteme* – does not seem to trouble this identification of Lacan's theory of the subject as difference, with a theory of historical difference. Recent work in cultural materialism has addressed the question of the relation between the various modes of difference which can operate in desire.

Beyond desire and subjectivity: contemporary cultural materialism

From a more Foucaultian perspective, which does not see desire as an excess which escapes signification, Jonathan Dollimore (1991) has also investigated the production of the modern subject. In particular, his focus on sexual 'dissidence' – the forms of subjectivity marked as 'other' or deviant – demonstrates the ways in which desire is produced through specific forms of discursive legitimation and exclusion. In his early work on Shakespeare, Dollimore had already argued that Shakespeare's *Measure for Measure* reveals that transgressive forces are not pre-discursive and then represented. On the contrary, power is achieved by *producing* a threat, chaos, otherness or transgression which then enables the very law opposed to that threat. Transgression, then, is not some pure force waiting to be liberated or released once power is overthrown. On the contrary, any transgressive 'other' is already part of the discursive system of power and is produced in that power. One of the main concerns of the Duke in *Measure* for *Measure* is that sexual desire might exceed social limits and constraints. At one level, Dollimore argues, the play reveals that power works by demonising desire in order to present law as legitimate (Dollimore 1985b: 74). The Duke speaks of a sexual groundswell which could at any moment destabilise the State; through his rhetoric the Duke constructs an 'other' which will justify his power. However, there is a further discursive strategy revealed in the Duke's rhetoric. By marking out *sexual* deviancy as other (alongside witchcraft and political insurrection) the authority of the State now concerns itself with internal discipline. The State produces, within its own boundaries, an otherness, which will enable an exercising of force or law. This law is not an externally imposed order on a pre-existing desire; rather, law and desire are mutually constitutive and immanently related effects of the distribution of power. Power is not just directed against physical disruption but concerns 'internalised discipline' (Dollimore 1985b: 75). A concern with sexual deviancy concerns all subjects who must become self-disciplining; the other is also within. Where the possibility of transgression emerges, then, is not in the inherently liberating character of desire but in ideology's own rhetoric. In order to produce itself as legitimate the Duke's power must constantly produce a deviant other; in so doing a site of disruption is constituted alongside authority's own articulation:

> At the same time in this period, in its laws, statutes, proclamations and moralistic tracts, the marginalised and the deviant are, as it were, endlessly recast in a complex ideological process whereby authority is ever anxiously relegitimating itself. *Measure for Measure*, unlike the proclamation or the statute, gives the marginalised a voice, one which may confront authority directly but which more often speaks of and partially reveals the strategies of power which summon it into visibility. (Dollimore 1985b: 84)

What this interpretation demonstrates is a move typical of cultural materialism. Desire is not something to be explained; but is, rather, produced according to historically-specific textual procedures. There is a Lacanian emphasis on the necessarily *excessive* nature of desire; but this is seen to be produced and effected through particular discursive practices. There is no desire in general, only a series of prohibitions, regulations and exclusions of desire.

The specifically cultural materialist debate of desire and containment exceeds the terms of Foucault's work on sexuality. In particular, the concern with transgression – and this is where cultural materialists most often differ from new historicists – has led many critics to supplement the theory of power with a theory of desire. In many ways both Foucault and Lacan preclude any positing of desire as natural or given: desire is always the effect of a law which demarcates a boundary between order and transgression. But Foucault's theory of power and sexuality is thoroughly immanent; both law and transgression are instances of power. The specific condition of modernity, in which the subject is established as an individual with an interior depth and unconscious is, for Foucault, part of a network of practices (including psychoanalysis) which produce the subject as an object of knowledge and normalisation. From a Lacanian perspective, on the other hand, the subject is not a positive object of knowledge; on the contrary, the subject is a necessary lack which is the effect of law's symbolic character. Because law, for Lacan, is the symbolic order (a system of signs and a system of differences) the subject can never coincide with or fulfil the law. There will always be some remainder – some point at which desire cannot be given an adequate object or representation. It is this lack, this essentially lawless character of desire, which demonstrates the closure or limit of the symbolic order and produces the possibility of law's disruption. Desire is, from this perspective, essentially impossible (Dollimore 1991: 335–6).

It is not surprising, then, that the most recent cultural materialist work (which has attempted to overcome the perceived impasse of Foucault's theorisation of power) has turned to the site of desire as the locus of possible transgression. While Catherine Belsey (1989), one of the main exponents of theories of desire, has distanced herself from the avowedly cultural materialist work of Dollimore and Sinfield, desire has still been a central topic of concern within cultural materialism. (Dollimore and Sinfield (1990) have also responded by arguing that Belsey's work is, in fact, not so different from cultural materialism as she believes.)

If there is a difference to be drawn between the card-carrying cultural materialism of writers like Dollimore and Sinfield and the work of other critics who have been associated with the movement, then the use of post-structuralism (a certain reading of Lacan and Derrida) probably marks the clearest point of disagreement. Writers like Anthony Easthope and Catherine Belsey, while arguing for a form of historical specificity, have also drawn on what they see to be certain key insights of post-structuralism regarding the possibility of meaning. According to Catherine Belsey, who sets her own work against a new historicism which she believes 'legitimates no political intervention' (Belsey 1991: 30), postmodernism has enabled a new form of Marxist critique. For Belsey, the postmodern loss of general norms of liberation enables, rather than precludes, a reinvigorated political critique. Marxism can be renewed as a 'postmodern project' by looking for the inevitable contradictions in texts. Reading Shakespeare's history plays 'otherwise' (attending to the textual construction of history) will, according to Belsey, show the ways in which any attempt at the historical representation of a unified past 'ends in indeterminacy' (Belsey 1991: 32). Postmodernism's critique of grand meta-narratives (stories of historical progress and liberation, such as Marxism and enlightenment progress) can, according to Belsey, be grafted onto a contemporary political reading practice. By showing that there are no pre-given and stable meanings or representations of history, the writing of history itself becomes a highly politicised project. Furthermore, because of the necessarily unstable character of meaning, texts will always be sites of struggle (Belsey 1991: 33).

Catherine Belsey's work on Milton, for example, has extended the new historicist theory of the performance of power by arguing that seventeenth-century masques were not only a production of the aristocracy's ideal self-image; as royal power began to wane in the 1630s masques desperately sought to sustain the earlier historical mode of power. While the ostensibly natural and moral character of monarchy was coming under question, Milton's Comus (1637) had a political function in the recreation or 'reaffirmation of the Jonsonian mode' of performing power (Belsey 1988: 48). Whereas the Jonsonian masques had represented royalty as part of a natural and harmonious moral order in which royal power was at one with natural and religious law, Milton's masque marks a new form of the performance of power. In Comus, power arrives from without in an absolutist sense; no longer natural and divinely-ordained, power appears as an arbitrary imperative, a force to be obeyed rather than a benevolent sense of general order. The masque's moral struggle between the seducing Comus and the virginal lady is traditionally interpreted as an affirmation of Milton's Christian account of the virtues. Belsey's politicisation of the masque, on the other hand, proceeds by seeing the affirmation of the lady's moral power as part of the stabilisation of power in general. Like cultural materialist readings, then, Belsey sees the representation of personal, moral and inward virtue as part of a general political dynamic. But, drawing on her reading of post-structuralism, Belsey also goes on to argue that any sense of stable meaning and certainty – and not just individualism – will reinforce political stability. After their moral debate Comus is persuaded by the lady's assertion of virtue; he sees 'Her words set off by some superior power'. According to Belsey:

The superior power is of course, divine, the transcendental signified, anchor and guarantee of meaning and truth, the Logos, God. But its human mouth-piece is the Lady, cast as virtue resisting intemperance. Contrary to all expec-tation, in consequence of the moral and political imperatives of the text, the eloquence of a woman fuses word and Word, politics and religion, in a pro-gramme for personal virtue and the social organization of the Christian com-monwealth. (Belsey 1988: 50)

Belsey's reading of Milton's masque has the historical subtlety of recognising that the performance of power may vary according to differ-ent political configurations. Milton's masque, she argues, is 'more abso-lutist' (1988: 48) than its Jonsonian forebears. However, Belsey's equation of the stability of meaning with a 'transcendental signified' which is then seen as the cement of political power might be seen to rest on a rather naive reading of post-structuralism. Belsey's reading of Milton is typical of a certain British appropriation of post-structuralism which argued that texts which were *semantically* stable and unified reinforced *political* stability. Anthony Easthope in *Poetry as Discourse* (1983), for example, saw the steady iambic pentameter of traditional English poetry as reinforcing a stable sense of subjectivity and meaning which was then linked to humanism and political stability. Poetry which disrupted meter and meaning was then seen as potentially transgressive. This argument led Easthope to favour the work of Ezra Pound's modernism over Pope and Wordsworth. According to Easthope:

Modernism, defined as the modernism of Eliot and especially Pound, com-prehensively challenges the English poetic tradition, even if it does not suc-ceed in overthrowing it. The whole field of the inherited discourse is subverted in one way or another. ... At stake in modernism, once again, is the definition of subject position. ... Modernist poetry can be seen as denying a position for the transcendental ego. By insisting on itself as production it asserts the subject as made, constituted, relative, rather than absolute. This view is explicit in both Pound and Eliot. (Easthope 1983: 134-35)

Like Belsey, Easthope associates stable meaning with reactionary politics and semantic indeterminacy with political transgression. According to Belsey, a demonstration of the plurality of meaning will be inherently rad-ical precisely because it overthrows questions of truth in favour of ques-tions of politics: 'meaning is plural, not fixed, not rooted in intention, experience, the world, or the mind, not guaranteed by reason, science or law, but the material of ideology, produced in the interests of power, and open to contest in the interests of politics' (Belsey 1984: 27–8). There are, of course, several problems with such interpretive manoeuvres, not the least of which is the conclusions which such an approach has yielded (where the Fascist poetry of Ezra Pound is seen to be politically liberating, while Milton's poetics are 'absolutist'). If, as critics like Belsey and Easthope argue, post-structuralism has demonstrated that texts 'cannot make present, even in imagination, a single, full, masterable meaning which-is-truth' (Belsey 1988: 24), then it is difficult to see how their own readings can identify a stability in certain texts (which is then equated with authority's stability). If texts *are* unstable then their meaning is either radically indeterminate (in which case the cultural materialist has nothing to work on) or the very act of reading, interpretation, performance or production must be seen as a quite particular and inevitable *determination* of meaning with specific political and ethical effects. Many new historicist and cultural materialist readings have the value of demonstrating that a text's political import is nothing other than its various articulations and productions; a text's history and meaning lie in the configuration of forces which converge upon any particular production. To argue that a text is essentially transgressive (or absolutist) is not only to make an unjustified conflation between semantic and political stability, it is also to forget that texts are events – of reading, production, performance and interpretation. Readings, such as Belsey's *John Milton* (1988), which argue that an appeal to a 'transcendental signified' is an appeal to 'social organization' have missed the point of Derridean post-structuralism.

If, as Belsey (following Derrida) argues, meaning's stability can only be achieved by appealing to some referent outside the text, then the invocation of a transcendental signified cannot be identified with a particular (absolutist) configuration of power. The appeal to such a signified would be the condition for the possibility of any meaning, rather than a locatable and condemnable political decision. A text can never exist in a state of pure free play and indeterminacy but must always be given in particular and specific ways. According to Derrida, a text is never indeterminate; but its determination (its specificity, its force, its articulation) can never be anchored in a general or pre-textual authority (Derrida 1988: 148). What Derrida's own readings seek to reveal is *how* the determination of specific texts is achieved. Belsey's reading which identifies and criticises a general authority (the transcendental signified, Logos or Word) implies that a text could do otherwise than invoke authority; for she sees this invocation of power as that which marks Milton's text as 'absolutist'. But, we might ask, how could a text ever be written if it did not locate or determine itself in some way? Power or determination is not a repressive force which is imposed from without but is, rather, the condition for the possibility of any production of meaning.

This returns us to the problem in Belsey's work of the status of theory in relation to (historical or cultural) difference. Belsey argues that the use of general claims, the force of 'truth' or an appeal to transcendental signifieds has a repressive or absolutist character. But, as can be seen in her own work, there cannot be a position of pure indeterminacy. Her own argument depends upon a moral dichotomy between those (good) positions of historical and cultural relativity and (bad) claims to truth, meaning and determinacy. This is not to say that we simply have to accept the truth claim of a single theory, but it may be better to recognise that – as Derrida and Foucault both argue – truth claims are effects of determination. Critical procedure must work with such acts of determination, rather than condemning determinacy as absolutist and celebrating indeterminacy as a politically self-evident good.

For Belsey, however, desire is *always* in excess of the particular significations through which it is expressed. While arguing that she will be interested in the specific historical articulations of desire and not in the idea of desire as a pre-cultural given, Belsey also sees desire and sexuality as inherently excessive:

> Desire, I believe, is the location of the contradictory imperative that motivates the signifying body which is a human being in love. Desire is in excess of the organism; conversely, it is what remains unspoken in the utterance. In consequence it has no settled place to be. And moreover, at the level of the unconscious its objects are no more than a succession of substitutes for an imagined originary presence, a half-remembered 'oceanic' pleasure in the lost real, a completeness which is desire's final unattainable object. Perhaps, therefore, desire itself, the restlessness of it, and not our inadequacy is the heart of the problem. (Belsey 1994: 5)

This notion of desire as an unconscious 'desire itself' which is prior to signification can be set against those more Foucaultian approaches which see desire as an effect of law and prohibition. Recent cultural materialist work has differed from the Belsey/Easthope style of post-structuralism by arguing for the specificity of particular textual effects and by refusing to identify any factor (such as desire, indeterminacy, or anti-humanism) as necessarily transgressive. The disruption of identity is not seen as politically liberating in general. Like new historicist readings, cultural materialists have focused less on textual undecidability and more on the particular interpretive and institutional decisions which surround textual production and reproduction. Dollimore's work on desire and its representation in *Sexual Dissidence* (1991) is typically eclectic in its combination of both Lacanian and Foucaultian insights: desire is both institutionally and politically constituted (Foucault) but it is also essentially incapable of fulfilment or adequate representation (Lacan). By examining texts which concern themselves with the articulation of homosexual desire, Dollimore negotiates the relation between desire's transgressive force and its institutional containment. For Dollimore, desire is neither essentially transgressive nor is desire solely an effect of institutional production. Desire has a contradictory and politically ambiguous status (Dollimore 1991: 334). Dollimore's work continues to examine the containment/subversion problem but does so by refusing to see any factor as purely subversive or purely ideological. This is most clearly evidenced in his discussion of the question of 'otherness'.

Within what has come to be known as 'postcolonial' criticism the question of the other has been of central concern. The West, it is argued, has continually functioned by representing the non-West as 'other'. All those features which are seen to define Europe and civilization (reason, order, enlightenment) are achieved by excluding and negating opposing features which are then identified with Europe's others. As Edward Said (1985) has argued, the very self-identity of the West is only possible once the otherness of the Orient has been actively produced through a process of representation. Colonialism has as its condition of possibility the creation, through representation, of the non-West as other. It might be seen to follow, then, that otherness as such, might contain some transgressive potential. But as Dollimore's work on desire has demonstrated, otherness, like desire, has a multiple and contradictory character. There is not an 'other' in general. Various configurations of exclusion and inclusion create quite complex political effects in the representation of otherness (Dollimore 1991: 331). In his work on Gide, Dollimore demonstrates that Gide (himself an 'other' in so far as he was a homosexual) harboured a nostalgic desire for the racial 'other'. Africa was depicted in Gide's fiction as a site where the system of sexual exclusion was not in operation. Gide figured the otherness of Africa as a utopian site where desire had fewer boundaries. Is Gide's work, then, ideological or transgressive? According to Dollimore it is both. In aestheticising the other in the pastoral mode Gide's writing displaces the actual 'plight of the other' onto a personal epic about the essential impossibility of desire (1991: 343). However, the utopian element which represents the otherness of homosexual desire as no longer radically other can also be seen, in part, as liberatory: 'in Gide's

189

case image and fantasy do indeed figure transgressively on the borders of history and the unconscious' (1991: 347). At the same time, the use of the cultural other to fulfil a desire of the West (where the other represents a possibility of erotic plenitude) is yet one more example of colonial projection (1991: 338). Both otherness and desire have to be located according to their specific historical and cultural specificity.

Furthermore, whereas 'humanism' has frequently been associated with ideological containment, Dollimore's reading of desire and otherness shows how humanism can be seen to harbour a radical potential. The very nostalgia of Gide's figuring of the other, where the other is seen to embody the integrity, fulfilment and self-identity which Gide has been unable to find in the West, is according to Dollimore a form of 'oppositional humanism' (Dollimore 1991: 348). Once the impossibility of desire is projected onto the racial other, then the West has already exposed its limits and destabilised its self-identity. The specific encounter between an estranged desire (Western homosexuality) and its imaginary fulfilment in the racial other enacts a movement where, according to Dollimore, the 'existential becomes social' (Dollimore 1991: 349). In the work of Franz Fanon, for example, it is the very figuration of the homosexual's lover as an embodiment of some timeless, eternally valuable and incorruptible human essence that grants the other integrity and identity. In so doing both Fanon and Gide adopt a form of humanism; but not only does this humanism have a strategic value, it is also capable of being read (as Dollimore does) as the effect of quite specific social and historical conditions. The humanism of Gide and Fanon must be read, according to Dollimore, as both containing and transgressive; and it has this character precisely because it expresses a moment of intersection between dominant and emerging ideologies: 'the social and psychic realities from which transformation will come are also those which require transformation; the dominant which the emergent contests always already informs the emergent; in short, there is no outside from which to make a totally new start' (Dollimore 1991: 350).

To this extent Dollimore's work remains faithful to the broad tradition of cultural materialism: no category (neither desire, nor otherness, nor humanism) has an essential political meaning. Each term is investigated according to its particular location and representation. Alan Sinfield has similarly argued that literature exists along 'faultlines'; literary texts are sites of contestation both in their production and their interpretation (1992: 5). A 'faultline', according to Sinfield, is a point at which a culture's contradictory moments occur. Shakespeare's Merchant of Venice and its portrayal of Shylock is such a site of 'cultural contest'. It is not a question of deciding, once and for all, whether Shakespeare's play is or is not anti-semitic. On the contrary, the play, its productions and subsequent inter-pretations provide ways for cultures to produce and legitimate any number of attitudes to the depiction of Shylock as a Jew. Rewritings and reproductions of the play (including cultural materialist readings) can be seen as acts of political intervention precisely because they take a culture's most prized icons and contest dominant meanings. Drawing upon Gram-sci's idea of hegemony, Sinfield argues that a culture's contradictory char-acter enables dissident reading (Sinfield 1992: 25), where the very status of what constitutes a 'great' text, such as Shakespeare, can be challenged by questioning whose interests such texts (and its dominant interpreta-tions) serve (1992: 28).

There is, then, a sense in which cultural materialism can be defined against both new historicism and other forms of British contemporary cultural criticism (such as that of Belsey) according to its emphasis on the political determination of language. For Belsey, language in general is an effect of difference; but, she argues, her own use of theoretical paradigms can be neither legitimated nor carry trans-historical force:

> The theories I invoke will be supplanted in due course. In the mean time they make it possible to reopen issues that seem closed, and to reread texts that appeared transparent. The authority I claim for them tentatively, hesitantly, is no more than that. And if Lacan and Derrida seem to me to be right, to tell it like it is, that proves nothing, except that I am an effect of a specific cultural and historical moment. (Belsey 1994: 16)

While the cultural materialism of Dollimore and Sinfield does recognise the historically- and culturally-specific nature of texts, this cultural speci-ficity is seen as a way of determining meaning and is also seen to be more than an arbitrarily adopted theory of difference and desire. History and politics provide language with its force and character; and many cultural materialist readings still rest upon some final limiting horizon of inter-pretation (such as class, race or sexual boundaries). Meaning is not an effect of signification in general (contra Belsey): the negotiation and exchange of symbols is always limited by social norms and boundaries. According to Sinfield, who argues against a certain uptake of post-struc-turalism, 'the post-structuralist vein in recent cultural work, including new historicism, has also helped to obscure the importance of collectivi-ties and social location' (Sinfield 1992: 38). This emphasis on the ulti-mately political character of meaning can be seen as a legacy of cultural

191

materialism's Marxist heritage which sustains a greater emphasis upon the location of meaning within historical and political wholes. At the same time, the status of texts has been rendered far more complex than in previous theories of ideology. There is no *single* political dynamic (neither class, nor race, nor sexuality); nor do texts possess a single meaning, an ideological sub-text or latent content which is there to be demystified by the critic. However, the plurality of meanings and the possibility of conflicting semantic possibilities is still located within a political horizon. The question of whether Shakespeare's comedies are transgressive or reactionary is discussed, for example, according to the specific interpretive, performative and historical conditions of particular plays and readings. The effect of difference is ultimately halted by the presence of power and ideology. Meaning and culture are mutually constitutive: cultures are the effects of stories and narrative production – this point would be shared by most new historicists. But a continued emphasis upon ideology enables cultural materialist readings to ground the configurations of those stories in a larger political narrative. Not only are cultures forms of 'traffic in significant symbols' (Geertz) or systems of exchange and negotiation of resonant objects (Greenblatt); these systems are *determined* by the character of a general ideology (however contradictory that ideology is seen to be). According to Sinfield the exchange of meaning and symbols is neither arbitrary nor unlimited; ideology provides boundaries to what counts as plausible within any given culture:

> Ideology is produced everywhere and all the time in the social order, but some institutions – by definition, those that usually corroborate the prevailing power arrangements – are vastly more powerful than others. The stories they endorse are more difficult to challenge, even to disbelieve. Such institutions, and the people in them, are also constituted in ideology; they are figures in its stories. At the same time, I would not want to lose a traditional sense of the power elite in the state exercising authority, through the ideological framework it both inhabits and maintains, over subordinate groups. This process may be observed in Shakespearian plays, where the most effective stories are given specific scope and direction by powerful men. (Sinfield 1992: 33)

If Shakespeare's plays are, in new historicist terms, forms of the 'performance of power' then it is also the case for cultural materialists like Sinfield that power is located in specific institutions and individuals. Against the Foucaultian idea that power is a general field of forces and relations and is *nothing other than its specific instances*, Sinfield's notion of ideology retains the idea of a social whole (ideology) within which power is distributed.

Power can be held, owned, surrendered and legitimated to ensure 'injustice and humiliation' (Sinfield 1992: 32). Power, here, retains its Marxist edge. Power is repressive and part of a 'dominant ideology' (1992: 32) which organises and limits social relations. Shakespeare's plays therefore enable an 'insight into ideology and power' (1992: 33) by showing the relations between dominant and residual stories.

Sinfield's reading of Othello shows how Othello himself narrates a story which reinforces the racist paradigms of his exoticism and otherness; his repetition of this story is ideological in so far as it reinforces dominant interests. Iago succeeds in bringing about Othello's demise precisely because he can successfully manipulate the narration of common stories. Othello regards Desdemona's love with suspicion primarily because he accepts the racist assumption that to love a moor is to already demonstrate an error of judgement: 'Othello 'recognizes' himself as what Venetian culture had really believed him to be: an ignorant, barbaric outsider – like, he says, the "base Indian" who threw away a pearl. Virtually, this is what Althusser means by "interpellation": Venice hails Othello as a barbarian, and he acknowledges that it is he they mean' (Sinfield 1992: 31). Shakespeare's plays, therefore, demonstrate or provide 'insight' into ideology. They show the ways in which certain stories are privileged over others and frame or present the workings of ideology. Also reading Othello, Dollimore has argued that the play – and its presentation of the way in which political conflict (colonialism) is displaced onto sexual conflict (Othello's relation with Desdemona) – can be read to show the way that 'authority legitimates itself by fastening upon discursively constructed, sexually perverse, identities of its own making' (Dollimore 1990: 171).

There is in both Sinfield's and Dollimore's accounts of Othello a clear and localised site of power (authority, ideology) as well as an argument that the text provides a way of representing this specifically political form of power. Their mode of criticism – because it explicitly adheres to a general explanatory narrative of power, norms and interests – does not encounter the theoretical impasse of a position like Belsey's which ultimately admits that her theory 'proves nothing' and is arbitrarily adopted. Dollimore and Sinfield can claim that their readings prove something, for on their reading of power and ideology there is something to prove. Power is not a general condition of possibility but is located in specific authorities and ideological forces. Because they have a moral project of emancipation – the overcoming of racial, sexual and class oppression – their theory can ultimately be legitimated by ethical justification. Their style of criticism can rest upon the hermeneutic foundation of liberation: if one can identify injustice and if there is an understanding of what emancipation would be, then a text can be read according to the (however multiple and complex) ways in which this possibility is represented or obscured.

As Sinfield argues, Shakespeare's plays show ideology in its production because they 'reveal' something about their historical location (Venetian culture and, by analogy, Renaissance power); they show the relations between stories and the network of power relations. The Foucaultian-derived reading of power in new historicism – where texts do not relate to or represent power relations but actively produce those relations – is given less emphasis here. For Sinfield the plays allow insight into ideology's dominating modes; and this insight also allows for the possibility that ideology, unlike power in the Foucaultian sense, can be delimited, subverted and resisted (Sinfield 1992: 35).

What both Dollimore and Sinfield share is a sense of a dividing line between 'dominant social formations' and its destabilising others (Dollimore 1990: 188). And it is precisely this presence of a culture's 'other', its production of an external threat, which provides the possibility of 'perversion as a strategy of cultural resistance' (Dollimore 1990: 193). Answering many of the feminist criticisms of new historicism and cultural materialism, Sinfield argues that his reading strategies enable resistance by appealing, not to an essential self which exceeds ideology, but to subcultures (Sinfield 1992: 37) in order to argue that dominant ideologies work against other social groupings. Here, he draws upon Gramsci as well as the recent work of Judith Butler.

For Butler, to argue that identity is an effect of discourse is not to abandon the possibility of resistance; resistance takes place from other points of social construction. By attending to marginalised identities (for Butler, the lesbian subject) the unity of discursive regimes can be disrupted. Dollimore's insistence that there can be strategic uses of humanism reinforces this point: if subjectivity is socially and discursively constructed then no subject position or representation is in itself either disruptive or stabilising. Rather, the politics of identity and representation will always depend upon the relations which inhere in any representational complex. It is not surprising, then, that one of the key debates which has emerged from the development of new historicist and cultural materialist criticism is the question of resistance. Because of the problematisation of the humanist subject and the Marxist economic base, post-Marxist criticism has struggled to find a legitimating ground from which its political critique can be launched. As a result, new historicism is often seen as a form of initially politicising critique (in its demonstration of texts as forms of power) which subsequently fails to offer any external position of resistance. In fact, one of the most common ways of differentiating cultural materialism from new historicism has been the presence of manifest political strategy in the residually Marxist cultural materialism (Felperin 1991). However, given the questioning of traditional Marxism's economic materialism and humanism's emancipatory paradigms, it is not surprising that political force is being sought from other critical movements. Sinfield's turn to Judith Butler's work is telling; cultural materialism, as well as new historicism, has tended to turn to feminist theory in order to regain the critical edge which has been vitiated by the attack on traditional forms of legitimation such as Marxism and humanism.

Not only have feminist critics claimed that new historicism's attention to the politics of historiography has long been a part of feminist scholarship (Newton 1989), it has also been claimed that feminist concerns provide new historicism with the only way of saving criticism from the postmodern destruction of historical engagement (Howard 1991: 101). It is not surprising, then, that criticisms of new historicism's political disengagement have come from feminist critics (Neely 1988). In fact, the problems of sustaining resistance, critique and agency in the wake of postmodern scepticism have long been concerns of feminist scholarship. Traditionally, and even within Marxism, the idea of a pre-social moral subject has been the cornerstone of ethical critique. If there is a subject to be liberated then criticism can regard literature as a site of expression, repression, struggle, resistance and emancipation. If, however, the subject is nothing other than its discursive construction then criticism is left with the problem of finding both a site of resistance as well as an object of liberation. The solution of critics like Belsey – that the very indeterminacy of discourse is itself politically destabilising – merely sustains, rather than addresses, the loss of political legitimation. Cultural materialist critics, like Dollimore and Sinfield have, as we have seen, responded to this crisis by maintaining a discourse of ideology and a sense of a determinate political project in response to determinate political objects such as capitalism and patriarchy (Dollimore and Sinfield 1990: 91).

The feminist response to postmodern critique may, however, provide the most forceful way of dealing with both the critique of traditional ideas of the subject and the charge of relativism that has been levelled against seeing discursive construction as originary. Judith Butler's (1993) work takes on the Foucaultian insight that if subjects are the effects of discursive construction, then it is also the case that such constructions produce possibilities of engagement and criticism. If there is no pure 'outside' to discourse this does not mean that discourse is a thoroughly coherent and closed system. In fact, discourse always constructs some putative ground, foundation, outside or origin in order for it to function as a discourse of some thing. Butler's main example is the construction of gender. The idea that gender distinctions are socially constructed – that masculinity and femininity are culturally produced – only works if there is some posited materiality or sexual nature which is there to be constructed. The pre-gendered or pre-discursive subject is an effect of discourse. So, while we always remain within the discursive boundaries of gender – we cannot appeal to some pure, pre-linguistic femininity – it is also the case that the idea of a pre-discursive sex or origin is produced by discourse as its own ground. The possibility of resistance or discursive disruption emerges, then, in the demonstration of the limits of discourse and its necessary positing of an origin: an origin which can always be revealed to be an effect of discourse itself.

Perhaps the clearest instance of this functioning of discourse is given in English Romantic poetry – a literary movement concerned specifically with origins, identity and textuality. The Romantic confrontation with Nature, according to traditional theories of the Romantic sublime, demonstrates the poet's attempt to contain Nature within the imagination: such an act of containment would overcome the division and disruption which characterises the subject's alienation. But such an act necessarily fails precisely because Nature always exceeds and surpasses the poetic imagination; there is an excess which marks the subject's limits. Romantic poems, then, succeed in their failure. The poet feels his imagination subdued or chastened by the 'return' of an origin which it cannot contain. But Butler's notion of discourse would carry the reading of the poem and identity further. The origin which the poem fails to represent is an effect of representation itself. Furthermore, the poet's identity is characterised and effected by its difference from this posited origin. Wordsworth's sense of a lost origin in the 'Intimations of Immortality' Ode (Wordsworth 1987: 460–62) creates a pre-discursive 'real' by continually invoking the limits of representation. Phrases such as 'The things which I have seen I now can see no More'; 'There hath past away a glory from the earth'; 'Both of them speak of something that is gone'; 'A Presence which is not to be put by'; and 'the primal sympathy' continually evoke an unrepresentable origin. But this origin is produced as unrepresentable from within representation itself. The origin is, therefore not original. It is determined by the form of discourse against which it is defined. As a result the Romantic 'subject' is an effect of this negation; the poet is at the limit of nature, the sublime and the 'eternal Silence'.

Butler has similarly argued that in psychoanalytic theory the masculine subject is characterised as other than its maternal origin – an origin which, again, is produced in discourse *as* pre-discursive. A reading practice which demonstrates the discursive construction of this origin, therefore exposes the origin as an effect. This form of critique does *more* than show the limits of representation, for Romanticism's discourse of the sublime had already done this. It also shows that the limit of discourse produces a particular 'outside' and that the non-representable origin is both an effect of representation and highly political. Wordsworth's 'eternal silence' produces a subject defined against Nature, plenitude, peace and glory. Such a discourse is both highly gendered in its definition of the subject as *other than* a feminised nature (as many feminist readings of Romanticism have revealed), as well as being historically specific: the subject is also other than the Enlightenment subject of reason, sense and social identity. Wordsworth's subject is discursively produced as that which precedes the 'exterior semblance' and 'endless imitation' of the worldly self.

What accounts like Butler's reveal is that discursive construction is never closed and that in its construction of identities there will always be points of excess which have a highly political function. Indeed it is the question of discourse's excess – whether that be in the form of desire, economic materiality, ideological determination, the body or (as we will see in Stephen Greenblatt) 'wonder' – that defines how the various historicist critiques operate. Cultural materialism, as practised by Dollimore and Sinfield, still relies on a general theory of ideology in order to engage with the politics of various discursive regimes. However, the turn to sexual identity as a site of political critique, particularly in Dollimore's work on sexual dissidence, manifests both a disruption of the general historical paradigms of ideology as well as an engagement with the traditionally feminist argument that politics is located primarily at the level of our sexual identity and that self-construction is the foundation of social organisation. Whereas cultural materialism in its post-Williams form began as a criticism of 'bourgeois' notions of identity, subjectivity and humanism and then later turned to the subject as a site of dissidence, new historicism began with a Foucaultian theory of self-formation only to turn increasingly towards the general systems of exchange and symbolisation within which such acts of fashioning occurred. This explains, perhaps, what has been perceived as new historicism's ultimate political quietism. The next chapter traces this movement in American new historicism.

9
Stephen Greenblatt and new historicism

Self-fashioning

Stephen Greenblatt's *Renaissance Self-Fashioning*, published in 1980, was one of the leading works which enabled new historicism to be discerned as a specific critical movement. Its central theme of self-fashioning became a point of convergence for many later new historicist enquiries. The idea of self-fashioning was, in many ways, a typically new historicist reaction against previous historical narratives. In Marxist and neo-Marxist histories the transition from feudalism to capitalism was marked by the 'rise' of the bourgeois individual (and concomitant literary forms such as the novel, lyric poetry, biography and autobiography). According to this picture, pre-modern societies were characterised by a hierarchical system of feudal relations where selves were solely defined by their social role. Capitalism, on the other hand, placed an emphasis upon individuals rather than communities, and upon competitive interests and social contracts rather than due reverence and divine right. Literary forms such as the novel, it was argued, expressed this newly-born individualism, just as epic and tragedy had expressed the pre-modern emphasis upon social coherence.

Rather than accepting the idea of the seamless 'emergence' of individuals, new historicist critics sought to show the contradictions and ruptures of historical change. Greenblatt's study of More, in *Renaissance Self-Fashioning*, demonstrates the ways in which conflicting notions of the self – as both authentic individual essence *and* as social performance – operated in Renaissance texts. Rather than seeing a nascent individualism reflected by these texts, Greenblatt demonstrates the ways in which literature itself played a part in the production of individuals. The process of self-fashioning was poetic or literary. An individual did not 'arise' in the capitalist era. Ideas of selfhood were highly problematic and needed to be worked out and contested. Such contestation was not *revealed* by literature;

rather, various performances, writings and theatricalisations *produced* the self. Running against the Marxist and humanist idea of a human spirit which would be alienated or de-humanised by modernity, the idea of self-fashioning showed the inextricable link between the formation of subjects and power. There are no pre-social selves who are *then* governed by a repressive or dominating authority. On the contrary, the self is the product of power. In the Renaissance, Greenblatt argues, it was the ability to produce the most persuasive or captivating fictions or perfomances of self which was the most efficacious form of social and political power.

The attention to self-fashioning as the hallmark of the Renaissance led new historicist critics to take on concerns which had once seemed marginal or insignificant for literary interpretation. Whereas previous critics had seen disguise plots as transitions from an original disorder to a final and natural harmony, new historicist critics saw such 'external' items as dress, misrecognition and disguise as *producing* that very sense of natural order. In Shakespeare's comedy *Twelfth Night*, for example, disguise creates a disorder and confusion which the end of the play sees resolved in a seemingly inevitable return to harmony, which is also a return to the natural order of the state. Sebastian and Viola recognise themselves as brother and sister; true gender categories and identities are restored, and the final marriage is also a celebration of the just and rightful rule of the state by the royal couple. But to take on this reading of a transition to inevitable order is to *accept* the fiction of Renaissance harmony, a fiction which the play itself constantly threatens to expose. Renaissance texts, new historicist critics argue, are themselves partly aware that such a natural order is an enabling and necessary fiction. For the final sense of order in plays such as *Twelfth Night* is produced by the very magic, deceit, confusion and conspiracy which are ostensibly excluded at the beginning of the play as unnatural and chaotic. The seemingly inevitable resolution appears as natural only because the forces of representation at work in the play produce certain states of affairs as legitimate and natural. In this process representation itself becomes a powerful political act.

In Stephen Orgel's *The Illusion of Power* (1975), the royal masque is read as a concrete social act in which the king, by acting a certain role, produces himself as a powerful subject and establishes authority. This feature of the royal masque is explicitly thematised, Orgel argues, in later Shakespearean drama. In *The Tempest* the contending claims of power between Prospero and Caliban are resolved by Prospero's claims to justice; but such claims are validated by the power and persuasiveness of Prospero's perfomance as legitimate ruler. Orgel was one of the first critics to see *The Tem-*

pest as a statement about the power of art and representation. In doing so he inaugurated what became a feature of new historicist criticism: the *recognition* of new historicism's own theory in the very texts it studies. There are certain critical motifs at work in new historicism (in this case, the power of performance) which the critic frequently sees as already thematised by Renaissance texts themselves. In *Renaissance Self-Fashioning* Greenblatt does not just *apply* a modern or Foucaultian theory of power to Spenser's *The Faerie Queene*; rather, he sees Spenser (along with Marvell, Marlowe and Freud) as himself a theorist of power. In doing so Greenblatt's work 'finds' in Renaissance texts those very theories of meaning and power which his own work articulates. Such acts of critical recognition are directly opposed to forms of critical 'demystification' or interpretation which seek to 'know' the work from a distanced and privileged position of commentary. The fact that the distinction between the literary work's meaning and the theory of the critic is so blurred is an indication of the extent to which such criticism is a 'history of the present'. Ideas flow freely between critic and text; there can be no detached 'theory' of the text. Present theories are themselves produced by the history of texts under examination; while those texts are re-produced in every act of (theorised) reading. The choice of the Renaissance as one of new historicism's privileged domains of examination is significant here. If the Renaissance is the beginning of both capitalism and modernity, then any critical reading of the Renaissance will also be a critique (and recognition) of the present.

The Tempest, which is often considered as the statement of the Renaissance awareness of the power of performance, is resolved when Prospero gives up the overtly coercive powers of magic and moves to more subtle modes of performance: a royal masque and the staged performance of a royal pardon for Caliban and the conspirators. What we see in *The Tempest* is a certain allegory of history and power. Prospero's transition from coercive power – in the form of magic and illusion – to power as a shared narrative, mirrors the transition from feudal power as spectacle to modern power as internalised legitimation. *The Tempest*, and Shakespeare's exploration of power and its varying forms, becomes the vehicle for reading different historical formations and their representation. A similar argument regarding the performance of power has been made in relation to *Measure for Measure*. In public performances (such as pardons, trials and proclamations) the ruler produces himself as a figure of authority. The idea of a natural order is not only something which Renaissance plays represent; natural or justified rule is also produced as part of the performance. These plays, it is argued, recreate, draw upon, and study the social energy or 'anxiety' surrounding Renaissance culture's most central and visible model of self-fashioning: royal power. They are themselves forms of literary analysis; the plays 'read' the texts and performances of political power. In so doing the plays are already historically self-reflexive, theoretical and effective. The performance of power through self-fashioning is at once effected and reflected upon in Renaissance drama.

The idea of the self as the product of performance has also profoundly influenced the way in which gender has been read, both in Renaissance dramas and in other texts. Such studies move away from the traditional Marxist and 'history of ideas' accounts in which a uniform 'individual' emerges in the Renaissance, determined by the general demands of capitalism. The 'subjects' which new historicist criticism sees as being produced in the Renaissance are formed through highly particular discursive procedures. Differences in gender and ideas of gender identity are one of the central ways in which individuals are fashioned. Again, by focusing on the cross-dressing plots which dominate the Renaissance, critics have shown that sexual identity, as well as political identity is not an entity ready to be represented but is the result of social acts of representation. When desire is finally 'restored' to its harmonious and socially acceptable form at the end of a disguise comedy, this order (as much as the initial disorder) has been the result of attire, dress and the performance of gender. Ideas of a natural and gendered self have to be worked at and can only be achieved by such 'unnatural' means as clothing and performance. Sexual desire is profoundly ambivalent; it underscores those practices of social cohesion (marriage and gender roles) at the same time that it undermines those practices (desire can always miss or misinterpret its 'proper' object). The mutability of sexual identities is particularly apparent in Renaissance drama. Not only do characters frequently resort to disguising their gender in order to achieve their ostensibly 'natural' sexual aims; the dependence of sexual identity upon dress was also foregrounded by the English practice of using boys to play female characters. Consequently, it was only dress or performance which could differentiate between genders; and much of the drama's energy was gained by playing upon the inevitable confusion of this practice. Stephen Orgel (1989) has even argued that the use of boys to play women's roles was motivated by a cultural fear of the malleability of sexual identity. Boys were used on stage, Orgel argues, because there was an anxiety that the visual presence of women could 'effeminate' the theatre's audience. Once again, this interpretation shows the ways in which the most ostensibly 'natural' phenomena – gender boundaries, sexual identity and sexual orientation – were both profoundly political and dependent upon ritualised social performance or self-fashioning.

Also tracing the textual production of modern selfhood, Jonathan Goldberg's work on Milton (1986) showed how the sense of an essential self depended upon textual inscription. Only by continually writing about the self, and then claiming that the self was always *other* than any act of writing was modern subjectivity produced. If, as authors like Greenblatt have argued, the Renaissance subject was produced through social and public performance, then the post-Renaissance subject of modernity relied on a quite different form of self-fashioning. Milton's production of himself as a unique individual, as a private self quite distinct from public performance and textual represention, is only achieved through texts that gesture to some pre-textual moment of production. Reading Milton's commemorative poem, 'On Shakespeare', Goldberg argues that Milton posits a self and an interior life that precedes the author's printed works. In *denying* that Shakespeare's memory requires a memorial poem, Milton produces the idea of a non-textual 'life', an interior voice that will always exceed the text. Milton's anxiety about printing – no text will be adequate to Shakespeare's memory and so the commemorative poem does not need to be written – is also an anxiety about his own relation to Shakespeare. Milton at once asserts and denies both Shakespeare's and his own identity's dependence on textual inscription. According to Goldberg, the modern self is a textual performance achieved through the denial of text. Only by claiming the inadequacy of text and inscription is the non-textual self able to emerge. For Goldberg, 'this text does not say "I", but emerges buried in the otherness to which it consigns Shakespeare – and itself. Appropriated, objectified, as the recipient of voice – as auditor – the text places, displaces (dislodges – no tomb for those bones) its subject' (Goldberg 1986: 129).

As a result of this interest in self-fashioning, new historicist critics began to concentrate on all those aspects of Renaissance drama which had once seemed so peripheral: cross-dressing, performance practice, disguise plots and the fact that boys played women's roles. Because the self is now seen as an effect of social production it makes sense to attend to all those features which enable differentiation to take place. In the Renaissance the self is produced publicly through performance, dress, visual display and public appearance. In post-Renaissance literature, however, subjectivity is produced as *other than* its textual or social performance. Rather than being a public role, the self of modernity is constituted through the 'private' genres of lyric poetry, the novel, diaries and autobiography. The 'subject' of modernity is no less a performance than the Renaissance subject but is now seen as a textual performance. By defining the subject as a textual performance (as does Goldberg), the model of Renaissance self-fashioning was transposed onto subjectivity and poetry in general. This attention to the subject as a textual performance or production depends upon a certain reading of the Renaissance in which the conditions of Renaissance subjectivity are taken as the grounds for modern selfhood as such. The Renaissance emphasis on public performance and the theatrical nature of the self and power are only more explicit instances of the conditions for any possible self-production. The re-reading of the Renaissance as the beginning of modernity was also of central importance for literary criticism concerned with later periods. Self-fashioning was more than a particular literary motif; it was the primary explanation for all texts and selves. A reading of self-fashioning in the Renaissance was also a claim about power in general.

Behind new historicism's focus on self-fashioning were certain major arguments in social and political theory. The focus on power and the self as a performance of power owes a great deal to Foucault's post-Marxist theorisation of power. In The History of Sexuality, Volume 1 (1978) Foucault rejected what he referred to as the 'repressive hypothesis'. This usual idea of power was entirely negative; it saw power as repressing or working against some pre-existing force or entity. Using the modern example of the discourse of sexuality, Foucault described the modern notion of sexual freedom as one in which a subject should work against all the repressions, interdictions and prohibitions which had inhibited his or her desire. But such discourses of liberation were, according to Foucault, actually productive of the very 'sexuality' which they sought to uncover. There would be no sexuality to liberate if the rules and procedures which both produce and regulate sexuality did not already exist. Power is positive; it produces its own objects. In the case of sexuality, subjects would have no sexual identity if there were not rules to describe, define and give a character to that identity. Furthermore, subjects themselves are produced by taking part in the discursive practices of sexuality. Consequently, any discourse of sexual liberation would also play a role in producing and ordering a supposedly 'authentic' sexuality. There can be no simple opposition between power and resistance. There are, rather, competing forces operating against each other.

New historicist criticism, which has drawn upon Foucault's theorisation of the connection between power and the formation of subjectivity, has varied in the extent to which it focuses upon the subject as a site of resistance or legitimation. *Renaissance Self-Fashioning* is perhaps typical in its stress upon the instability or ambivalence of any performance of subject identity. While the production of a culture depends upon the successful performance of subjects, the process of self-fashioning can also produce anxieties (in the case of More) or declarations (in the case of Marvell) that the self is nothing other than theatrical display. There can, Greenblatt suggests, be no general or trans-historical theory of the subject; rather, each act of critical investigation seeks to determine the particular subject-formations at work in any text or performance of texts. The concept of self-fashioning is therefore a general explanation of how texts and cultures interact, at the same time as it works to undermine any general theory of culture. Self-fashioning takes a number of forms due to its intimate connection with the modalities of power. Despite the fact that the idea of self-formation through power gained a general critical currency, Greenblatt's own work turned away from the centrality of the question of the subject towards the processes of representation of which selves were the effect.

Representation, negotiation and exchange

In addition to self-fashioning, one of the most consistent features of new historicism has been its refusal to accept a culture's dominant self-representation. Because recent anthropology and ethnography have resisted positing any latent system of rules of which cultural participants themselves would not be aware, there has been a tendency to read cultural formations at face value. In the absence of any deeper ideological meaning one simply 'describes' a culture's norms as forms of enabling procedure. But in so far as literary criticism is, institutionally, a practice of reading, it is more likely to sustain the task of interpretation rather than description. What is literary criticism to do if it is to avoid interpreting a text according to some pre-textual or extra-textual order but nevertheless wants to go beyond a text's manifest content? In response to these sort of questions literary criticism has taken up the idea that cultural analysis of texts is not so much the discovery of a latent order as it is a recognition of what texts *do* or how they work. Rather than accepting certain representations of political order as descriptive, new historicists see such representations as *productive* of order. Furthermore, it is argued, for any text there will always be other representations, other stories as well as disruptions and contradictions in the dominant or empowered representations. The text's production of order is also marked by the disorder it excludes and the possibility that its ordering strategies may misfire.

At the same time as there has been a distrust exercised towards dominant representations, there has also been an equal refusal to ignore or disregard as merely illusory a culture's own explicit presentation of itself. Rather, a culture's self-representation is viewed as a symbolic and effective practice. Political manuals, stage-plays, histories, travel accounts and acts of self-description are not dismissed as propaganda or ideology; they are seen to perform an effective part in producing the culture they describe. Representation plays an active role in the production of social wholes and is dynamically effected by, and efficacious in, the transformation of social networks. Static psychological totalities like 'world-views' or 'mind-sets' are rendered problematic by seeing the realm of representation as a multiple arena of discourses which operate in processes of exchange and circulation. Seamless representative wholes, such as the 'great chain of being' or the 'Elizabethan world-picture' are symbolic attempts to integrate and regulate conflicting systems of images and expressions. In this sense, we could see Tillyard's idea of Elizabethan order as the result of an acceptance of certain particular and interested Renaissance representations of order as both real and exhaustive. Writing of his own approach to ideas of Elizabethan 'order' Stephen Greenblatt argued that such 'visions of hidden unity seemed like anxious rhetorical attempts to conceal cracks, conflict and disarray' (Greenblatt 1988a: 2). Any general homogenisation of symbolic networks – even a certain use of Foucault's theory of power – would, Greenblatt argues, miss the multiple uses, resistances and positions which characterise any culture. Capitalism, in particular, is characterised by a remarkable proliferation of representational networks. With the development of ever-larger markets, there is also an increasing trade and circulation of images. In this process of circulation 'other' representations and images are taken up, transferred across domains (or 'negotiated') and recirculated in an expanding and contradictory network of signs. According to Greenblatt, 'it is with capitalism that the proliferation and circulation of representations … achieved a spectacular and virtually inescapable global magnitude' (Greenblatt 1988b: 6). Greenblatt's work charts a genealogy of this circulation of images and shows the ways in which representation, as much as any other more overtly material commodity, is invested with both value and power.

The nascent capitalism of Renaissance culture can only be understood, according to Greenblatt, by registering the resistances, contradictions, tensions and transformations which operate *against* the dominant representational positions. In his essay, 'Murdering peasants', for example, Greenblatt shows how Dürer's engravings act strategically to draw social boundaries. Dürer's engraving of a possible monument to a successfully suppressed peasant rebellion has to work within a genre of heroic monuments at the same time as it has to acknowledge the particularly unheroic, or farcical, character of the peasant-opponent. Dürer's column has to represent valiant honourable victory and opposition while concurrently figuring the absence of threat, power or force in the rebellious peasant. To represent the peasant as other than entirely pathetic would be to grant the rebellion a sense of force or legitimacy. Dürer manages to create a successful resolution to this representational-economic problem in which honour has to be attributed to the victory, but not to the vanquished, by combining two distinct genres – the heroic and the pastoral. But in doing so a tension and dissonance haunts the work. Greenblatt's essay seeks to show the ways in which Dürer's task (the representation of victory) takes place within certain defined discursive practices, the conjunction of which threatens to subvert the overt strategy of the column:

> A victory column, like any other artistic genre, is a received collective practice, but the social conditions of this practice – both the circumstances that make the genre possible and the objects that the genre represents – may change in such a way as to undermine the form. (Greenblatt 1988c: 3)

By processes of 'semiotic contamination' the symbols used by Dürer can intersect with conflicting and subversive meanings: here the pathetic defeat of the peasants also comes dangerously close to the recognisable figurations of Christ's innocence. Consequently, Dürer's column is a negotiation of an historic event through the dominant modes for dealing with such events. The discordance between the contingency of the event (this particular rebellion) and the formality of representational modes (pastoral, georgic and tragic) creates a complex of forces; intention, event, genre and history are so many factors contributing to the representational complex:

> We have constructed then a reading of Dürer's design based upon the complex interplay of three forces: the artist's intention, genre, and the historical situation. By the latter I mean both the particular objects of representation and the specific structure of ideology and event that renders something – person, place, institution, thing, idea, or action – sufficiently notable to be represented. Neither intention nor genre can be reduced to this historical situation: a given genre, as Dürer's design powerfully demonstrates, may have great difficulty accommodating a particular representational object, and artistic intention has an arsenal of strategies – including irony, laughter, open revolt, and subversive submission, to name but a few – designed to differen-

tiate it from the surrounding world. But this differentiation is not the same as autonomy, and the most important lesson to be learned from our discussion of Dürer's design is that intention and genre are as socially contingent, and ideological, as the historical situation they combine to represent. (Greenblatt 1988c: 13)

Dürer's column can be seen as an intersection of certain representational expectations (the heroic representation of victory set alongside the pastoral domestication of the peasant). While each symbolic practice may have a role to play in the maintenance of social boundaries, Greenblatt's reading draws attention to the active *drawing* of those boundaries, rather than accepting them as hidden facts which the text reveals or represents. It is this treatment of representation as an active play of forces which characterises much new historicist work.

The question of the meaning of the text, the idea that there is a 'signified' (however complex) 'behind' the work, is displaced in favour of an examination of the text's labour. Instead of seeking a richer and more complex hermeneutic depth to the work, new historicist criticism asks how the text functions. Questions are not directed to what lies beneath the text but to those other texts and events which surround the work. The answers to such questions are necessarily multiple given the various situations in which a text can be read and performed, as well as the various historic events to which the work can be considered adjacent. Seeing the multiplicity of a text's functions is a direct effect of the new ways of thinking about history brought about this century by figures such as Foucault and de Certeau. If history is no longer a single and linear narrative characterised by a progressive development towards a meaningful end, then the simple 'context' and meaning of history is exploded. The literary work can no longer be referred to a single context which it in some way 'represents'. 'History', as Foucault has argued, is itself a historical phenomenon and the connectedness of our historical narratives is a function of the questions we ask, the uses we seek history to serve and the information we choose to make meaningful.

New historicist critics are, then, critically aware of the ways in which their history is a 'history of the present' – the active creation of connections which serve to question and problematise our own critical circumstances. If new historicism has been charged with a certain depoliticisation of history (Lehan 1990; Lentricchia 1989), this has been because of its refusal of a traditionally Marxist history which would be directed by a single political meaning. However, the awareness that any representation, including the representation of history, is always already a political and social act only emphasises the ways in which the 'political', like the 'historical' cannot be treated as an unproblematic given. The foregrounding of the representational work which occurs in literature can just as legitimately be directed to the texts of history, travel writing, science and literary theory itself.

The distinction which has traditionally divided the literary from the non-literary has tended to focus on the mode of representation: literary texts are those which take the act of representation, rather than what is represented, as their subject. This was the dominant argument of American new criticism which focused on literary works as self-reflexive. Modernist literature (with its explicit thematisation of art) provided new criticism with a paradigm for self-reflexive aesthetics. But Renaissance drama – where plays foreground both their own fictionality and the 'theatre' at work in everyday life – could also be seen as literary precisely because of its focus on the fictive and performative. New historicism has taken this explicit foregrounding of the literary work and applied it to traditionally non-literary texts. In doing so, it has been accused of taking conservative literary formalism into the domain of history and politics (Liu 1989; Porter 1989). This criticism, however, misses the point of the ways in which representation has been rethought.

To begin with, the idea of the self-reflexive art work which dominated American new criticism enabled a distinction between works which represented or referred and those which were manifestly 'poetic'. This elevation of the literary text as an isolated and self-contained whole (or 'verbal icon') implicitly granted those non-literary texts a privileged relation to the 'real'. Not only has new historicist criticism shown that realist texts such as those of history, reportage, science and political theory are inextricably involved in the negotiation of literary form and representation; it has also shown that the practice of representation, the phenomenon of formal or literary qualities, is itself political and concerned with power.

Secondly, this relationship with power is not one in which literary form is used for political ends. On the contrary, the distinction between the political and the aesthetic, as well as the boundaries in the political domain itself, take place through the representational or symbolic field. To accuse new historicism of bringing 'literary formalism' into the domain of history and politics and thereby depoliticising these domains, is to grant the literary an apolitical space. It is precisely the challenging of this distinction which typifies new historicism as a movement. This is not to say that all historical or political phenomena are reduced to the level of the text; it is, rather, to see the textual as one of the central ways in which the political operates. When Louis Montrose (1986) refers to the 'historicity of texts and the textuality of historicity' this blurring of functions does not amount to turning history and politics into literary formalism. It disavows the possibility of a purely aesthetic formalism at the same time as it problematises the idea of history or politics as a simple referent.

To take, again, the example of Shakespeare's The Tempest: the traditional reading of Prospero as an image of the consummate Renaissance artist is given a new inflection in new historicism. Prospero's artistic achievements are seen to be the means through which colonial power is perpetuated. The 'self-reflexiveness' of The Tempest does refer to the play's own recognition of the role of art; but art is seen to be an already political practice. Prospero is powerful precisely because he controls the means of representation. Caliban and Miranda are his loyal subjects because they accept and repeat Prospero's stories regarding their origins, watch his entertainments and speak his language. New historicist readings of The Tempest show that political power is bound up with representational practice. Prospero must perform the role of the monarch (a performance he had failed to undertake in Milan) while Caliban must accept the language in which this performance takes place. The stories Prospero tells legitimate and constitute his power. The narratives Prospero recounts in the first acts of The Tempest are those which situate him as a character of authority; he becomes the author of the island's history and a typification of the forms of legitimation that occur through narrative. Such reflections on the power of telling are not just allegories of colonialism. They do not just suggest that the monarch is like an artist who performs stories of authority. In various ways new historicists have shown that art and its performance is power. Political hegemony is achieved through persuasive performances, effective display and narratives which can pass themselves off as 'real'. Interpretations of The Tempest and its processes of representations are also acts of politics and representation; in each reading a decision is made regarding the status of the text, representation and its specific power. The Renaissance is a privileged interpretive object precisely because it connects power with persuasion and rhetoric. The reading of the Renaissance is used, quite explicitly, to challenge our modern notion that power, subjectivity and justice can be legitimated beyond rhetorical force.

By exposing the presence of rhetoric and performance in all forms of political power, the traditional moral divisions which have dominated criticism have become problematic. Ethical oppositions such as good and evil are seen to be strategic. The interpretation of Iago in Othello as a morally reprehensible and ruthless manipulator of rhetoric depends upon setting Iago against characters who have a more virtuous and legitimate relation to power. But on a new historicist reading the distinction between Iago on the one hand and Cassio and Othello on the other is not so much an opposition between good and evil, as one between explicit and naive uses of rhetoric. Whereas Iago is a flagrant and self-confessed performer and dissimulator, Othello and Cassio commit themselves to the performance of a single and consistent character. Their virtuous 'selves' are no less dependent upon rhetoric and performance, but their self-fashioning is less overtly artful. Iago is not an evil and extraneous accident in Renaissance society (as in the humanist reading); he is, instead, the consummate performer of self and the epitome of Renaissance self-fashioning. The powers of narrative and performance pervade all aspects of the play and cannot be marginalised in the character of Iago. In Othello Desdemona is won from her father by Othello's capacity to narrate tales. But Othello is himself undone by the more persuasive narrative powers of Iago. It is no longer the case that we can see Iago as evil simply because he feigns or dissimulates; for, in general, there is no true self or authentic ethic behind social performances. The 'art' of Iago is simply more explicit and calculating than the art of a supposedly more legitimate power. The distinction between the real and authentic power of the monarch and the theatrical power of imposters and dramatists is itself a performance, a performance of sincerity.

If ethics is now conflated with rhetoric and art this raises the question of new historicism's own ethical legitimacy. New historicism's relation to the past it reads is perhaps the question which surrounds the movement. It could be argued that the Renaissance is not characterised by the sophistry which Greenblatt and others uncover in characters like Iago. There has been a long history of performance and criticism which accepted characters like Iago as evil and went on to discuss the problem of evil accordingly. The play certainly offers a reading in which Iago's use of rhetoric – his rampantly individualistic, self-seeking, destructive and manipulative use of language – is seen as less worthy than Cassio's concern for social role, performance and 'reputation'. Shakespeare's Othello might be read as critical of the (modern, emergent) attitude to ethics which Iago's opportunism represents. New historicism's argument that power and value are nothing other than representation, persuasion and performance can then be seen as acts of historical projection. It is only after post-structuralism or Nietzsche that all values are seen as effects of the force of language, rather than language being used to express ethical norms. The question of whether *Othello* really is a demonstration of the all-pervasive character of representation as power, or whether this 'insight' is read back onto the text is a question of historical interpretation. Does new historicism miss the point in seeing its own (contemporary) beliefs about language in the texts it studies? (If this were the case new historicism would not really be historical at all but a reflection of the present.) Or, does Shakespeare's Iago represent another way of thinking which typified the Renaissance – a belief that all ethics is really power and representation – which is then obscured and misrecognised in a subsequent history of moral interpretations? Interestingly, new historicist criticism moves through both sides of this interpretive dilemma. The past is both other – and serves to show the limits of our present – and the same: through the past we recognise the limits of our present. The 'undecidable' character of new historicism's past has been severely criticised. It is not clear whether new historicism is asserting its own beliefs or revealing the meaning of a historically specific text. But this recognition effect goes some way towards thinking through the strange divide between theory and criticism. Theory is a statement about meaning in general, while literary criticism is an interpretive location of statements. Literary theory, essentially, has this double nature of being both a set of claims and a critical reading of those claims. The undecidability of new historicism brings this out explicitly.

New historicist criticism seeks to unmask the distinctions which set one performance or representation off as fictional and manipulative and another as natural, theoretical or legitimate. It also seeks to show the ways in which this distinction between the authentic and the derivative itself relies on certain powers of representation. The Renaissance is seen as both a time when modern theories of power as performance were emerging (in Machiavelli and Marlowe) as well as a time when power was set off against more 'legitimate' and 'natural' forms of authority. New historicism 'reads' the Renaissance by taking various representations of power (as both performance and legitimate authority) and noting an *ambivalence* in most texts. The sense that power is nothing other than performance pervades the Renaissance, but at the same time there are various competing attempts to establish more foundational or natural forms of order and control. Stephen Greenblatt's *Renaissance Self-Fashioning* is typical of new historicist readings of the period in its favoring of the Machiavellian theory of power, which is seen to contaminate and over-turn earlier ideas of authority as just rule.

Such critical insights into power and representation have been used to read texts from the Renaissance other than those which are explicitly literary or dramatic. In Greenblatt's reading of the European encounter with the New World, for example, the idolatry of the native Americans has to be set against the true faith of the invading Spaniards. But this very distinction is enabled by valorising certain forms of representation (writing, scripture, documents) and excluding others (symbols, performances). Greenblatt's work on the New World has revealed the representational work and power that underlies such distinctions and exclusions: the ways in which the rhetoric and symbolism of the invader is taken as 'real' while the culture of the native Americans is dismissed as fantastic and fictional. Every invader acts as a Prospero by imposing a representational complex and then disavowing the status of that complex as representation or artifice. At the same time, this mode of representation can draw upon and appropriate the very imagery it seeks to disempower. By doing so it reduces the threatening otherness of its opponent and weakens its disturbing effect. Representation becomes a social practice with a ritualistic function. If ritual is a way of creating distinctions and borders and warding off threats, then European art and texts are no less ritualistic than those of the cultures it dismisses as primitive. To see traditional literary texts as referring directly to a world (or historical context) is to accept the eurocentric logic that while other cultures work within a symbolic and effective logic, European culture has access to a rational and pristine real. The work of cultural anthropologists and ethnographers of this century has problematised the notion of the impartial European observer who can rationally explain the symbolism of other cultures. The observer is no less culturally embedded than the observed. The very practices of ethnography, historiography and literary theory are also culturally determined symbolic practices.

History, as Greenblatt notes, is one of the West's dominant modes of representation. It is itself an exercise of power and cannot be appealed to as some pure outside or 'context' which could adjudicate a conflicting field of representations. The narratives of history are just further ways of creating borders, boundaries and exclusions. Drawing upon the work of de Certeau, Greenblatt shows how Columbus's encounter with the New World used the writing of history as a way of inscribing boundaries. Columbus's seemingly futile recitations of various acts of Spanish law to the native Americans were, Greenblatt argues, 'linguistic acts'. They enabled the Spanish to legitimise their act of dispossession by drawing a distinction between their written, legal and historically grounded codes and the world of the Americans. It is not just that the Spanish denied the indigenous Americans their rights; on the contrary, Columbus's performance of acts of treaty, legal negotiation and authority performed a historical subsumption of the Americans who were immediately included and set within the Spanish history and tradition of rights. Both the recitation of words and their subsequent inscription produces a history which can make an event acceptable, ethical and in keeping with the symbolic values of Western imperialism:

> Columbus's journal mentions that naked people were sighted on shore before the Spanish landed, but it is not altogether clear that the ritual of possession took place within earshot of these people who subsequently approached in large numbers. Ceremonies take the place of cultural contacts; rituals of possession stand in for negotiated contracts. Columbus acts entirely within what Michel de Certeau calls 'the scriptural operation' of his own culture, an operation that leads him not simply to pronounce certain words or alternatively to write them down but rather to perform them orally in the presence of the fleet's named and officially sanctioned recorder. Writing here fixes a set of public linguistic acts, gives them official standing, makes them 'historical' events. (Greenblatt 1988b: 58)

We can conclude, then, that while works of art (such as The Tempest and Measure for Measure) can take as their subject the performances and representational practices which produce the divisions of power, these very works can also play a role in redrawing those boundaries. Furthermore, overtly political practices, such as kingship and judicial proceedings, themselves take part in performance and symbolic display. The distinction between these domains (the literary, the political, the historical, the theoretical), like the distinction between the true faith of the Spaniards and the idolatry of the native Americans, is a function of representational practice. Representation is, then, not mimetic but an effective practice which seeks to domesticate an other through misrecognition, to order a culture by inscribing boundaries and to perform social acts which attribute identity.

The 'strong' emphasis on representation, however, also tends to preclude the task of cultural understanding. If representation is not a minor practice but the condition for any possible thought or action, then the encounter of 'other' cultures is already determined as an instance of competing representation. Greenblatt's distinction between the writing of the conquistadores and the symbols of the native Americans still includes the two cultures within the common domain of representation. While representation has been retheorised as a form of practice, and now includes a large variety of non-linguistic phenomena, it could still be argued that the focus on representation upholds a desire to interpret all events within a

213

single system. Representation may have been used by Greenblatt to demonstrate the limits of Western culture, but the use of representation and its concomitant metaphors of exchange and economy still sustains a desire to think of single interpretive condition or ground. While Western metaphysics is often interpreted precisely as the inability to think otherness beyond the 'closure' of representation, there has also been – from philosophy's inception – an attention to wonder as that which opens or disrupts the totality of thinking. Greenblatt's later work is characterised by an attempt to think the wonder of that which exceeds any interpretive enterprise.

Resonance and wonder

In his work on the New World and in an important essay, 'Resonance and wonder', Stephen Greenblatt moved away from the Foucaultian emphasis on power towards the notion of wonder. In keeping with Greenblatt's description of representation, wonder is considered as part of an economy of encounters and responses. It is at once specific to the European imagination as well as providing a way of thinking about cultural difference in general. While wonder is part of the colonising strategy which seeks to contain the radical difference of the New World (Greenblatt 1988b: 14) it is also the recognition of a difference so radical that it will resist any attempt at complete comprehension: 'The experience of wonder seems to resist recuperation' (Greenblatt 1988b: 17). Greenblatt's rejection of any totalising concepts such as 'world-view', 'context' or 'ideology' in the traditional sense is revealed and enabled by his repeated use of wonder which concentrates on the specificity and particularity of objects, events and texts. The use of 'wonder' also marks a critical departure from early new historicism's emphasis on the system of power and representation. In fact, wonder – like Foucault's notion of the event or de Certeau's silent histories – is a term which works with the closure of theoretical analysis only to reveal its limit.

If wonder registers the absolutely strange, and the ambivalent response to that strangeness, then resonance, for Greenblatt, is both its opposite and its counterpart. In order for a sign to be meaningful it must be repeatable. A word can only signify if it is recognised, and recognition occurs with familiarity and repetition. Any single or random complex of letters cannot communicate; signs can only mean when they become part of an organised system of exchange. 'Resonance' is precisely the passage of a sign's meaningfulness, the uses and instances which have produced its meaning. While no particular instance can be identical to another, it is the recognition of a certain identity which enables meaning to take place (Greenblatt 1988b: 36). The experience of resonance is closely tied to 'circulation'. The economic metaphors which underpin Greenblatt's descriptions of representation serve to show the *material* basis of signs – the fact that meaning always resides in actual tokens, objects, pictures and so on which are regularly exchanged. Stories are circulated, exchanged, re-produced and re-circulated. It is this process of circulation which pro-duces resonance. A story will gain in resonance with increasing circulation. A sign or symbol is not meaningful in itself; it only becomes meaningful through social circulation.

The vicissitudes of this process of circulation are charted by new his-toricist criticism which focuses upon aspects of performance, printing, framing, consumption, institutionalisation, binding, reading – anything, in fact, which is contiguous to the text. Just as Michel Foucault's notion of archaeology sought to disrupt the linearity of history and show the mul-tiple series of connections and discontinuities which could prevail over any single phenomenon, so the idea of resonance can reveal any number of events, icons and exchanges which can bear upon the meaning of a work. There is no single meaning, nor is there a single medium for mean-ing (such as context, ideology or intention). Various forces are at work in making any text or object resonant; such forces can be figured in the form of practices, other texts, journeys, dreams, diagrams, buildings, cata-logues or letters. An emphasis upon contiguity – an emphasis apparent in Foucault's concept of archaeology – enables the new historicist critic to bring to bear, as 'resonant', any phenomenon which has intersected with the circulation of the text. Consequently, stories, as much as weapons, can become the physical facts which enable acts of power to take place. Stories circulate and enable a culture to represent itself as legitimate, moral, valu-able and authoritative. In an encounter with the New World, for example, it will be the resonance attached to certain texts (treaties, the Bible, letters) which provides a form of power. This is not to say that colonialism is a purely linguistic phenomenon, but it is to acknowledge that the power of imperialism is tied up as much with the forces of representation as it is with the material tools of invasion (Greenblatt 1988b: 64). Even the seemingly fundamental economic imperative which drives the colonial project – the acquisition of gold – is, according to Greenblatt, itself depen-dent upon the fact that gold as a material substance has been invested with a *symbolic value*.

Drawing attention to the processes of circulation which produce res-

onance, new historicist critics often begin their readings with the mini-
mal narrative unit available for circulation – the anecdote. Instead of referring to a homogenous whole which would characterise or represent a
culture, the anecdote is a local and highly particular instance. It acts out a
point between a pure and unmediated historical event (some moment
prior to representation) and the point at which that event becomes represented (Greenblatt 1988b: 3). We can see the use of anecdote as enabling
a history which is non-linear and sensitive to discontinuities and disturbance. The anecdote is not a pre-discursive 'real'; on the contrary, it is one
of those stories or symbols which can circulate in a culture and gain resonance. But the anecdote is also the recording of an event at its most simple and particular level – prior to the interpetive work of the critic,
dramatist or novelist. Focusing on anecdotes reveals both that the 'raw
material' of history is not some pure statistically-measureable data but an
already narrativised event and that these particular stories and events resist
any easy inclusion within a seamless historical context. Just as Foucault's
Discipline and Punish opens with the story of the torture of Damiens the regi-
cide (and thereby shows the ways in which this culture tells its very different stories to itself), so Greenblatt's focus on anecdote highlights the
difference and contingency at work in the stories which circulate at any
historical moment. Anecdotes provide both a form of historical evidence
and a resistance to the historical 'real' in so far as they are other and
strange, characterised by a contingency which resists recuperation
(Greenblatt 1990: 5).

Wonder

According to Greenblatt, while any experience of wonder must occur
at a historical moment and can only be understood in terms of historically
and culturally specific relations, it cannot be explained through a notion
of context; this is precisely because wonder is the mark of historical contingency. The seamless and naturalised world of Renaissance Europe is
torn apart and dislocated in the encounter with the New World. The alterity of the indigenous American form of life presents both a fascination and
a challenge to the representational economy of the European invaders. The
attempts to contain, delimit, order and incorporate the other are figured
in the colonialist representation of the native Americans within European
imagery. At the same time the Western economy of representation breaks
down before the strangeness and opacity of the other culture. The sense of
wonder expressed in the writings of the New World records the failure of

the European representational arsenal to remain the ordered, natural 'whole' it would see itself as (Greenblatt 1988b: 19).

Whereas traditional historiography shows European culture developing from within itself, formulating new ways of dealing with its own internal problematics, Greenblatt's focus on wonder places an emphasis upon historical contingency. Events occur which disturb the integrity of the European imagination. While events can only be experienced from a particular cultural position which has *already* ordered and made the world meaningful, historical contingencies reveal to a culture the limits of its world. If, as Foucault's work makes clear, continuous histories fail to deal with the event – the breaks and discontinuities which are the stuff of history – then Greenblatt's use of 'wonder' provides a way of thinking beyond a linear and developmental history. Wonder reveals the limits and fragilities of a culture. It shows the dynamism and hybridity which characterise history and culture. Renaissance culture continually had to work to overcome the strangeness of the strange – whether this presented itself as the New World, the monstrous or the rebellious. Its dominant presentation of itself as an ordered whole necessitated a representational practice that continually recuperated all forms of otherness. However, the very process of recuperation can be evidenced in those texts which present, ostensibly, the coherent totality of the Renaissance world. If encountering the other evokes a sense of wonder, then the process of representational domestication which works to tame wonder can always be re-read in any text. (This is Greenblatt's project in *Marvelous Possessions* which focuses on the wonder of Renaissance travel literature.)

Consequently, new historicist readings seek neither to show that a text is revolutionary nor conservative. Texts are, rather, strategic; their processes of working upon the historically contingent are not left behind to leave a single and coherent meaning. On the contrary, the text is the document of a certain labour. Representational complexes have to be re-worked, re-ordered and renovated to cope with historical contingency or cultural alterity. But in such re-working the traces of this labour, the challenges to the given representational materials are still apparent. Greenblatt's reading of Dürer shows the vestiges of a comfortable signifying economy (the heroic valedictory column) coming to terms with a new historical event (the peasant rebellion). Because meaning is always dependent upon the cultural materials which allow it to take place (words, images, symbols, gestures), all attempts to make an event meaningful come up against the resistance of these materials. Wonder registers an event outside available forms of representation. While wonder is itself a

217

representation it is a representation which registers the limits of representation.

Greenblatt's theory of wonder takes as its explicit theme that which most new historicist readings presuppose: that texts are neither the reflection nor the effect of stable and static structures. Texts are, rather, forms of cultural labour which work upon heterogeneous materials from within received symbolic practices. To emphasise heterogeneity and hybridity does not necessarily demand a gesture toward some pure and pre-textual data. It is, on the contrary, to show that while all experiences are mediated through some form of representation, those representations work in dynamic systems of exchange. A language is something to be passed around and used; but in its travels it re-combines and meets with different uses. Wonder is one of those limit cases which reveals that while language may make a world and history possible it can never exhaust that world. It is through the Renaissance texts examined in *Marvelous Possessions* that we are given a sense of that which lies beyond Renaissance understanding. Wonder is ambiguous because it both registers radical difference at the same time that it prefigures the need to re-incorporate and make meaningful the event of wonder. Wonder is, then, that fleeting moment prior to discursive recuperation which is still only ever discursive. (Greenblatt 1988b: 20).

Greenblatt's emphasis upon the ineffability and radical otherness of wonder demonstrates both the historical changes in new historicist work, and the diversity of its theory and practice. From an early Foucaultianism which stressed the productive nature of power – and hence resisted any pure 'outside' to discourse – Greenblatt's work shifted towards the contradictory and contestatory forms of representation. Rather than seeing the Renaissance as dominated by a single representational network, of either 'power' or the individual, Greenblatt's work in *Shakespearean Negotiations* saw representation as a dynamic and contested process of circulation and exchange. The later emphasis upon wonder in *Marvelous Possessions* and 'Resonance and wonder' attempts to think through the exteriority which lies outside the system of representational exchange. In doing so Greenblatt departs from the earlier Foucaultian idea that power as discourse is productive of all forms of 'exteriority'. The transition from an emphasis upon power to an emphasis upon wonder is also marked by a shift in Greenblatt's focus and influences. Ideas of the 'other' are enabled by thinking through work in ethnography; representation as a social symbolic practice is theorised using various forms of social and anthropological and social theory.

The idea that wonder is that which resists recuperation – however fleetingly – perhaps returns us to all those notions of the unique and ineffable value of aesthetic works which recent forms of criticism have done so much to challenge. The fact that a notion like wonder runs directly against the 'discursive' arguments of Foucault's work demonstrates the ways in which Greenblatt's work uses, rather than remains faithful to, its theoretical sources. The contradictory nature of wonder – its mysterious and indefinable ability to resist domination and incorporation – can perhaps best be explained by looking at new historicism's critical relation to post-structuralism. This will be the subject of the final chapter.

10
Conclusion: new historicism and contemporary criticism

Although new historicism has often been seen as a reaction against the supposedly ahistorical character of post-structuralist criticism, it is also the case that new historicism's theoretically self-aware revision of historiography owes much to the insights of post-structuralism. The idea that new historicism provides a political grounding after the putative relativism of post-structuralism cannot be sustained once it is recognised that post-structuralism, at least in its Derridean form, has consistently demonstrated the *impossibility* of relativism. Post-structuralism is a demonstration of the 'play' of textual difference, but it is also an attention to the continual redetermination of play. New historicism may have initially appeared as an 'answer' to the interpretive insecurity precipitated by post-structuralist theories of textuality. But new historicism itself continually encountered the problem of its own legitimation. History in general could not be retrieved as some pre-textual ground so attention was directed to all those local devices and instances from which history was formed: anecdotes, artefacts, specific materials and contingent events. While new historicism proceeded with the recognition that history was itself already textually determined, it also attempted to grasp some non-textual exteriority – power, culture, wonder, materiality, specificity – in order to enable historical interpretation. The textualisation of history, as well as an attempt to think beyond history as text, is perhaps the clearest identifying feature of new historicism. Greenblatt's theorisation of wonder, as that which resists discursive recuperation, is exemplary of the ways in which new historicism, rather than being an 'overcoming' of post-structuralism, encounters the same problems. This chapter examines new historicism's relation to post-structuralist literary theory in order to explain the common concern with the limit of representation.

From new criticism to post-structuralism

In many ways, literary criticism in the United States has been dominated by the movement of new criticism which emerged in the 1930s. Even those theoretical movements which might ostensibly appear to be entirely antithetical to new criticism can still be seen to bear the marks of new criticism's continued influence. American post-structuralism is perhaps the best example of the ways in which new criticism has continued to exert its power over literary criticism in the United States.

New criticism was formed in the 1930s and 40s as a self-consciously rigorous reaction against traditional literary scholarship which had been concerned with evaluation, biography and the annotation of sources and influence. New criticism's two central arguments – against the 'intentional fallacy' and the 'affective fallacy' – served to isolate the text which was no longer seen as a sign of something else (such as intention, expression, history or feeling). The text was, rather, a self-contained object with its own meaning, form and function. The 'intentional fallacy', according to Wimsatt and Beardsley (1946 and 1949), lay in confusing a text's meaning with what was going on inside the author's mind. Against the idea that the author's life, thought or circumstances should be the object of literary criticism, Wimsatt and Beardsley argued that a text's meaning could (and should) be determined without reference to the external circumstances of the text's creation. One would not study Emily Dickinson's poetry by referring to Dickinson's religious beliefs, her isolation, or her other works (either literary or non-literary). On the contrary, the text was to be considered only in relation to itself. Individual units of the text were seen in relation to each other in terms of 'tension', 'paradox', or 'irony'.

Similarly, the argument against the 'affective fallacy' proceeded by rejecting the relevance of the reader's emotional response when assessing the meaning of a text. To describe a poem's affect (the ability, say, to move a reader to tears) had nothing to do with the text's meaning. Once again, it was argued that the text should be seen as an autonomous object rather than an act of communication or the expression of feeling. Cleanth Brooks's (1947) description of the text as a 'well-wrought urn' or W. K. Wimsatt's (1954) idea of the 'verbal icon' aptly illustrate the extent to which texts were considered to be like objects of fine art which were self-contained, autonomous and non-referential. Such criticism was formalist; it considered the text itself in terms of its own form and did not refer to extraneous phenomena (other texts, the author, history or readers).

221

New criticism was not just a literary critical theory; it was also, in many ways, a moral programme. At the heart of new criticism was an attempt to resist reducing literature to any values other than those of literature itself. Literature, it was argued, had its own edifying power; the study of literature would cultivate sensitivity, awareness and refined sensibility. A text was not a historical document, nor was it a window into an author's mind; even less was it an object of pleasure or feeling which existed to produce a certain effect. In so far as texts were irreducible and autonomous wholes, the study of literature had to be seen as an end in itself. The function of criticism would not be to discover some historical or authorial meaning or referent. If literature were not to be reduced to history, expression or mere pleasure it would have to have its own specifically literary value. For the new critics this value lay in the heightened awareness that the particularly non-referential use of language in literature provided. Not surprisingly, poetry was the favoured genre of new criticism as it demonstrated more clearly than drama or prose fiction the non-referential power of literary works.

While there were many challenges to American new criticism throughout the twentieth century – forms of feminism, reader response criticism and Marxism – certain motifs of new criticism still operate in many of the most trenchant anti-formalist theories in the United States. Post-structuralism in its American form sustained, at the same time as it problematised, many of the formalist inclinations of new criticism. At the centre of American post-structuralist literary criticism was Jacques Derrida, whose work was interpreted, expanded and disseminated by critics of the Yale school – Paul de Man, Barbara Johnson, Geoffrey Hartman and J. Hillis Miller. While an extended consideration of American post-structuralism lies outside the domain of this study, it is worth noting some of the more significant transformations made to Derrida's 'deconstruction' through its importation into the United States.

At its broadest level post-structuralism worked as a radicalisation of structuralism. Saussure's structuralist linguistics argued that language was a system of signs and that no individual unit of language could have meaning without being defined against all the other units in the language. Language was not a collection of names for a pre-given and already-meaningful reality. On the contrary, language was a system of differences; meaning was an effect of the divisions made by language. Structuralism could, then, be seen as another mode of formalism. A text was not to be considered in regard to its world or referent, but as a set of relations. However, the radicalisation of structuralism in post-structuralism broke open the 'closure' of this structuralist paradigm of language as a delimited system of signs.

If, as Saussure had argued, language works by differences, then no sign could be meaningful in itself. Derrida's radicalisation of this insight lay in asking *how the system of differences itself was possible*. If the meaning of a sign can never be self-present, because meaning is an effect of the entire system, then the system will always exceed or go beyond any act of analysis or interpretation. In so far as the structure is a field of differences it must be a consequence of a differential production. But because this differential production produces the structure it can never be known or experienced from within the structure. Derrida refers to this radically anterior production of difference or structure in a number of ways: trace, *différance*, *écriture*, supplement, untamed genesis, etc. If structuralism posited the idea of a system of signs as an objectivist gesture which would enable an almost scientific consideration of language as a closed system of signs, Derrida's deconstruction exploded that closure by asking the question of the 'structurality of structure' (1978b: 163). Most importantly, Derrida's critique of structural totalities precluded the possibility of any general account of meaning. Any term – such as culture, history, representation or structure – was already itself an effect of structural difference and could not locate itself in some transcendental 'outside' from which it could exhaustively explain difference. However, the abandoning of general explanations is equally impossible. In so far as we offer any meaningful statement or explanation we draw upon the force of conceptual generality; relativism or complete indeterminacy is impossible. Consequently, for Derrida metaphysics – general truth claims – is a necessary impossibility.

While the consequences of the deconstruction of structuralist closure led to the *undecidability* of a text's meaning, they did not lead to relativism. To say that the text's meaning can never be finally secured and self-present is not to say that a text can mean anything at all. In fact, Derrida has been a tireless critic of those who misread his work. The point of deconstruction is not that a text can have just any meaning. Rather, Derrida's deconstruction works by showing that any text, as a system of signs, will always have to be based on a certain determination which, because it produces the text, cannot be exhaustively known by the text itself. This determination will remain, then, necessarily undecideable (1988: 148).

Derrida has insisted upon the ethical force of deconstruction by demonstrating the ways in which considerations of the text's limits will always open any text or statement for ethical consideration; for the text will always be the effect of a specific determination and cannot have any transcendental authority. Despite this insistence, post-structuralism – particularly in the United States – has been seen to harbour an apolitical, ahistorical and dangerously conservative relativism. Many critics have taken deconstruction's demonstration that no text can be exhaustively determined to mean that no meaning is possible and that all moral claims are unsustainable (Lehman 1991). In order to see how this criticism is made it is worth considering the American version of post-structuralist ethics.

The most explicit American defence of post-structuralism as an ethical enterprise is J. Hillis Miller's *The Ethics of Reading* (1987). According to Miller, because a text's meaning is itself radically undecidable, every act of reading will have to proceed by deciding the meaning of the text. Because the burden of decision is shifted away from the text and back to the reader, reading becomes an ethical task; it consists of freely-chosen and undetermined decisions. Because a truly *ethical* decision is not motivated by a desire for pleasure or profit and cannot be forced or prompted, the free and undetermined act of reading provides a paradigm for all those ethical decisions which, necessarily, take place in a field of undecidability. Because texts are themselves undecidable, but are then determined in any act of reading, reading provides the model of ethical thinking. Literary texts, in so far as they foreground textual undecidability, are for Miller the epitome of ethical practice.

Furthermore, narrative or storytelling is also seen by Miller as essential to ethics because it is the free and unmotivated creation of stories which demonstrates the ethical faculty *par excellence* – choice. Narrative is a demonstration of specificity and particularity. There can be no general or universal ethical law which is not demonstrated or given in a particular instance. While ethics cannot be reduced to any particular statement of the law, it can only ever be articulated within a specific and local statement. Narrative gives an account of the ethical law at the same time as it points to narrative's inability to fully exhaust the law:

> Storytelling is the impurity which is necessary in any discourse about the moral law as such, in spite of the laws's austere indifference to persons, stories, and history. There is no theory of ethics, no theory of the moral law and of its irresistible, stringent imperative, its 'Thou shalt' and 'Thou shalt not', without storytelling and the temporalization (in several sense of the word) which is an intrinsic feature of all narrative. (Miller 1987: 23)

From all this it follows that what makes a literary text important, or literary, is what *exceeds* the social and historical determinants of a text. The text's literary value lies in the undecidable 'ethical moment' (the freedom which precludes the text from being decidable, determined or lawfully secured). And the foregrounding of the freedom of reading (as free inter-pretation) awakens the reader to ethics in general. It is this freedom which resists the inclusion of a text within a historical or political context:

> This ethical 'I must' cannot, I propose to show, be accounted for by the social and historical forces that impinge upon it. In fact the ethical moment contests these forces or is subversive of them. The ethical moment, in all four of its dimensions [author, narrator, characters, reader], is genuinely productive and inaugural in its effects on history. (Miller 1987: 8–9).

The ethics of a text, on this picture, is not to be found in its content (its ideology, discourse or representational effect); in fact, the text itself is eth-ical precisely because what it means remains undecidable until deter-mined through the act of reading. If undecidability is seen by Miller to be the very essence of the ethical, it is also the case that post-structuralism's foregrounding of undecidability was more frequently interpreted as a retreat from ethics, politics and history. For all its radical claims, it was argued, post-structuralism was just another form of closed formalism (Lentricchia, 1980: 180–3). Not surprisingly, the way out of this formal-ist dead-end was seen to be a reconsideration of history. For it was not only deconstruction in its highly theoretical Yale School formulation which was subjected to the charge of ahistorical conservativism. Post-structural-ist Marxists – such as Fredric Jameson – and the postmodern theory of Jean-Francois Lyotard were also seen as having failed to consider the spe-cific historical circumstances of textual production. This is, in fact, the charge that Stephen Greenblatt levels against Jameson and Lyotard in 'Towards a poetics of culture' (1989).

According to Greenblatt, no general theory, neither Jameson's critique of capitalism as atomising nor Lyotard's picture of totalisation, can account for the contradictory, particular and historically specific features of capi-talism. In this sense Greenblatt's new historicism can be seen as a 'return' to history and historical particulars. But if new historicism demands a more historical and local account of texts in contrast to the general theo-ries of meaning offered by post-structuralist philosophy, it is also the case that the 'new' of new historicism marks a certain critique of traditional historicism which owes much to post-structuralism. We have already seen how Foucault's reaction against nineteenth-century historiography has enabled a more critical historical methodology. New historicism also bears a complex and contradictory relationship to the work of Derrida and post-structuralism in general.

New historicism and post-structuralism

Like Foucault, Derrida's early work was concerned with the question of historicism and (again like Foucault but in different ways) this early work was concerned with the critique of historicism in favour of a more radical historicity (Derrida 1989). But it was not the anti-historicist aspect of Derrida's work which marked the theoretical self-awareness of new historicism. In fact, Derrida's critique of historicism is at odds with some of new historicism's most consistent features. (We will return to this point later.)

If post-structuralism did have a positive bearing on the revival of historical studies it lay in the problematisation of the relations between the literary (considered as purely 'fictive') and other texts or events which were granted a greater authority or reality. Both Greenblatt and Montrose have invoked post-structuralism as an important factor in breaking down the division between literary and non-literary texts. For Montrose, the consequences of this questioning of boundaries enabled a move away from formalism towards 'the historicity of texts and the textuality of history' (Montrose 1986: 8). For Greenblatt (1990) the post-structuralist critique of the distinction between literary and non-literary texts led to 'an intensified willingness to read all of the textual traces of the past with the attention traditionally conferred only on literary texts'. At the same time, both Greenblatt and Montrose expressed anxieties about the supposedly overly-formalist character of post-structuralism. While acknowledging the value of the questioning of the division between literature and history, Greenblatt also wants to maintain the referential character of historical texts. While they should be read as literary texts, historical texts should also be seen as significantly different from those texts: this difference 'fundamentally alters our mode of reading texts and changes our ethical position' (Greenblatt 1990: 15). For Greenblatt:

> The traditional paradigms for the uses of history and the interpretation of texts have eroded – this is a time in which it will not do to invoke the same pathetically narrow repertoire of dogmatic explanations – but any history and any general textual interpretation worth doing will have to speak to this difference. (Greenblatt 1990: 15)

Similarly, Louis Montrose, following Frank Lentricchia's argument against 'the antihistorical impulses of formalist theories of literary criticism', situates his own work against 'various structuralist and post-structuralist formalisms that have seemed, to some, to put into question the very possibility of historical understanding' (Montrose 1986: 5).

The association of post-structuralism with antihistoricism is not surprising if we consider Miller's particular version of post-structuralism and
its invective against historicist reading. Of course, post-structuralism in
general cannot be equated with either formalism or antihistoricism. Derrida has frequently argued that his statement, 'There is nothing outside the
text', refers to the pervasiveness of textuality and not the absence of the
world or a reality outside the text considered in the narrow sense. Furthermore, much of Derrida's recent work has also reinvigorated the question of historicity (Derrida 1994). There have, in fact, been many
convincing attempts to mark important differences between the work of
Derrida and a certain American appropriation of his work (Nealon 1992;
Norris 1985). Indeed, Derrida's early and recent critiques of historicism
sought to think of a radical historicity which could not be reduced to the
representations or discourses of conventional historiography. Derrida's
work demonstrated that any writing of history would involve general
repeatable or meaningful concepts: history would, therefore, always miss
the historicity of the event. Once the event was historically represented it
would become part of the writing of history and lose its temporal specificity (Derrida 1978a: 61).

While new historicism's appeal to history has tried to avoid any totalising use of concepts such as 'world-view', 'era' or 'mind-set', it has relied
on the notion of representation as an almost fundamental given of human
experience. The notion of representation is used to show the ways that
cultures form or represent themselves; to focus on representation is, as we
have seen, to refuse to accept any culture as a simple and given object, but
to see its production as a process of self-creation (through self-representation). Historical enquiry, in dealing with such productive and dynamic
representations, is also aware of its own acts of representation. To the
extent that new historicism concerns itself with representation, it brackets
any questions of an originary presence which would be the basis for subsequent re-presentation. There are no pre-cultural facts which a culture
then goes on to clothe in representation; cultural analysis is not a practice
of decoding or demystifying a symbolic logic. On the contrary, representations are seen to produce or present a reality which is already representational.

This problematisation of the origin owes much to post-structuralist
theory. If an event is to be experienced as meaningful it must be considered in terms of some idea, concept or representation; but such an idea or
concept, in so far as it makes sense and must be applicable in more than
one instance, must always miss the unique specificity of the event. To

227

experience an event as, say, a 'revolution' I must have some idea of what a revolution is; but I can only have that idea through past experience or some general concept which covers more than one case. The first or 'originary' event would only be understood as a 'revolution' in terms of a subsequent event. The 'origin' would, then, be an effect of the second time, or an effect of re-presentation.

But if to focus entirely on representation/re-presentation is to acknowledge post-structuralism's problematisation of the origin, it is also to abandon some of the force of post-structuralism's critique of historicism. Much of the critical power of Derrida's work lay in demonstrating that the iterability (or repeatability) of any representation would already miss the historicity or 'untamed genesis' of any event (Derrida 1978b). In his early essay on Foucault, Derrida argued that any attempt to write a history was also an exercise in representation. History was inextricably intertwined with the Western metaphysics of presence whereby everything that is is thought in terms of its meaning or re-presentation for a self-present subject (Derrida 1978a). Against the historicism of re-presentation Derrida called for a more radical sense of historicity, a historicity which would not be exhausted by historical representation. In the work which followed *Madness and Civilization* (1970) Foucault himself also embarked on a critique of historicism. History could not be seen as some final ground of human life; the practice of historicism was itself a part of modernity's project of humanist self-understanding. In ways quite different from Derrida's call to think a more radical historicity, Foucault posited the notion of positivity. Historicism was a positive fact of our modern existence which could not be recuperated in a final moment of trans-historical self-understanding and self-representation. To see that the movement of historicism was itself a historically specific phenomenon did not mean that we could step outside historical understanding in a moment of transcendental understanding. To accept historicism as itself a fact of history is to accept the 'positivity' of our being – our always-specific and particular location.

Derrida's critique of historicism took another tack. By demanding that we think the limit or event of any historical representation, Derridean post-structuralism remained (critically) within the modern enterprise of thinking the systemic ground or condition of any event. While a pure representation of this condition was impossible, the question of the condition should still be asked – precisely because only this question would reveal the limit or the event of thinking. Derrida sets himself against Foucault's historicisation of reason by arguing that the question of reason – the question of the general condition which enables any event – must be asked. The necessity of this question follows, Derrida argues, because all texts are already metaphysical. Whatever attempt we make to grasp a pure particular or event is always conceptually determined. History cannot be outside reason because history itself is a meaningful concept. We cannot step outside history but only solicit its structures from within. The task of thinking the event, that which exceeds historical representation, characterises Derrida's work. His interventions in the history of philosophy have focused on marginal instances – such as metaphors, errors, ambiguities and the framing of utterances – to show that any determination of context is the effect of a certain decision. By attending to those devices which delimit a context we also attend to that exteriority or 'abyss' beyond the limit, even if this is only perceivable through the limit. To this extent his work might seem to overlap with new historicist attention to the contingent events and marginal cases of literary history. There is, however, an important difference which can be identified in Derrida's assertion of the theoretical imperative. We cannot, he argues, just attend to the specific and material circumstances which enable any general theory. A theory will always be 'contaminated' by the particular circumstances of its utterance; but any focus on this particularity will also always be a theory. A clear example is given in his theory of the frame or *parergon*. A text or work – any meaningful item – has to have its meaning determined. Meaning, therefore, has a prior condition. In the case of the work of art, there has to be a frame which delimits the work, enables its reading *as* a work and delimits its context. The frame itself then has a productive effect in producing meaning. From this, however, we cannot conclude – as new historicism might – that we can just attend to the local and particular instances of 'framing' which make a text possible. For any description of the frame is itself an act of framing which determines the frame as a frame. And for Derrida it is necessary to ask the question of the condition for any posited condition, such as framing, history or representation:

> No 'theory,' no 'practice,' no 'theoretical practice' can intervene effectively in this field if it does not weigh up and bear on the frame, which is the decisive structure of what is at stake, at the invisible limit to (between) the interiority of meaning (put under shelter by the whole hermeneuticist, semioticist, phenomenologicalist, and formalist tradition) *and* (to) all the empiricisms of the extrinsic which, incapable of either seeing or reading, miss the question completely. (Derrida 1987: 61)

Because we can have neither a pure theory nor an empiricism of particulars, Derrida employs a double method which asks the question of the condition, frame or context of any text at the same time as it reveals that condition to be itself the effect of a condition, an abyssal framing. But the attention to this condition or frame is precisely what enables the sense of the event of that which exceeds framing.

In his recent work, Stephen Greenblatt has suggested that it is just such a concern for exteriority which has come to occupy his attention. If we return to the concepts of 'resonance' and 'wonder' we can see how this question of what precedes representation is played out. Like Derrida and other post-Saussurean theorists, Greenblatt recognises that meaning can only be an effect of both difference and repeatability. His use of economic tropes (such as 'negotiation', 'exchange', 'circulation' and 'capital') shows how signs work in an economy: a differential system of relative values. There is no meaning without an entire system: just as monetary values are determined relationally, so language is a system which creates or produces concepts by marking differences. Similarly, ideas of circulation and negotiation also show that meaning is an effect of repeated exchange. If monetary values only work by their use as exchanged tokens, it is also the case that language only *means* because of its repeatability. Although Greenblatt's use of 'resonance' is not an economic metaphor it, too, refers to repeatability; the meaning generated through resonance is an effect of repeatability and exchange. Resonance characterises the representation as such, as a re-presentation.

But Greenblatt also emphasises the extent to which repeated use also alters the meaning of any sign: in doing so he draws attention to that which differs from the sign's present or original meaning (Greenblatt 1990: 163). And so, resisting the closure of conventional historiography, Greenblatt argues that new historicism focuses on what lies outside traditional historical representation:

> Traditional formalism and historicism, twin legacies of early nineteenth-century Germany, shared a vision of high culture as a harmonizing domain of reconciliation based upon an aesthetic labor that transcends specific economic or political determinants. What is missing is psychic, social, and material resistance, a stubborn, unassimilable otherness, a sense of distance and difference. (Greenblatt 1990: 169)

While Greenblatt's new historicism is concerned with resonance – the ways in which the meanings of the present are created by the repetition of signs from the past (Greenblatt 1990: 170) – it is also concerned with the event which precedes resonance, and the openness of resonance to changes in meaning. The historical object's meaning becomes dynamic.

The present culture is an effect of the circulation of signs; if criticism focuses not just on the meaning of those signs, but on the process and production of that meaning, then the contingency, or historicity, of history may be restored:

> For the effect of resonance does not necessarily depend upon a collapse of the distinction between art and non-art; it can be achieved by awakening in the viewer a sense of the cultural and historically contingent construction of art objects, the negotiations, exchanges, swerves, exclusions by which certain representational practices come to be set apart from other representational practices that they partially resemble. (Greenblatt 1990: 172)

Greenblatt's notion of 'wonder', then, might be considered as a way of thinking the exterior or outside of representation. Whereas the dynamic concept of resonance acknowledges that no sign is stable (because any use or exchange will always effect or differ from the original meaning), wonder attempts to think the outside of representation more radically. For Greenblatt no sign or object can exhaust its origin – to this extent he would be in accord with the post-structuralist refusal to reduce the 'event' to its representation. But Greenblatt's concept of wonder which is 'partly independent' of the economy of representation returns us to an origin of feeling or experience. Speaking of the work of Dürer he writes:

> It would be misleading to strip away the relations of power and wealth that are encoded in the artist's response, but it would be still more misleading, I think, to interpret that response as an unmediated expression of those relations. For Dürer gives voice to an aesthetic understanding – a form of wondering and admiring and knowing – that is at least partly independent of the structures of politics and the marketplace. (Greenblatt 1990: 179)

Greenblatt's confidence that what lies outside resonance and representation can be experienced and named as 'wonder' runs against the post-structuralist argument that meaning and experience are effects of difference and repetition. Derrida always refers to the condition or origin of representation as a 'non-origin' and argues that any such condition would have to be radically anterior to experience, because it produces and enables experience. Derrida, therefore, gives a variety of names to anteriority or exteriority: trace, écriture, différance (which is 'not a concept'), the supplement, etc. Similarly, Foucault's critique of the idea of origin acknowledged that there could be no experience or knowledge of the conditions of discourse or representation. Unlike Derrida, Foucault did not posit a radical anteriority; he argued that we accept our position within discourse, accept that positivity and give up the search for transcendental conditions. Rather than problematise or solicit the logic of conditions – as do both Derrida and Greenblatt – Foucault suggests that we start to ask different questions. His own work in the later volumes of *The History of Sexuality* represents just such an attempt: to think of selves not in terms of their intentional horizons but as located within practices. New historicism in its early form, which explored modes of historical interpretation without theorising the general condition of such interpretive manoeuvres, might be likened to the Foucaultian enterprise of not asking transcendental questions. But Foucault still set himself the task of 'thinking otherwise' and as a result, not surprisingly, often suggested that there were certain 'limit' experiences (such as avante-garde literature or desire) which might dislodge us from our anthropological sleep. As long as the theoretical terrain occupies itself with the notion of a limit it is likely that it will sustain the problem of 'exteriority'. The trajectory of Greenblatt's own thought – from a concern with power and representation to wonder – demonstrates that it is perhaps the question of the event as such which sustains the problems of system, condition and origin. Greenblatt's later idea of 'wonder' as an experienced and meaningful origin or presence runs counter to his own post-structuralist use of economic tropes and his focus on the power of representation. Wonder functions as an ineffable 'other' to representation at the same time that wonder is seen as experienceable, present and representable:

> Someone witnesses something amazing, but what most matters takes place not 'out there' or along the receptive surfaces of the body where the self encounters the world, but deep within, at the vital, emotional center of the witness. This inward experience cannot be marginalized or denied; wonder is absolutely exigent, a primary or radical passion. (Greenblatt 1988b: 17)

The point of questioning Greenblatt's use of wonder is not to suggest that he ought to have been more faithful to his post-structuralist influences. On the contrary, perhaps notions like 'wonder' (which attempt to think the limit of representational closure) should lead us to question the premises of closure itself. The concern which has dominated all the approaches considered in this study – how to interpret the other without incorporation in one's own paradigm of understanding – has led to an increasingly intensified scrutiny on the limits and conditions of experience. The attempt to explain the conditions for cultural meaning refer to a number of terms – culture, discourse, symbolic exchange, power, representation, difference – only to then recognise that no such term could remain undetermined by that which it seeks to explain. The condition which supposedly explains experience is itself seen to be conditioned. The attempt to think beyond this condition yields a number of responses: from de Certeau's invocation of silent history to Greenblatt's wonder. There is also an attempt to refuse to think any grounding condition: from Geertz's avoidance of the question of how culture itself might be culturally located to Belsey's assertion that her position 'proves nothing'.

If Greenblatt's early work in *Renaissance Self-Fashioning* concerned itself with power and the dominance of representations in the production of power, then his latest work shifts towards that wonder which lies outside or before representation and the structures of power. The motivation for this shift can be understood, at least in part, as a similar concern with the exteriority or anteriority of representation which sustains post-structuralist critique. At the same time, however, the argument that this exteriority is the irreducible 'primary or radical passion' of wonder would seem to return us to the domain of sensibility and response which was at the heart of the old new criticism. While Greenblatt's new historicism resists the reduction of the text or object of art to historical resonance; it does so by returning to a notion of feeling which, in so far as it resists the structures of political and semantic economy, provides that aesthetic autonomy so cherished by the new critics.

The newness of new historicism lies in its critical force: its refusal to see the text as a sign of some prior and stable context; its refusal to see history as a single and coherent line of progress; its acceptance of the literary historian's own position within the historical narrative he or she charts; and in its emphasis on the dynamic and productive character of representation. Foucault's concept of genealogy and the productive nature of power, de Certeau's argument that texts are actively consumed and that historiography itself is an effective practice, Bourdieu's demonstration that representations are bearers of symbolic value, as well as an emphasis on culture, cultural difference and cultural production: all these theoretical moves have enabled a problematisation of traditional literary studies and literary history. At the same time, it would be inappropriate to think of these recent developments as a final demystification of conventional historiographical blindnesses. Greenblatt's use of 'wonder' and the problems it harbours leave the question of history and its relation to representation as contentious and open as ever. If wonder has returned us to something like the new critical valorisation of the independent experience of the aesthetic object, it has also raised the question of the possibility of thinking otherwise: towards a possible other of both historicism and formalism.

For it is perhaps only with the premises of historicism – however critically adopted – that we arrive at the position of interpretive closure which then forces us to think the (impossible) limit of that closure. Only if we accept that meaning and culture is produced though conditions and limits (cultural, historical, representational) do we then have the problem of interpreting that limit. The Marxist problem of surmounting ideology, the feminist obstacle of patriarchy, and the idea that experience is bounded by the structures of meaning all depend upon locating the givenness of the world *within some other condition* which it is the task of the critic to interpret. Perhaps the aim should not be to think of some condition – such as wonder, representation, discourse or culture – which would both enable and undermine the task of explanation through general conditions. What new historicism as a literary critical movement has revealed is the rhetorical specificity of any text or interpretation. This explains why new historicism proceeded for so long without developing an autonomous body of theoretical justification. The 1970s, on the other hand, provided the opposite paradigm; there were no shortage of books written in English departments on Derridean philosophy but when these theories were occasionally 'applied' what they yielded was a demonstration of the 'truth' of this philosophy through a reading of literary texts. There was a clear case of disciplinary subordination whereby the philosophical claims were accepted and then demonstrated through reading. Literary theory was more theory than literature and concerned itself with general problems of how meaning is possible. J. Hillis Miller's *The Ethics of Reading* is a theory about reading and meaning in general. The claims Miller makes for his cited authors (Trollope, Eliot, Kant and James) by the logic of his own argument apply to any text. New historicism, on the other hand, has largely been literary critical. Renaissance power, a text's peculiar circumstances, performance procedures and other contingent factors have been objects of interpretive labour. The theory of this movement then argued for the value of particular considerations of general definitions and theoretical foundations. At the same time, new historicism was also – despite its claims for interpetive specificity – articulating general concerns about power, subjectivity and representation.

The problem of new historicism is the problem of literary theory itself. What Greenblatt's use of 'wonder' demonstrates is that any theory of particulars is still a theory and to that extent will always have determined the particular in advance. The literary critical enterprise – to read the text and to be open to the text rather than repeating one's own meaning and assumptions – implies, however, that whatever our theory may be, the point of *reading* is not to confirm our theory but to read something other. What we may need to question is the enterprise of theories of cultural or historical specificity which have been shown to be so problematic in all the approaches considered in this study. There has been a continual project of overcoming the notion that cultures are rule-bound totalities, coherent systems or organised wholes. But perhaps what needs to be challenged is not the character of social organisation but the notion of the *cultural and historical* limit itself.

Foucault's history of historicism in *The Order of Things* suggested that this particular problem of interpretation and finitude was peculiar to modernity. Only if we accept that human life occurs as finite within an infinite horizon – such as history or culture – are we left with the problem of the closure and interpretation of that horizon. Nineteenth-century historicism with its assertion of epochs and world-views would be the starting point, rather than the radical other, of theories of culture, ideology and interpretive limits. This is not to say that theories of historicism are incorrect; but that other approaches might be possible. New historicism's *ad hoc* procedure of reading, its attention to contiguity and circumstance is perhaps the best strategy literary criticism has produced to disrupt the notions of general interpretive horizons, limits and justifications. Only when we ask the *condition* for this procedure are we then obliged to offer a term, like wonder, which immediately undermines the critically effective force of the attention to particulars. Thought from this perspective we can see that the task of literary theory – of asking how meaning and reading are possible – both produces the limit of meaning and the terms, like wonder, which try to think beyond that limit.

References

Abrams, M. H. (1971), *Natural Supernaturalism: Tradition and Revolution in Romantic Literature*, New York, Norton.

Addison, J. (1773), 'An account of the greatest English poets', in *The Poetical Works of the Right Honourable Joseph Addison, Esq.* Edinburgh.

Althusser, L. (1971), 'Ideology and ideological state apparatuses', in *Lenin and Philosophy and Other Essays*, trans. B. Brewster, London, New Left Books.

Anderson, P. (1977), 'The antinomies of Antonio Gramsci', *New Left Review*, 100, 5–78.

Bakhtin, M. (1984), *Rabelais and His World*, trans. H. Iswolsky, Bloomington, Indiana University Press.

Baldick, C. (1983), *The Social Mission of English Criticism: 1848–1932*, Oxford, Clarendon.

Barker, F. (1984), *The Tremulous Private Body: Essays on Subjection*, London, Methuen.

Belsey, C. (1980), *Critical Practice*, London, Methuen.

——(1984), 'The politics of meaning', in *Confronting the Crisis: War, Politics and Culture in the Eighties*, ed. F. Barker, P. Hulme and D. Loxley, Colchester, University of Essex.

——(1986), 'The romantic construction of the unconscious', in *Literature, Politics and Theory: Papers from the Essex Conference: 1976–84*, ed. F. Barker, P. Hulme, M. Iversen and D. Loxley, London, Methuen.

——(1988), *John Milton: Language, Gender, Power*, Oxford, Basil Blackwell.

——(1989), 'Towards cultural history – in theory and practice', *Textual Practice*, 3.2, 159–72.

——(1991), 'Making histories then and now: Shakespeare from *Richard II* to *Henry V*', in *Uses of History: Marxism, Postmodernism and the Renaissance*, ed. F. Barker, P. Hulme and M. Iversen, Manchester, Manchester University Press.

——(1994), *Desire: Love Stories in Western Culture*, Oxford, Blackwell.

Blake, W. (1966), *Complete Writings*, ed. G. Keynes, Oxford, Oxford University Press.

——(1975), *The Marriage of Heaven and Hell*, ed. G. Keynes, London, Oxford University Press.

Blanchot, M. (1982), *The Space of Literature*, trans. Ann Smock, Lincoln, University of Nebraska Press.

Bloom, H. (1973), *The Anxiety of Influence*, Oxford, Oxford University Press.

——(1976), *Poetry and Repression: Revisionism from Blake to Stevens*, New Haven, Yale University Press.

Bourdieu P. (1977), *Outline of a Theory of Practice*, trans. R. Nice, Cambridge, Cambridge University Press.

——(1983), 'The philosophical establishment', in *Philosophy in France Today*, ed. A. Montefiore, Cambridge, Cambridge University Press.

——(1985), 'The market of symbolic goods', *Poetics*, 14, 13–44.

——(1990), *The Logic of Practice*, trans. R. Nice, Cambridge, Polity.

——(1991), *The Political Ontology of Martin Heidegger*, trans. P. Collier, Cambridge, Polity.

——(1993), *The Field of Cultural Production: Essays on Art and Literature*, ed. R. Johnson, Cambridge, Polity.

Brooks, C. (1947), *The Well Wrought Urn: Studies in the Structure of Poetry*, New York, Harcourt, Brace and World.

Butler, J. (1993), *Bodies That Matter: On the Discursive Limits of 'Sex'*, New York, Routledge.

Camus, A. (1957), *L'Etranger*, Paris, Gallimard.

Certeau, M. de., (1984), *The Practice of Everyday Life*, trans. S. Randall, Berkeley, University of California Press.

——(1988), *The Writing of History*, trans. T. Conley, New York, Columbia.

——(1991), 'Travel narratives of the French to Brazil: sixteenth to eighteenth centuries', trans. K. Streip, *Representations*, 33, 221–6.

Clifford, J. (1986a), 'Introduction', in *Writing Culture: The Poetics and Politics of Ethnography*, ed. J. Clifford and G. E. Marcus, Berkeley, University of California Press.

——(1986b), 'On ethnographic allegory', in *Writing Culture: The Poetics and Politics of Ethnography*, ed. J. Clifford and G. E. Marcus, Berkeley, University of California Press.

Colebrook, C. (1994), 'The end of redemption and the redemption of ends: apocalypse and enlightenment in Blake's prophecies', *Southern Review*, 27, 79–92.

Cooper, J. F. (1826), *The Last of the Mohicans: A Narrative of 1757*, Albany, State University of New York Press 1983.

Creed, B. (1993), *The Monstrous Feminine: Film, Feminism, Psychoanalysis*. London, Routledge.

Crosby, C. (1992), 'Dealing with differences', in *Feminists Theorise the Political*, ed. J. Butler and J. W. Scott, New York, Routledge.

Danielson, D. (1982), *Milton's Good God: A Study in Literary Theodicy*, Cambridge, Cambridge University Press.

Davis, L. J. (1983), *Factual Fictions: The Origins of the English Novel*, New York, Columbia.

Deleuze, G. and Guattari, F. (1986), *Kafka: Toward a Minor Literature*, trans. D. Polan, Minneapolis, University of Minnesota Press.

——(1994), *What is Philosophy?*, trans. G. Burchell and H. Tomlinson, London, Verso.

Derrida, J. (1978a), 'Cogito and the history of madness', in *Writing and Difference*, trans. A. Bass, London, Routledge.

——(1978b), 'Genesis and structure' and phenomenology, in *Writing and Difference*, trans. A. Bass, London, Routledge.

——(1987), *The Truth in Painting*, trans. G. Bennington and I. McLeod, Chicago, University of Chicago Press.

——(1988), 'Afterword: toward an ethic of discussion', in *Limited Inc.*, trans. S. Weber, Evanston, Northwestern University Press.

——(1989), *Edmund Husserl's Origin of Geometry: An Introduction*, trans. J. P. Leavey, Lincoln, University of Nebraska Press.

——(1994), *Specters of Marx: The State of Debt, the Work of Mourning and the New International*, trans. P. Kamuf, New York, Routledge.

Descombes, V. (1980), *Modern French Philosophy*, Cambridge, Cambridge University Press.

Dilthey, W. (1976), *Selected Writings*, Cambridge, Cambridge University Press.

Dollimore, J. (1984), *Radical Tragedy: Religion, Ideology and Power in the Drama of Shakespeare and his*

Contemporaries, Chicago, University of Chicago Press.

——(1985a), 'Introduction: Shakespeare, cultural materialism and the new historicism', in *Political Shakespeare: New Essays in Cultural Materialism*, ed. J. Dollimore and A. Sinfield, Ithaca, Cornell.

——(1985b), 'Transgression and surveillance' in *Measure for Measure*, in *Political Shakespeare: New Essays in Cultural Materialism*, ed. J. Dollimore and A. Sinfield, Ithaca: Cornell.

——(1990), 'The cultural politics of perversion: Augustine, Shakespeare, Freud, Foucault', *Textual Practice*, 4.1, 170–96.

——(1991), *Sexual Dissidence*, Oxford, Clarendon.

Dollimore, J. and Sinfield, A. (1985), 'History and ideology: the instance of *Henry V*', in *Alternative Shakespeares*, ed. J. Drakakis, London, Methuen.

——(1990), 'Culture and textuality: debating cultural materialism', *Textual Practice*, 4, 91–9.

Douglas, M. (1966), *Purity and Danger: An Analysis of Concepts of Pollution and Taboo*, London, Routledge.

Dreiser, T. (1965), *Sister Carrie*, London, Oxford University Press.

Dummett, M. (1993), *Origins of Analytic Philosophy*, London, Duckworth.

Dumont, L. (1988), *Essays on Individualism: Modern Ideology in Anthropological Perspective*, Chicago, University of Chicago Press.

Eagleton, T. (1976a), 'Criticism and politics: the work of Raymond Williams', *New Left Review*, 95, 3–23.

——(1976b), *Criticism and Ideology: A Study in Marxist Theory*, London, New Left Books.

Easthope, A. (1983), *Poetry as Discourse*, London, Methuen.

——(1993), *Wordsworth Now and Then: Romanticism and Contemporary Culture*, Buckingham, Open University Press.

Eliot. G. (1903), *The Mill on the Floss*, London, Oxford University Press.

Eliot, T. S. (1934), *Selected Essays*, London, Faber and Faber.

Empson, William (1965), *Milton's God*, rev. ed., London, Chatto and Windus.

Felperin, H. (1991), '"Cultural poetics" versus "cultural materialism": the two new historicisms in Renaissance studies', in *Uses of History: Marxism, Postmodernism and the Renaissance*, ed. F. Barker, P. Hulme and M. Iversen, Manchester, Manchester University Press, 1991.

Fielding, H. (1749), *The History of Tom Jones, a Foundling*, 2 vols, ed. F. Bowers, Oxford, Clarendon, 1974.

Fineman, J. (1986), *Shakespeare's Perjured Eye*, Berkeley, University of California Press.

——(1994), 'Shakespeare's ear', in *The New Historicism Reader*, ed. H. Aram Veeser, New York, Routledge.

Foucault, M. (1965), *Madness and Civilization: A History of Insanity in the Age of Reason*, trans. R. Howard, New York, Vintage.

——(1970), *The Order of Things: An Archaeology of the Human Sciences*, London, Tavistock.

——(1972), *The Archaeology of Knowledge and The Discourse on Language*, trans. A. M. Sheridan Smith, New York, Pantheon.

——(1973), *The Birth of the Clinic: An Archaeology of Medical Perception*, London, Tavistock.

——(1977a), *Language, Counter-Memory, Practice: Selected Essays and Interviews*, ed. D. F. Bouchard, trans. D. F. Bouchard and S. Simon, Ithaca, Cornell.

——(1977b), *Discipline and Punish: The Birth of the Prison*, trans. A. Sheridan, New York, Pantheon.

——(1978), *The History of Sexuality: An Introduction*, Vol. 1, trans. R. Hurley, New York, Pantheon.

——(1985), *The History of Sexuality: The Uses of Pleasure*, Vol. 2, trans. R. Hurley, New York, Pantheon.

——(1988), *The History of Sexuality: The Care of the Self*, Vol.3, trans. R. Hurley, Harmondsworth, Penguin.

Freud, S. (1973), *Civilization and its Discontents*, trans. Joan Riviere, London, Hogarth.

Froula, C. (1984), 'Pechter's spectre: Milton's bogey writ small: or, why is he afraid of Virginia Woolf', *Critical Inquiry* 11, 171–8.

Frow, J. (1995), *Cultural Studies and Cultural Value*, Oxford, Clarendon.

Gallagher, C. (1989), 'Marxism and the new historicism', in *The New Historicism*, ed. H. Aram Veeser, New York, Routledge.

Gatens, M. (1996), *Imaginary Bodies: Ethics, Power and Corporeality*, London, Routledge.

Geertz, C. (1973), *The Interpretation of Cultures*, New York, Basic Books.

——(1995), *After the Fact: Two Countries, Four Decades, One Anthropologist*, Cambridge, Harvard University Press.

Goldberg, J. (1986), *Voice Terminal Echo: Postmodernism and English Renaissance Texts*, New York, Methuen.

Goldmann, L. (1975), *Towards a Sociology of the Novel*, trans. A. Sheridan, London, Tavistock.

Gossman, L. (1986), 'History as decipherment: Romantic historiography and the discovery of the other', *New Literary History*, 18.1, 23–57.

Graff, G. (1989), 'Co-optation', in *The New Historicism*, ed. H. Aram Veeser, New York, Routledge.

Gramsci, A. (1971), *Selections from the Prison Notebooks of Antonio Gramsci*, ed. and trans. Q. Hoare and G. Nowell Smith, London, Lawrence and Wishart.

Greenblatt, S. (1980), *Renaissance Self-Fashioning: From More to Shakespeare*, Chicago, University of Chicago Press.

——(1987) 'Invisible bullets: Renaissance authority and its subversion', *Glyph*, 8, 40–60.

——(1988a), *Shakespearean Negotiations: The Circulation of Social Energy in Renaissance England*, Oxford, Clarendon Press.

——(1988b), *Marvelous Possessions: The Wonder of the New World*, Oxford, Clarendon Press.

——(1988c), 'Murdering peasants: status, genre, and the representation of rebellion', in *Representing the English Renaissance*, ed. S. Greenblatt, Berkeley, University of California Press.

——(1989), 'Towards a poetics of culture', in *The New Historicism*, ed. H. Aram Veeser, New York, Routledge.

——(1990), *Learning to Curse: Essays in Early Modern Culture*, New York, Routledge.

Grosz, E. (1994), *Volatile Bodies: Toward a Corporeal Feminism*, Bloomington, Indiana University Press.

Habermas, J. (1987), *The Philosophical Discourse of Modernity: Twelve Lecture*, trans. F. Lawrence, Cambridge, Polity.

Hall, S. (1981), 'Notes on deconstructing "the popular"', in *People's History and Socialist Theory*, ed. R. Samuel, London, Routledge.

Hegel, G. W. F., (1807), *The Phenomenology of Spirit*, trans. A. V. Miller, Oxford, Clarendon 1977.

——(1830), *Logic: Being Part One of the Encyclopaedia of the Philosophical Sciences*, trans. W. Wallace, Oxford, Oxford University Press, 1975.

Heidegger, M. (1967), *What is a Thing?* trans., W. B. Barton, Jr. and V. Deutsch, Lanham, University Press of America.

Howard, J. (1991), 'Towards a postmodern, politically committed historical practice', in *Uses of History: Marxism, Postmodernism and the Renaissance*, ed. F. Barker, P. Hulme and M. Iversen, Manchester, Manchester University Press.

Iser, W. (1978), *The Act of Reading: A Theory of Aesthetic Response*, London, Routledge.

Jameson, F. (1981), *The Political Unconscious: Narrative as a Socially Symbolic Act*, Ithaca, Cornell University Press.

——(1984), 'Postmodernism, or, the cultural logic of late capitalism', *New Left Review*, 146, 53–92.

Jauss, H. R. (1982), *Toward an Aesthetics of Reception*, trans. T. Bahti, Minneapolis, University of Minnesota Press.

Johnson, S. (1781), *The Lives of the Poets*. London, Oxford University Press, 1906.

Kant, I. (1949), *Kant's Critique of Practical Reason and Other Writings in Moral Philosophy*, trans. L. White Beck, Chicago, University of Chicago Press.

Kristeva, J. (1980), *Desire in Language*, trans. L. Roudiez, New York, Columbia University Press.

——(1984), *Revolution in Poetic Language*, trans. M. Waller, New York, Columbia University Press.

Kuhn, T. (1962), *The Structure of Scientific Revolutions*, Chicago, University of Chicago Press.

Lacan, J. (1977), *Ecrits*, trans. A. Sheridan, London, Tavistock.

Lacoue-Labarthe, P. and Nancy, J. L., (1988), *The Literary Absolute: The Theory of Literature in German Romanticism*, trans. P. Barnard and C. Lester, Albany, State University of New York Press.

Lawrence, D. H. (1928), *Lady Chatterley's Lover*, Harmondsworth, Penguin, 1973.

Leavis, F. R. (1936), *Revaluation*, London, Chatto and Windus.

——(1960), *The Great Tradition*, 2nd edn, London, Chatto and Windus.

——(1964), *D. H. Lawrence: Novelist*, Harmondsworth, Peregrine.

Lehan, R. (1990), 'The theoretical limits of the new historicism', *New Literary History*, 21, 533–53.

Lehman, D. (1991), *Signs of the Times: Deconstruction and the Fall of Paul de Man*, New York, Poseidon.

Lentricchia, F. (1980), *After the New Criticism*, London, Athlone.

——(1989), 'Foucault's legacy: a new historicism?', in *The New Historicism*, ed. H. Aram Veeser, New York, Routledge.

Levinson, M. (1986), *Wordsworth's Great Period Poems: Four Essays*, Cambridge, Cambridge University Press.

Liu, A. (1989), 'The power of formalism: the new historicism', *ELH*, 56, 721–71.

Lovejoy, A. O. (1924), 'On the discrimination of Romanticisms' *PMLA*, 39, 229–53.

——(1964), *The Great Chain of Being: A Study of the History of an Idea*, Cambridge, Mass., Harvard University Press.

Low, L. and Harding, A. J. (1994), *Milton Metaphysicals and Romanticism*, Cambridge, Cambridge University Press.

Lukacs, G. (1981), *Essays on Realism*, ed. R. Livingstone, trans. D. Fernbach, Cambridge, Mass., MIT Press.

Lyotard, J. F. (1984), *The Postmodern Condition: A Report on Knowledge*, trans. B. Massumi, Minneapolis, University of Minnesota Press.

——(1994), *Lessons on the Analytic of the Sublime*, trans. E. Rottenberg, Stanford, Stanford University Press.

Macherey, P. (1978), *A Theory Of Literary Production*, trans. G. Wall, London, Routledge.

MacIntyre, A. (1981), *After Virtue: A Study of Moral Theory*, London, Duckworth.

MacPherson, C. B. (1964), *The Political Theory of Possessive Individualism: Hobbes to Locke*. Oxford, Oxford University Press.

Marx, K. (1867) *Capital*, Vol. 1, trans. S. Moore and E. Aveling, London, Lawrence and Wishart, 1970.

Mauss, M. (1970), *The Gift: Forms and Functions of Exchange in Archaic Societies*, trans. I. Cunnison, London, Routledge and Kegan Paul.

McGann, J. (1976), *'Don Juan' in Context*, London, J. Murray.

——(1983), *The Romantic Ideology: A Critical Investigation*, Chicago: University of Chicago Press.

Miller, J. H. (1987), The Ethics of Reading: Kant, de Man, Eliot, Trollope, James, and Benjamin, New York, Columbia University Press.

Milton, J. (1667), Paradise Lost, ed. A. Fowler, London, Longman, 1971.

Montrose, L. (1986), 'Renaissance literary studies and the subject of history', English Literary Renaissance, 16, 5–12.

——(1988), '"Shaping fantasies": figurations of gender and power in Elizabethan culture', in Representing the English Renaissance, ed. S. Greenblatt, Berkeley, University of California, Press.

——(1989), 'Professing the Renaissance: the poetics and politics of culture', in The New Historicism, ed. H. Aram Veeser, New York, Routledge.

——(1991), 'The work of gender in the discourse of discovery', Representations, 33, 1–41.

Nealon, J. T. (1992), 'The discipline of deconstruction', PMLA, 107, 1266–79.

Neely, C. (1988), 'Constructing the subject: feminist practice and the new renaissance discourses', English Literary Renaissance, 18, 15–18.

Newton, J. Lowder. (1989), 'History as usual? Feminism and the "new historicism"', in The New Historicism, ed. H. Aram Veeser, New York, Routledge.

Nietzsche, F. (1873–76), 'On the uses and disadvantages of history for life', in Untimely Meditations, trans. R. J. Hollingdale, Cambridge, Cambridge University Press, 1983.

Norris, C. (1985), 'Philosophy as a kind of narrative: Rorty on post-modern liberal culture', in Contest of Faculties: Philosophy and Theory After Deconstruction, London, Methuen.

Orgel, S. (1975), The Illusion of Power: Political Theater in the English Renaissance, Berkeley, University of California Press.

——(1989), 'Nobody's perfect: or why did the English stage take boys for women?', South Atlantic Quarterly, 88.1, 7–29.

Paine, T. (1791–92), Rights of Man, Harmondsworth, Penguin, 1984.

Patterson, A. (1988), '"The very age and body of the time his form and pressure": rehistoricizing Shakespeare's theater', New Literary History, 20, 83–104.

Pechter, E. (1987), 'The new historicism and its discontents: Politicizing Renaissance drama', PMLA, 102, 292–303.

Percy, T. (1765), Reliques of Ancient English Poetry, ed. J. V. Prichard, London, G. Bell 1976.

Porter C. (1989), 'History and literature: after the new historicism, New Literary History, 253–81.

——(1990), 'History and literature: After the new historicism', New Literary History, 253–81.

Richardson, S. (1740) Pamela: or, Virtue Rewarded, ed. T. C. Duncan Eaves and B. D. Kimpel, Boston, Houghton Mifflin, 1971.

Said, E. (1985), Orientalism, Harmondsworth, Penguin.

Scholes, R. and Kellogg, R. (1968), The Nature of Narrative, London, Oxford University Press.

Shelley, P. B. (1970), Poetical Works, ed. T. Hutchinson, Oxford, Oxford University Press.

Showalter, E. (1977), A Literature of Their Own: British Women Novelists from Bronte to Lessing, Princeton, Princeton University Press.

Sinfield, A. (1985), 'Royal Shakespeare: theatre and the making of ideology', in Political Shakespeare: New Essays in Cultural Materialism, ed. J. Dollimore and A. Sinfield, Ithaca: Cornell University Press.

——(1992), Faultlines: Cultural Materialism and the Politics of Dissident Reading, Berkeley, University of California Press.

——(1994), Cultural Politics – Queer Reading, London, Routledge.

Spengler, O. (1926), The Decline of the West, trans. C. F. Atkinson, New York, A. A. Knopf.

Stallybrass, P. and White, A. (1986), The Politics and Poetics of Transgression, London, Methuen.

Taylor, C. (1989), *Sources of the Self: The Making of Modern Identity*, Cambridge, Cambridge University Press.

Tillyard, E. M. W. (1943), *The Elizabethan World Picture*, London, Chatto and Windus.

——(1944), *Shakespeare's History Plays*, London, Chatto and Windus.

Veeser, H. Aram, ed. (1989), *The New Historicism*, New York, Routledge.

Warton, T. (1774–81; Vol. 4 1824), *History of English Poetry from the Close of the Eleventh to the Commencement of the Eighteenth Century*, ed. W. C. Hazlitt, Hildesheim, G. Olms (1968).

Watt, I. (1957), *The Rise of the Novel: Studies in Defoe, Richardson and Fielding*, London, Chatto and Windus.

White, H. (1973), *Metahistory: The Historical Imagination in Nineteenth-Century Europe*, Baltimore, Johns Hopkins.

——(1987), *The Content of Form: Narrative Discourse and Historical Representation*, Baltimore, Johns Hopkins.

Willey, B. (1940), *The Eighteenth-Century Background: Studies on the Idea of Nature in the Thought of the Period*, London, Chatto and Windus.

——(1949), *Nineteenth-Century Studies: Coleridge to Matthew Arnold*, New York, Columbia University Press.

——(1950), *The Seventeenth-Century Background: Studies in the Thought of the Age in Relation to Poetry and Religion*, New York, Columbia University Press.

Williams, R. (1961), *The Long Revolution*, London, Chatto and Windus.

——(1963), *Culture and Society 1780–1950*, Harmondsworth, Penguin.

——(1968), 'Introduction', in *From Culture to Revolution: The Slant Symposium 1967*, ed. T. Eagleton and B. Wicker, London, Sheed and Ward.

——(1970), *The English Novel: From Dickens to Lawrence*, London, Chatto and Windus.

——(1973), *The Country and the City*, Oxford, Oxford University Press.

——(1976), 'Notes on Marxism in Britain since 1945', *New Left Review*, 100, 81–94.

——(1977), *Marxism and Literature*, Oxford: Oxford University Press.

Wilson, R. (1992), 'Introduction: Historicising new historicism', in *The New Historicism and Renaissance Drama*, ed. R. Wilson and R. Dutton, London, Longman.

Wimsatt, W. K., Jnr (1954), *The Verbal Icon: Studies in the Meaning of Poetry*, Lexington, University Press of Kentucky.

——and Beardsley, Monroe C. (1946, 1949), 'The intentional fallacy' [1946] and 'The affective fallacy' [1949], in *Twentieth-Century Literary Criticism: A Reader*, ed. D. Lodge, London, Longman, 1972, 334–58.

Wittreich, J. A. (1975), ed. *Milton and the Line of Vision*, Madison, University of Wisconsin Press.

——(1979), *Milton's Tradition and his Legacy*, San Marino, Huntington Library.

——(1987), *Feminist Milton*, Ithaca, Cornell University Press.

Wordsworth, W. (1987), *Poetical Works*, rev. ed. T. Hutchinson and E. de Selincourt, Oxford, Oxford University Press.

Young, R. (1990), *White Mythologies: Writing History and the West*, London: Routledge.

Index

243